Scribal Secrets

Scribal Secrets

Extraordinary Texts in the Torah and Their Implications

by JAMES S. DIAMOND

Edited by Robert Goldenberg
and Gary A. Rendsburg,
with editorial assistance provided by Charles W. Loder

☙PICKWICK Publications · Eugene, Oregon

SCRIBAL SECRETS
Extraordinary Texts in the Torah and Their Implications

Copyright © 2019 Judith Diamond. All rights reserved. Except for brief quotations in critical publications or reviews, no part of this book may be reproduced in any manner without prior written permission from the publisher. Write: Permissions, Wipf and Stock Publishers, 199 W. 8th Ave., Suite 3, Eugene, OR 97401.

Pickwick Publications
An Imprint of Wipf and Stock Publishers
199 W. 8th Ave., Suite 3
Eugene, OR 97401

www.wipfandstock.com

PAPERBACK ISBN: 978-1-5326-4799-4
HARDCOVER ISBN: 978-1-5326-4800-7
EBOOK ISBN: 978-1-5326-4801-4

Cataloguing-in-Publication data:

Names: Diamond, James S., author. | Goldenberg, Robert, editor. | Rendsburg, Gary A., editor.

Title: Scribal secrets : extraordinary texts in the Torah and their implications / James S. Diamond, edited by Robert Goldenberg and Gary A. Rendsburg, with editorial assistance provided by Charles W. Loder.

Description: Eugene, OR: Pickwick Publications, 2019 | Includes bibliographical references and index.

Identifiers: ISBN 978-1-5326-4799-4 (paperback) | ISBN 978-1-5326-4800-7 (hardcover) | ISBN 978-1-5326-4801-4 (ebook)

Subjects: LCSH: Bible. Pentateuch—Criticism, interpretation, etc. | Bible. Old Testament—Criticism, Textual. | Masora

Classification: BS1136 D53 2019 (paperback) | BS1136 (ebook)

Manufactured in the U.S.A.   04/05/19

Contents

Copyright Notices | vii
Figures and Tables | viii
Editors' Preface | xi
Editors' Acknowledgments | xiii
Preface | xv

Introduction | 1
Chapter I. The Scribal Tradition in Israel | 10
Chapter II. The Extraordinary Texts in the Torah | 29
Chapter III. Reading the Torah Today | 155

Bibliography | 173
Index of Scriptural Passages | 177
Index of Ancient and Medieval Sources | 181
Index of Authors | 185

Copyright Notices

Figure 1   Photo © The Israel Museum, Jerusalem, by Ardon Bar-Hama.

Figure 2   Photo © The Israel Museum, Jerusalem, by Ardon Bar-Hama.

Figure 3   Torah scroll by scribe Rabbi Gustavo Surazski. Scroll image courtesy of Temple Aliyah, Needham, Mass.

Figure 4   Used with kind permission of the Bodleian Libraries, University of Oxford. Photo: © Bodleian Libraries, University of Oxford.

Figure 5   Torah scroll by scribe Rabbi Gustavo Surazski. Scroll image courtesy of Temple Aliyah, Needham, Mass.

Figure 6   Torah scroll by scribe Rabbi Gustavo Surazski. Scroll image courtesy of Temple Aliyah, Needham, Mass.

Figure 7   Image © Mordechai Pinchas (Marc Michaels), *Sofer STaM*, used with kind permission (www.sofer.co.uk).

Figure 8   Photograph by Bruce and Kenneth Zuckerman, West Semitic Research, in collaboration with the Ancient Biblical Manuscript Center. Courtesy Russian National Library (Saltykov-Shchedrin).

Figure 9   Used with kind permission of the Bodleian Libraries, University of Oxford. Photo: © Bodleian Libraries, University of Oxford.

Figure 10 Torah scroll by scribe Rabbi Gustavo Surazski. Scroll image courtesy of Temple Aliyah, Needham, Mass.

Figure 11 Photograph by Bruce and Kenneth Zuckerman, West Semitic Research, in collaboration with the Ancient Biblical Manuscript Center. Courtesy Russian National Library (Saltykov-Shchedrin).

Figure 12 Torah scroll by scribe Rabbi Gustavo Surazski. Scroll image courtesy of Temple Aliyah, Needham, Mass.

Figures and Tables

Figure 1　A portion of the Great Isaiah Scroll (1QIsaᵃ), cols. 34–37, containing Isaiah 40:28—44:23, found amongst the Dead Sea Scrolls, written c. 100 BCE, as an indication of the ancient Jewish scribal tradition. | 33

Figure 2　The Great Isaiah Scroll (1QIsaᵃ), col. 29, written c. 100 BCE, with line 10 (the third line in this image), including the dots above the word בירושלים in Isaiah 36:7. The word is missing in the later Masoretic text, as adumbrated here by the dotted letters, indicating that the word was written in error and should be deleted. | 36

Figure 3　Deuteronomy 29:28 as represented in a contemporary Torah scroll. Note the dots above the letters לנו ולבנינו and above the following ע. The same image appears later, as Figure 10, regarding the large letter named in the preceding verse. | 56

Figure 4　Cairo Geniza document listing the large and small letters in the entire Bible (not just the Torah). MS Bodl. Heb. d. 66, fol. 134a/134b. | 82

Figure 5　Genesis 1:1 as represented in a contemporary Torah scroll. Note the large *bet* which commences the verse and indeed the entire book of Genesis. | 87

Figure 6　Genesis 2:4 as represented in a contemporary Torah scroll. Note the small letter *he* in the sixth line of text in this image. | 93

Figure 7　The word שלום (*shalom*, "peace") in Numbers 25:12, written with the broken letter *vav*. | 123

Figures and Tables

Figure 8 Deuteronomy 6:4–9, the Shemaʿ paragraph, as represented in the Leningrad (St. Petersburg) Codex, written 1009–1010 CE, Tiberias, Israel. Note the large ʿayin in the first word of the first line and the large *dalet* in the second word of the second line. See Figure 9 for greater scribal/artistic accentuation of the two large letters. | 130

Figure 9 Deuteronomy 6:4–9, the Shemaʿ paragraph, as represented in the Kennicott Bible, written 1476 CE, La Coruña, Spain, fol. 103r (upper-left portion of the page). Note the beautifully illuminated large ʿayin and large *dalet,* each of which extends to three lines of regular text. | 131

Figure 10 Deuteronomy 29:27 as represented in a contemporary Torah scroll. Note the large letter *lamed* in the word וישלכם. The same image appears as Figure 3, regarding the dotted letters in the next verse. | 133

Figure 11 Numbers 10:35–36, as represented in the Leningrad (St. Petersburg) Codex, written 1009–1010 CE, Tiberias, Israel. The two verses are set off from the preceding text and the following text with the inverted *nun*s (or in this case, an approximation thereof) set within the white spaces which surround the passage. | 138

Figure 12 Numbers 10:35–36, as represented in a contemporary Torah scroll. Note the inverted *nun*s that demarcate the two verses. | 138

Table 1 Letters Large and Small in the Torah. | 86

Editors' Preface

Rabbi James S. Diamond enjoyed a long and fruitful career in the American rabbinate, largely as Hillel director at a succession of distinguished universities. His final posting was at Princeton University, and when he retired from there in 2004, he stayed in town and continued his other work as a prolific writer and teacher. Alas, our dear colleague was tragically killed in an automobile accident on March 28, 2013 (the first intermediate day of Passover, 5773). As Rabbi Diamond was walking to his car on a quiet street in a residential neighborhood in Princeton, he was struck by a passing vehicle and died instantaneously. Rabbi Diamond left behind the manuscript of the current book, *Scribal Secrets*, which he had shared with both of us for comments and feedback.

We undertook to prepare the manuscript for publication. The first two parts were essentially complete, in need only of editorial tightening and clarification. Unfortunately the third part, where the author's own thoughts would have come to the fore, was still in rudimentary form; we whose own academic background did not equip us to do more, decided to clarify the writing as best we could, but not to carry the content of the material beyond the point where Rabbi Diamond had left it. "Woe for that which is lost and cannot be found."

This has been a labor of love, an expression of our deep affection for Rabbi Diamond and our admiration for his many contributions to American Jewish life and to the academic world. It is our hope that Rabbi Diamond's family, colleagues, and other admirers will find the result worthy of him.

Robert Goldenberg
Emeritus Professor,
History and Judaic Studies
Stony Brook University

Gary A. Rendsburg
Blanche and Irving Laurie Professor
of Jewish History
Rutgers University

Editors' Acknowledgments

We gratefully acknowledge the editorial assistance of Charles W. Loder (Southern Baptist Theological Seminary), without whom this book would still be in progress. The inclusion of his name on the title page is a small token of our appreciation for his superb and efficient work.

Sally Freedman (Princeton University), personal friend of the late author, lent her keen editorial eye to the final stages of the book's preparation; every page bears the marks of her contribution.

The Blanche and Irving Laurie Chair in Jewish History at Rutgers University enabled the production and publication of this volume with generous financial support, for which we wish to express our deepest gratitude.

We further thank K. C. Hanson and Matthew Wimer of Wipf and Stock Publishers, for taking on this project. It has been a pleasure to work with them and with other members of their staff.

Finally, we are especially grateful to Judy Diamond, who gave us full blessing to bring her husband's final book-length manuscript to the light of day.

Preface

When we read something, whether printed or written by hand, what is happening?

We look at the letters and the words and we begin to try to make some sense of them. We piece together from those letters and words the elements of a story or some kind of meaning. We construct this meaning out of the combination of various letters into words, and the assemblage of those words into sentences, and the organization of those sentences into whole passages.

But alphabet and phonetics are not the only means by which we construct this meaning. There are also things on the page that more subtly influence and guide our interpretation of what we are reading: periods, commas, semicolons, question marks, quotation marks, parentheses. This is as true when we are reading *Newsweek* or *The New York Times* as it is when we take in hand something like *Moby Dick* or *Harry Potter*. It is also true when we read the Torah or the Pentateuch, whether in a book with the Hebrew original and perhaps a translation beside it or from out of the Torah scroll itself.

This book is about some of the subtle devices that operate within and upon the writing in the Torah to impart to it a meaning or meanings beyond the textual surface. Let me be clear though: in the Torah's case I am not talking about punctuation marks. The signs that are my subject here are not found in every line or on every page of the Torah. They show up only occasionally, and when they do, they do so in quite unexpected ways. The aim here is to show you what these devices are, how and where to find them, and how to use them in your own encounter with this text that has served as the wellspring of Jewish religious expression since Judaism anchored itself in the written word.

Preface

Let me give a famous example of what I'm talking about: the words of the Shema' as they are written in a Torah scroll in their original place in the sixth chapter of Deuteronomy and as they are printed in virtually all *Humashim* (Pentateuchs) and *siddurim* (prayer books):

שמע ישראל יהוה אלהינו יהוה אחד

Hear O Israel! The LORD is our God, the LORD alone.
(Deut 6:4)

Do you see—it's hard not to—how two letters here, the 'ayin and the *dalet,* are written larger than the others? They have been written that way for a very long time, possibly as much as two thousand years.

Why?

Attempts to answer this question are as many as they are profound. They break down into two schools of thought, about each of which I shall have a lot more to say in this book. One school holds that the reason the two letters need to be written large is to make sure that they are not mistaken for another letter that may look alike, or for another consonant that may sound alike. This will ensure that one is reading exactly the right words with the right theological intentions, and not near-homographs or near-homonyms that have other meanings with insidious and even heretical implications. Thus:

- The large 'ayin guarantees that the word will be read and pronounced as *shema'* (שמע, which means "hear" or "comprehend"), and not *shemma'* (שמא, which means "perhaps" or "maybe"). We don't want to say "Maybe, O Israel, the Lord is our God . . . "—a statement that, as an affirmation of Jewish creed, would be, shall we say, problematical.[1] In this case the letters do not look alike, but they sound very like one another.

- Likewise, because the difference between the letter *dalet* ד and the letter *resh* ר is slight, writing the *dalet* large ensures that we will say that God is *'eḥad* (אחד), "One," i.e., "unique" or "singular," and not *'aḥer* (אחר), "another." It would, to say the least, be undesirable for a Jew to proclaim the existence of a deity other than or in addition to the God of Israel. In this case the letters do not sound alike, but they look very similar.

---

1. Samson Raphael Hirsch (exact work not given) in Ron, *Sefer Qaṭan ve-Gadol*, 177.

Preface

A second school of thought explains the large letters in terms that are less doctrinal. They are to be written that way as mnemonic devices, visual triggers that should serve to initiate a range of thoughts and associations in the mind of the one saying the Shema‛ so as to expand, deepen, and enhance the experience of saying these words that are so foundational for Judaism. Thus:

- The large ‛*ayin* (which is the Hebrew word for "eye") intimates that one should open his or her eyes to the natural world and thus come to contemplate the One who created it.[2]

- Alternately, the numerical value of the letter ‛*ayin* being 70 points to the 70 names the midrash says that God has for Israel. Or the numerical hint is about the 70 faces of the Torah, i.e., the 70 modalities by which it can be interpreted.[3]

- Likewise with the letter *dalet*, the numerical value of which is four. The large *dalet* signifies that when we say the Shema‛ we should keep in mind the four directions, or, in modern scientific terms, the four dimensions of reality—of time and space—that God's domain encompasses.[4]

- Taken together, the two enlarged letters can be seen to bracket the verse, a function that points to other significations. The framing letters thus serve to remind the one saying the verse to concentrate on the words that lie between them. Together they also form the Hebrew word ‛*ed* (עד, "witness") and thus concretize the idea that in reciting the Shema‛, a Jew is bearing witness to the reality and the authority of the unique and incomparable God and is living out the words of Isaiah (43:10): "*You are my witnesses, says the LORD*." (And here I cannot but cite the amazing midrashic gloss on this verse: "if you are my witnesses, says God, then I am God; if you are not my witnesses, then I am, so to speak, not God"!!!)[5]

This is the kind of thing we'll be exploring in the pages that follow.

---

2 Ovadiah Sforno (Italy, 1475–1550), commentary on Deuteronomy 6:4.

3 Ba‛al HaṬurim (Jacob ben Asher, Germany and Spain, ca. 1269-ca. 1343), commentary on Deuteronomy 6:4.

4 Keli Yakar (Shlomo Ephraim of Luntschitz, Poland, 1550–1619) on Deuteronomy 6:4.

5 Midrash Tehillim 123:2 and Pesiqta de Rav Kahana 12:6.

Preface

* * *

You may be wondering: Do I need to read Hebrew to read this book?

My answer is "yes" and "no." Knowing Hebrew will certainly help. A lot of what is involved in understanding the signs and letters treated in the following chapters does indeed turn on the intricacies of Hebrew grammar and syntax.

But a knowledge of these intricacies, while a plus, is not a prerequisite. This is because much of what I do with Hebrew in this book will focus on the visual aspects of the Hebrew letters in the Torah's text—their shape or size—and not on their semantic denotation or connotation, as we have just seen with the two enlarged letters of the Shema'. So even if you do not know Hebrew you should be able to follow most of the discussion, because often the meanings I will be pointing towards are independent of the grammatical or syntactical issues in the words with which I will be dealing. When they are not, and a working knowledge of Hebrew is assumed, I suggest you skip the part in question and move on.

In any case, I do translate and/or transliterate all Hebrew words and quotations. I would, though, recommend having the Hebrew along with an English translation handy, so that you can see for yourself in the text the signs I'll be discussing and the full context in which they occur.

That said, here are some particular details that will be helpful for you to know—or review—before you begin:

- For use in the synagogue, the five books of the Torah are written out consecutively on one very long scroll of parchment. Each Torah scroll is handwritten by a qualified scribe (called a *sofer* in Hebrew) with a special quill in a special ink.

- The Hebrew alphabet contains 22 letters, and they are all consonants.[6] There are vowel signs in Hebrew, but they are visible only when they are inserted beneath, above, or into the consonants. We call such marking "pointing." A text with vowels inserted is said to be pointed.

- The consonantal text is original, that is, from the time of authorship and/or early scribal copying in ancient Israel. The vowel markings are a product of the Middle Ages.

---

6 Five of the 22 letters have special forms that are used at the end of a word.

PREFACE

- The text of the Torah as it is written on the scroll is unpointed. It contains only consonants, no vowels. In printed Hebrew Bibles the text is pointed.
- Some of the textual oddities that are the subject of this book are visible in all Torah scrolls; some are not. Many of them, not all, can be seen in printed Hebrew Bibles.

Finally, a few notes on style and usage.

Unless otherwise indicated, biblical citations in translation follow the New Jewish Publication Society version (NJPS).

Citations from the Talmudim are labeled b. Tractate or y. Tractate, with the former referring to the Babylonian Talmud and the latter referring to the Talmud of the Land of Israel (the so-called Talmud Yerushalmi, or Jerusalem Talmud, or Palestinian Talmud).

Midrash capitalized refers to a specific collection of rabbinic interpretation of Scripture—Midrash Rabbah or some other work; *midrash* uncapitalized refers to the general body of such interpretation or to the hermeneutical process by which it is carried out.

God is obviously beyond gender. Hopefully my recording here of this awareness will obviate the need to jump through verbal hoops each time God's attributes and actions are invoked. My usage of the conventional masculine forms "He," "Him," or "His" follows the practice of the biblical writers.

Introduction

THE CENTRAL PART OF this book tells the story of some extraordinary texts in the Torah (the five books of Moses): certain letters, words, and verses that are marked or written in unusual ways. Some have strange-looking dots over them. Some are written differently than the rest of the letters in the text. How these scribal anomalies came about is told in Chapter I, out of which the central part, Chapter II, proceeds. Chapter III deals with what emerges from our exploration of these strange textual phenomena. It will hold up some larger issues that they raise about how we read the Bible, especially the Torah, in our time.

Each of these three themes has a backstory. I will tell them so as to explain more fully what goes on in the following pages.

1. BACKSTORY #1

Sometimes, when you read the Bible, you see things you never noticed before. This happened to me a long time ago—I forget exactly when.

I was reading Genesis and came to the part where Jacob is about to re-encounter his brother Esau; Jacob had fled from Esau twenty years earlier in the wake of his filching the birthright from his older twin. Jacob had gone back to the family ranch in Paddan-Aram to lie low with his uncle Laban until his brother's anger would cool.

During the two decades there, he has prospered. He has found his wives Leah and Rachel, not to mention his two concubines Bilhah and Zilpah, and has fathered children with all of them. Now he is on his way back to Canaan. Enroute, he learns that Esau is advancing toward him with 400 men. Ominous news, but Jacob reacts coolly. He dispatches men to ride out and meet the oncoming Esau with a gift, an impressive shipment

Scribal Secrets

of choice sheep and cattle. Maybe that will blunt Esau's vengeful feelings. Jacob divides his camp, thinking that if Esau attacks, one half of the family can escape. He also beseeches Heaven to protect him from harm so he can continue the line of his grandfather Abraham and his father Isaac. That night, sleepless, he wrestles with a mysterious being. As dawn breaks, he extracts from his antagonist a blessing: the name Israel.

And then it is morning, and in the clear light of day the fateful moment arrives: there is Esau advancing toward his brother Jacob. What is going to happen? I read:

וַיָּרָץ עֵשָׂו לִקְרָאתוֹ וַיְחַבְּקֵהוּ וַיִּפֹּל עַל־צַוָּארָו וַיִּשָּׁקֵהוּ וַיִּבְכּוּ

> *And Esau ran to greet him. He embraced him and, falling on his neck, he kissed him; and they wept.* (Gen 33:4)

As I read this verse, caught up as I was in the high drama it narrates, my eyes were drawn to something unusual: *over each of the six letters of the Hebrew word for "kissed" were—are—dots*. Six dots.

What are these? I wondered. Why are they there? Who put them there? It can't be a mistake. A Torah scroll can't have mistakes.

The more I looked at the verse, the more those dots intrigued me. They seemed to be telling me something, *something that was not in the text*. The text says that Esau embraces Jacob and kisses him. That is remarkable enough. The dots suggest that this is not only or merely remarkable, but something to which I should pay close attention. The dots seemed almost to be calling out to me. "Dear reader: Do you see what Esau is doing here? Ponder it. Investigate."

Subsequently, I had this same experience with another verse in the Torah, this one near the end of Deuteronomy. As Moses is winding up his valedictions to the children of Israel, he says:

הַנִּסְתָּרֹת לַיהוָה אֱלֹהֵינוּ וְהַנִּגְלֹת לָנוּ וּלְבָנֵינוּ עַד־עוֹלָם לַעֲשׂוֹת אֶת־כָּל־דִּבְרֵי הַתּוֹרָה הַזֹּאת

> *The secret things belong unto the LORD our God; but the things that are revealed belong unto us and to our children for ever, that we may do all the words of this law.* (Deut 29:28)

Here again there are dots, this time over eleven letters. Here again, an evocative verse seems to be flagged. "Dear reader: Take note. Ponder this verse and the dotted words. What are they saying?"

INTRODUCTION

Indeed, what *are* they saying? What do the eleven dots mean? Are they part of the text, intrinsic and necessary to any interpretation of it? Or are they additions to the text, extraneous to its interpretation?

Over time it got curiouser and curiouser. I noticed that dots were not the only non-phonetic extra-lexical attention-getters in the Torah's text. There were many others:

- Enlarged letters. As in the very first word of the Torah:

בראשית

When God began to create . . . (Gen 1:1)

- Diminutive letters. As we find in the first word of the book of Leviticus:

ויקרא

The LORD called to Moses and spoke to him . . . (Lev 1:1)

- Reversed *nuns*. They appear at the end of chapter ten of Numbers, when the Israelites are about to march off into the desert:

׆ וַיְהִי בִּנְסֹעַ הָאָרֹן וַיֹּאמֶר מֹשֶׁה קוּמָה ׀ יְהֹוָה וְיָפֻצוּ אֹיְבֶיךָ וְיָנֻסוּ מְשַׂנְאֶיךָ מִפָּנֶיךָ:
וּבְנֻחֹה יֹאמַר שׁוּבָה יְהֹוָה רִבְבוֹת אַלְפֵי יִשְׂרָאֵל: ׆

When the Ark was to set out, Moses would say:
Advance, O LORD!
May Your enemies be scattered,
And may Your foes flee before You!
And when it halted, he would say:
Return, O LORD,
You who are Israel's myriads of thousands! (Num 10:35–36)

What are these extraordinary non-lexical markings? Why are they there? How did they get there? Do they serve any function, harbor any meanings?

One way to answer these questions is to proceed historically. We can inquire into how scribes in the ancient Near East typically marked the texts they wrote and what graphic devices they employed to call attention to certain features in them, features that impinged on how that particular text should be read or on what its plain sense is. Then we can see how these signifying practices relate to the texts in the Torah we are studying here. We must remember that the scribes who wrote out the Torah and the Bible needed to make sure that literally every jot and tittle was correct.

They regarded the scroll or scrolls they were writing as an authentic visual replication of what God had communicated to Moses at Sinai, and so that replication had to be read correctly.

We can also look at the various markings in a different way, as signifiers of another kind of meaning. In this perspective, the supralinear dots or the enlarged or diminutive letters or the reversed *nuns* might be understood not in their historical context as the product of scribal practices and conventions that obtained in antiquity for the practical purpose of guiding the reader to the plain sense of the text. Rather, we can see them as visual flags that tell the reader that the word or phrase or passage in question invites or requires special interpretation, that a special meaning was encoded therein which the reader had to ferret out, a meaning that lies beyond the plain sense of the text. Seen this way, the dots, letters, and reversed *nuns* are cues and opportunities for midrashic interpretation. The central part of this book explores all this. In it, we will examine how the different markings and signs were understood and interpreted over time, and what they might mean for us today.

2. BACKSTORY #2

I was hardly the first reader of the Torah to be confounded by the supralinear dots. The rabbis wondered about them too, as we see in the following vignette in the midrash:

> Ezra reasoned thus: If the prophet Elijah comes and asks me, "Why have you written these letters and words and passages?," I will reply "That is why I put dots over them." And if he says to me, "You have done well to write them," then I shall erase the dots over them.[1]

Ezra was a *kohen* or hereditary priest living in the Babylonian exile a little over a century after the First Temple was destroyed in 586 BCE. He was also an expert *sofer*, a scribe learned in Torah, maybe even the scribe who edited and/or wrote out the definitive version of the Torah as we have it today, an opinion that some, though by no means all, Bible scholars of today hold.[2]

---

1. Bamidbar Rabbah 3:13 and repeated in other rabbinic texts.
2. Friedman, *Who Wrote the Bible*, 223–25.

INTRODUCTION

In this passage the rabbis seem to think that it was Ezra who first put the dots in the various places in the Torah where we see them today. But why he did this is not at all clear from this passage. Did he put in the dots to indicate that the letters and words under them are spurious and do not belong in the text? Or to indicate just the opposite: that they do, in fact, belong? Or to indicate something else, something that has nothing to do with whether these particular letters and words belong in the text or not? Or perhaps there is some other completely different reason for their presence of which this midrash with its reference to Ezra is simply unaware? Whatever the answer, this passage suggests that if we want to understand the dots and, I would add, the other extraordinary markings in the Torah—their origin and their function—we need to know something about how the Bible's text came into being, how it went from being something communicated orally to a written text, and how that written text was transmitted. This is a story not much told.

The central figures in this story are the *sofrim* and the *ba'ale masora*. The *sofrim* are the generations of scribes who labored painstakingly and meticulously to inscribe the text of the Torah—each one of its 5,845 verses (consisting of 79,856 words in which there are 400,945 letters)[3]—onto a parchment scroll. The *ba'ale masora* are their successors, the Masoretes of the early Middle Ages who reviewed the Jewish textual tradition from its origins to their time; they standardized and, among other things, systematized the orthography, pronunciation, accentuation, and cantillation of every single word in the Hebrew Bible. Their story is the subject matter of Chapter I.

3. BACKSTORY #3

At the Shabbat morning minyan (prayer group) in which I participate, we follow a practice that is common to many such prayer-groups: after the weekly Torah portion and Haftarah have been read, we have a Torah discussion. Each week a different member of the minyan prepares some ideas and questions and facilitates the discussion. Some weeks the focus is on historical issues: What is the context of such and such events? How do the

---

3 These totals are the product of the later generations of Masoretes and they are, not surprisingly, contested; different manuscripts and different editions present different totals. The numbers here are those recorded in the Masoretic notes at the end of Tigay, *Deuteronomy*, 341.

events or laws or poems in the Torah reading relate to the societies and the literatures of the ancient Near East? How do we account for and resolve apparent contradictions in the text? On other weeks the discussion takes on a more midrashic cast: How do the rabbis and later commentators read such and such event? What do they make of this verse, that character, that dialogue between characters? What do the rabbinic or the medieval philosophical or the mystical traditions say about the events or the people or the laws in the Torah portion, and how does what they say relate to our lives as Jews? More often than not, the conversation goes back and forth between these two foci.

If one is present at these discussions over several weeks, one can observe an interesting phenomenon. When the issues raised are of an historical or cultural nature, some members of the minyan are energized, become voluble, and engage with the matters that have been put forward, while others tend to remain silent and listen respectfully. When literary or midrashic or larger spiritual issues are raised, it is the latter attendees who perk up and shape the discourse, and the former ones sit politely and wait patiently for the discussion to run its course. Value judgments on these different perspectives are seldom expressed—it is all very civil—but one can tell from the body language that there are two clear interpretive groups here.

This divide bespeaks two fundamentally different approaches to how we read the Torah: the historical and the midrashic. Chapter II will show us how these two approaches or interpretive codes play out with respect to the dots, the unusually written letters, and the reversed *nuns*. But this divide needs to be broadened out to consider what it implies for how we read the Torah and the Bible in general. What does critical historical reading give us that ahistorical midrash does not? How does midrashic meaning differ from historical meaning? How do these two approaches relate to the traditional distinction between *peshaṭ*, the plain meaning of the text, and *derash*, the meaning that accrues when various interpretive moves are applied to the text? Chapter III will deal with these questions.

Each chapter in this book is a discrete discussion and can be read separately from the others. Anyone who just wants to zero in on the primary subject in Chapter II can certainly do so and disregard Chapters I and III. Similarly, anyone who is not that interested in the larger interpretive issues of reading the Bible can focus on Chapters I and II and skip Chapter III. But my hope is that the reader who follows the itinerary of the book as a whole will come to see how Chapter I flows into Chapter II and how Chapter III flows forth from both of them.

4. A NOTE ON THE DIFFERENT MARKINGS

Technically speaking, what we are studying in this book are *graphemes*. The term *graphemes* broadly refers to anything written. This includes not only letters, which are transcriptions in writing of the spoken word (*phonemes, morphemes, lexemes*—that is, the individual sounds, grammatical forms, words, etc.), but all diacritical signs and markings in a written text. Phonemes, of course, communicate meaning, but non-phonetic graphemes do too. They just do it in a different way.[4] On a Torah scroll the best-known example of graphemes that are not phonemes are the *taggim*, the filigreed crowns that are inscribed over many letters. While they have no bearing at all on how the letters and words they embellish are read or pronounced, for Rabbi Akiva and his school of scriptural interpretation they certainly were of hermeneutic significance. The tradition records that they deduced "piles and piles of *halakhot*" from these jots and tittles.[5]

The non-phonetic or non-lexical graphemes that form the subject of this book are not uniform in origin or function. Dots over words are a different order of sign from the reversed *nun*s of Numbers 10:35–36 (though both kinds of markings are graphemes). The large and small letters are something else again. While they certainly represent phonemes—they are, after all, letters—their unusual size enables them to communicate meaning in a non-verbal way. It is that meaning which we will examine here. Their heterogeneity notwithstanding, what these three kinds of markings have in common is that they all were established in the Torah text relatively early on, prior to the major Masoretic enterprise, and they are all integral to the text and are visible in all Torah scrolls. They are the subject of this book.

Not integral are those graphemes that are not inscribed in Torah scrolls and are not part of the text. These include the vowel points, the *te'amim* (small markings with a triple function, marking accentuation, punctuation, and cantillation), and various other diacritical signs that we see in printed Bibles. These different graphemes control how the consonantal words are pronounced and chanted (knowledge that a Torah reader must already possess, since these signs are not inscribed on a Torah scroll). The vowel points

---

4 See Johnson, "Writing," 42.
5 b. Menaḥot 29b.

and the melodies of the cantillation signs go back to an early stage of the text's history, when it was orally declaimed in public and was not widely read silently. Early in the Middle Ages the Masoretes (of whom I will say more in Chapter I) inserted them into the manuscripts of the Bible which they prepared, in order to ensure that the text would be pronounced, accentuated, parsed, and chanted correctly. None of these concern us here because they are not integral to the Torah's text in its pre-Masoretic stage.

Also beyond the scope of the following chapters are the *taggim* referred to previously. While they are part of the text, their graphemic function was only recognized by Rabbi Akiva and his school and the later mystics. The meanings they extracted from them, case by case, are scattered throughout the vast canon of rabbinic and kabbalistic literature.

There is no question that the *te'amim* as punctuation marks also have an interpretive function; the rabbis of the Talmud already knew the effects of punctuation on the meaning of a verse, even if written signs had not yet been created and hence were not to be seen in the texts that lay before them. But because these signs are not included in the received consonantal text I do not treat them here.

5. A NOTE ON HOW I READ

Finally, let me say something about how I, as a reader of the Pentateuch, handle its text. My approach is multi-dimensional. I begin where most, if not all, contemporary Bible readers begin: with history and the historical.

The most distinctive feature of the modern study of the Bible is its emphasis on history: the attempt to uncover what the biblical texts meant at the time they were composed, rather than what they came to mean in later tradition, or how they might inspire the believer today.[6]

I take seriously the findings and insights of modern biblical scholarship, speculative as many of these may be. They ground me in the documented data of linguistic, cultural, and anthropological research into how our biblical forebears lived, thought, and wrote. But history is only a starting point. The 24 books of the Bible[7] offer much more than historical truth, important as that is. What its words came to mean in later tradition and how

---

6. Sperling, "Modern Jewish Interpretation."

7 In the traditional Jewish counting, the Bible contains 24 books. Samuel, Kings, and Chronicles are counted as one book each, as are Ezra and Nehemiah together, and the twelve so-called minor prophets are counted as a single book.

Introduction

they inspired believers is of no less concern to me. For believers the biblical text was more than an inert collection of words to which they applied their analytical faculties. It was a living entity that inspired them as they tried to make sense of their life in this world. And so it is for me. The text of the Pentateuch is for me a fit and absorbing object for close reading and various kinds of critical analysis. It is also a dialogical partner that addresses me in my subjectivity even as I interrogate it on the page. It addresses me with a distinct view of God, man, and the world—a distinct theology (though unformulated as such)—that by turns challenges me, qualifies me, enlarges me, uplifts me, and sometimes even upsets me. In the following pages the objective and the subjective are intermingled. I cannot say where one leaves off and the other begins. Sometimes I will speak of the five books of Moses the way biblical critics do, as the Pentateuch, and sometimes I will speak of them as Jews of faith do, as Torah. I often move from one to the other in the same paragraph and sometimes even in the same sentence.

The present book is thus neither a purely academic study of certain textual phenomena in the Pentateuch nor a personalistic interpretation of their existential import as Torah. At times it will read like the former, and at times it will sound like the latter. The determinations of meaning that history and midrash have arrived at cavort together here freely and licitly.

CHAPTER I

The Scribal Tradition in Israel

The Torah, i.e., the Pentateuch or five books of Moses, as well as the whole Hebrew Bible, the Tanakh, consists only of consonants. To our forebears, the text of the Torah was not of this world. To them it was—and to some Jews today it literally still is—effusions of the divine mind concretized into the letters and words of Hebrew consonants.

> The text of the Hebrew Bible, and that of the various books it includes, was handed down over a very long period, in the single form of a *consonantal text without addition of vowels or punctuation marks of any kind.*[1]

That is the fundamental fact from which the itinerary of concerns of this book proceeds.

Marc-Alain Ouaknin elaborates:

> The scriptural handing-down of the sacred texts, in their original form, was carried out—and is still carried out in our day . . . —in the form of . . . scrolls made of tanned leather or of parchmented leather. On these scrolls, made up of strips of skin sewn one to another and ruled horizontally and vertically with an awl, the sacred texts are copied with the use of a reed calamus in the East and a goose quill in the West. These copies are scrupulously executed according to the traditional rules and *without any particular signs being added to the consonantal text* that might have suggested to the reader a particular way of vocalizing and so of interpreting the

1. Ouaknin, *Burnt Book*, 131. Emphasis in the original.

The Scribal Tradition in Israel

text or of dividing the text into logical or semantic units, to make it perceptible to the reader. Any sign added to the body of a scroll would have expressed a particular exegetical choice that could be accepted as a possible exegesis of the text, but could not be considered as representative of rabbinical exegesis par excellence. As a result, traditional scribal rules have always *prohibited the adding of any graphical signs other than those reserved for the copying of the consonantal text*, and that alone. The oral knowledge of traditional exegesis passed on from the masters to their pupils has, alone, for a long time made up for the absence of a more elaborate graphical system.[2]

So when writing or copying a Torah scroll, no vowels, no periods, no commas, or anything else is added. Just the unpointed consonantal letters. Yet the fact is that there are certain signs in the text of every Torah scroll (visible in many printed Hebrew versions of the Pentateuch) that are not consonants. Nor are they vowels, for they are not pronounced.

These various signs, as I noted in the introduction, are not anomalies but part and parcel of the Torah's text even though they are not read. The traditional rules for writing Torah scrolls referred to the mandate that *these signs have to be written*. So, too, do other occasional irregularities, such as certain letters that have to be made larger than the others and some smaller. These rules, like the markings themselves, are the product of a scribal tradition that goes back to the earliest stages of Israel's history and spans not only centuries but millennia. As we've seen, linguists call the various signs we are considering graphemes; textual critics of the Bible call them "paratextual elements."[3] If we want to know what we can of their origins and history, in particular how they became integral parts of the Torah's text, we need to tell the story of the scribal tradition as it developed in Israel and in the Judaism that grew out of biblical tradition.

It is a story not easily told, and its details are known mostly to specialists in the history of the biblical text. In its widest sense, the scribal tradition I am talking about is called "the Masorah," a word I shall explain more fully in the course of this discussion. One of its foremost students, Israel Yeivin, has written:

> The Masorah consists of a mass of data collected over a long period by many scholars. It includes the work of different schools

---

2. Ouaknin, *Burnt Book*, 131–32. Emphasis in the original.
3. So Tov, *Textual Criticism*, 47–48 (and elsewhere in the book).

and individuals, with different opinions, but in general only the information itself was considered important, and its origin is not recorded. Despite recent discoveries of very ancient biblical texts and masoretic fragments, we still do not have information which shows clearly who produced the Masorah and how it was done. The outline of its development can only be sketched on the basis of vague hints, and with much speculation.[4]

What follows is a piecing together of bits and pieces of textual evidence about this scribal tradition that we find in the Bible, the Talmud, and other sources into a coherent picture that may appear more historically sequential than it is—or was.

1. THE SCRIBES OF THE FIRST TEMPLE PERIOD

When we think of scribes, we think of a culture in which the primary mode of literary expression is writing. But, as folklorists have known for a long time and contemporary biblical scholars have only recently begun to understand, scribes functioned in an oral culture too, where the primary mode of religious and artistic creation (there often was little difference between these) was oral.[5]

In his important study of the origins of the biblical text, David Carr cautions against thinking that these two modalities of literary expression, oral and written, were mutually exclusive or developed in strict chronological sequence. For a long time, the conventional view was that epics were first sung or declaimed orally to be received aurally, and only later written down to be read. Carr and others believe that the two modalities co-existed and overlapped. In fact the difference between them was smaller than modern students may suppose. Texts were written, to be sure, but they were not written to be read silently and privately by individual readers. They were written to be read aloud by the bard-teacher to an audience or to a group of students. They functioned, as Carr nicely puts it, "more the way a musical

---

4. Yeivin, *Introduction to the Tiberian Masorah*, 131.

5. Four key books explore the issues involved in the transition from oral to written cultures, and what that transition might mean for our understanding of the Bible. The first to deal with these issues in a substantial way was Niditch, *Oral World and Written Word: Ancient Israelite Literature*. In her wake have come three important studies: Schniedewind, *How the Bible Became a Book: The Textualization of Ancient Israel*; Carr, *Writing on the Tablet of the Heart: Origins of Scripture and Literature*; and van der Toorn, *Scribal Culture and the Making of the Hebrew Bible*.

score does for a musician who already knows the piece than like a book the reader has never encountered before."[6] Only in the latter centuries of the biblical period (approximately 300–165 BCE) were texts written to be read and explicated by individual readers. The period of the First Temple (ca. 960–586 BCE) was a transitional era. This was the time when parts of the Torah—think of the stories in Genesis—that had existed as orally performed narratives, or as crib-sheets for the bards who declaimed them, began to assume more polished written form through the work of scribes.

Let us note here, for it will be important for our later discussion, that the word Scripture uses for "scribe," *sofer*, has a convoluted history. Nowadays the word refers to someone who is trained to write out the Pentateuchal text onto Torah scrolls or onto the smaller pieces of parchment that go into *tefillin* or *mezuzot*. Ernst Würthwein, however, reminds us that: "During the Israelite kingdom the word *sopher* indicated the incumbent of a high political office."[7] With a different function in mind, the Talmud notes that "the ancients were called *sofrim* because they counted every letter in the Torah."[8] Counting the letters might have served as a way of ensuring that they had missed nothing in their copying and had produced a text that was not only accurate but complete.

Etymology confirms this double function. The Hebrew word *sofer* derives from the verb stem *s-f-r*, which means both to "count" and to "tell" or "recount" in the sense of "narrate." (Similarly in English a "teller" is someone who counts out money but also one who narrates a tale.) The Hebrew term *sofer* perfectly captures the double function of the scribe in this formative period of Israel's textual tradition: as a faithful steward of the sacred writ in both its graphic and its performative representations.

It is on this basis that we must understand the work of *sofrim* during the First Temple period. Here is how Karel van der Toorn, an important student of the scribal enterprise in the ancient Near East, describes it:

> Texts were for the ears rather than for the eyes ... To properly appreciate the role of the ancient scribes, it is necessary to take leave of the common conception of the scribe as a mere copyist ... In the words of James Muilenberg, scribes "were not only copyists, but also and more particularly composers who gave to their works

---

6. Carr, *Writing on the Tablet of the Heart*, 4.

7. Würthwein, *Text of the Old Testament*, 12. References to high-ranking scribes can be found, for example, at 1 Kings 4:3, 2 Kings 22:9, and Jeremiah 36:10.

8. b. Qiddushin 30a.

their form and structure, and determined to a considerable degree their wording and terminology."[9]

* * *

A momentous event occurred during a refurbishment of the Temple in the time of King Josiah (ca. 622 BCE). A mysterious scroll, described as "a scroll of the Teaching" (Hebrew: *sefer ha-torah*, ספר התורה) was "discovered" by the High Priest Hilkiah in the inner recesses of the Temple. He gave it to Shaphan the scribe, who read it and then took it to the king (see 2 Kings 22:8–10).[10]

In the present context, what is of interest in this incident is the three-way linkage among Temple, Torah, and text, and therefore the role of the scribes as writers and readers of that text. The Temple, we see, was something more than a place of sacrifice. It was a locus of textual activity, a place, maybe *the* place, where the Torah's text, such as it was, was written and copied and kept. Besides being the focal point of the relationship between the God of Israel and the people of Israel, the Temple served as a scriptorium and as the national library and archive. Within it the scribes were something more than clerical scriveners.

This understanding of how texts and scribes functioned in antiquity has direct implications for how we can explain some of the markings in the Torah that are to be discussed in the following chapters. To the scribes who wrote them, they were devices of graphic presentation that they used

---

9. van der Toorn, *Scribal Culture*, 12, 109. He further writes:

> It may be useful to sum up the characteristics of authorship in antiquity by contrasting them with modern notions of authorship. To us, the author is first of all an individual . . . But what does it mean to be an individual? We think of a human person as a unique individual distinct from all other human beings. This view is the outcome of a long historical process. Earlier cultures put much greater emphasis on the social role of the individual . . . The individual is indistinguishable from his or her social role and social status . . . In Mesopotamia and Israel, the author . . . is a particular character or role. The social group the author belongs to and identifies with is that of the scribes. His work expresses the common values, ideological and artistic, of the scribal community. The author is a craftsman. Individual talent, which would be as real a gift in antiquity as it is today, was not an instrument to express the private and the personal but was a way to attain the pinnacle of a collective art (*Scribal Culture*, 45–47).

10. The consequences of this discovery were significant. We believe that the scroll that Hilkiah found was the book of Deuteronomy, or, more likely, an early version thereof, and its reading led to a major reformation in how Torah was understood and practiced.

The Scribal Tradition in Israel

to encode something about the words or verses in or over or around which they were inscribed, something that the scribe would note or remember and communicate as he was declaiming the text. Non-verbal signs were there to communicate extra-verbal meanings.

But—and this is decisive—matters change, especially "when written texts supplant the oral tradition as the main channel of information."[11]

Oral traditions are characteristically in a state of flux; research in oral cultures shows that the alleged antiquity of the tradition does not inhibit its spokesmen from adapting and reshaping it as they see fit. The tradition is the preserve of the specialists who keep and maintain it; the audience is unable to check the version of the performing expert against the original, for there simply is no "original."

Once the knowledge of the experts has been put down in writing, the tradition obtains an existence outside the mind of the initiate. The transition from an oral to a written tradition is neither abrupt nor complete; for centuries the written tradition runs alongside the oral one, the one fructifying and supporting the other and vice versa. Yet at some point the written tradition takes the lead; from that moment on, new experts are formed on the basis of textual instruction. The oral lore does not die, but its authority is subordinate to that of the written texts.[12]

Since the written text has an objective existence outside its producers and consumers, it is a source of authority by itself. Where, before, religious specialists derived their legitimacy from the revelation they possessed in person, they now have to refer to the sum of knowledge laid down in a body of texts.[13]

In other words, when the culture of writing finally superseded the culture of oral performance, the whole understanding of revelation, how the will of God is disclosed to man, changed. It went from being the product of a mantic or visionary experience of a bard-scribe or a prophet to the result of the interpretation of a written text by a qualified reader. Revelation became the province of scribes and scholars; the art of interpretation supplanted the gift of intuition.[14]

By identifying revelation with a circumscribed group of texts, the scribes shifted the focus of the concept. Until then, revelation had been

---

11. van der Toorn, *Scribal Culture*, 206.
12. van der Toorn, *Scribal Culture*, 218.
13. van der Toorn, *Scribal Culture*, 207.
14. van der Toorn, *Scribal Culture*, 207.

understood as an interaction between superhuman beings and human individuals, in which the former imparted knowledge to the latter. In the conception developed by the scribes, revelation became an object rather than an interaction; it was coterminous with a set of texts.

> The consequences of the new concept of revelation have been tremendous. Once the text became a revelation instead of an aid to the expert or an archival record, *it turned into a store of hidden treasure and secret meanings. The scribal doctrine of revelation spawned an exegetical tradition in which the quest for meaning of a text came to resemble an oracular inquiry.*[15]

This was the situation that began to emerge in the last years of the First Temple. The function of the scribe was changing from textual performance to textual interpretation. In the early years of the Second Temple period, the figure who best embodies this shift is Ezra, but between the two Temple periods stands the critical interim era of the Babylonian Exile, the years between 586 BCE, when the First Temple was destroyed by the conquering Babylonians, and ca. 519 BCE, when its successor was rebuilt under Persian auspices. The Babylonian Exile was likely the time and place where the leaders of Israel engaged in a process of consolidating the displaced people's religious and cultural holdings. The key element of that process was quite probably the editing and redaction of the various strands and sources that make up the Pentateuch, and it is not too much to assume that the consonantal text of the five "books" and some of the para-textual elements we are examining here were known by then. Just which ones, we will note when we get to them.

2. THE SCRIBES OF THE SECOND TEMPLE PERIOD

In a classic study of the literary culture of the Second Temple era, Saul Lieberman writes that "according to the Rabbis, the Soferim pursued their literary activity ... during the domination of the Persians over Palestine [539–333 BCE] and the early years of the Hellenistic ascendancy" (after 333 BCE).[16] We know a lot less about the first of these periods than we do about the second. What we do know is that in 538 BCE, after the Persians had conquered Babylon, the Persian emperor Cyrus allowed those exiles

---

15. van der Toorn, *Scribal Culture*, 232. Emphasis mine.
16. Lieberman, *Hellenism in Jewish Palestine*, 26.

who wished to do so to return to their homeland and rebuild their Temple. That homeland, which before the Exile had been the southern kingdom of Judah (*Yehudah*), was now the tiny province of Yehud situated toward the remote western edge of the Persian empire. The returnees who came back from exile were *Yehudim*, whom we now call Jews. We also know that some time during the following century the Persian ruler Artaxerxes called upon Ezra to go to Yehud and help his fellow-Jews re-establish their local religious life. Ezra was a *kohen* and thus a scion of the priestly Temple ranks. But he is also described (in Ezra 7: 6) as a *sofer mahir be-torat moshe* (ספר מהיר בתורת משה), a "scribe expert in the Teaching of Moses [which the LORD God of Israel had given]."[17]

When Ezra arrived in Yehud he had with him a scroll of the Torah (possibly its first edition!). Ezra brought the scroll before the people assembled in the Jerusalem marketplace, and, together with his colleagues, he read it to them, interpreting it as he went along:

> *They read from the scroll of the Teaching of God, translating it and giving the sense; so they understood the reading.* (Neh 8:8)[18]

The text from which Ezra and his colleagues read consisted only of consonants—we see no vowels or any other punctuation in any version of the Pentateuchal text until much, much later. How did they know how to pronounce the words? How did they know that a given word was to be read and vocalized as "x" and not "y"?[19] How did they know where a sentence began and ended? Closer to our purposes, on what basis could they have determined what "the sense" of the text was to begin with?

We are forced to conclude, I think, what critical scholarship and Jewish religious tradition, two approaches to the Bible that are usually at odds, both affirm: that, as van der Toorn has stated, the written text from its inception was informed by an oral tradition, a tradition that determined the meaning of the Torah text by furnishing the following:

17. That same chapter provides a long list of Ezra's ancestors. Among the names is Hilkiah; is this the same Hilkiah who found that scroll in the days of King Josiah?

18. It should be noted that various modern editions render the word "translating" in a great variety of ways.

19. To be sure, Semitic languages are very often written without vowels, and people know how to read them; examples that may be familiar to readers of this book include the average Israeli newspaper and almost any traditional edition of the Mishnah or the Talmud. Still, with a holy text designed for public performance, things are different: in other cases one can misread a word, realize the error later on, and just correct the mistake in one's mind, but public reading of Scripture should be perfect on the first try.

1. vowels for the vocalization of the consonantal words;

2. punctuation of the verses;

3. interpretation or interpretations of the plain sense of the words.

These three prerequisites for oral performance were, at this stage, only oral; they were not written down, not yet.

Related to the third item was a fourth: the marking of specific words or passages whose plain sense was indeterminate or whose presence in the text was deemed problematic or even open to doubt. These markings might include dots over particular words and letters, or a few letters written larger or smaller. Rabbinic tradition ascribes them and their placement in the text to Ezra.[20] The oral tradition may also have preserved a particular understanding of the two verses of the "Song of the Ark" (Num 10:35–36); at some point these were encased in reversed *nuns*.

The Talmud calls all these components of the oral tradition the *masoret* (מסורת, "tradition"),[21] a word that, as we shall presently see, acquired an even broader resonance in the Middle Ages.

We see, then, that from the outset the oral and the written traditions existed symbiotically and synergistically, and their custodians were the *sofrim*. We have in Nehemiah 8:8, at that moment in the Jerusalem marketplace, the first documented moment when the two traditions came together performatively in the communal life of the Jews. It is not too much to say that at that moment Ezra was functioning not only as a *sofer* but as the first rabbi, and that moment of *exegesis*—interpretation of or commentary on the Torah—would energize the Jews and Judaism from then on; it continues in our own time.

The scribal role continued, indeed flourished, after Ezra. An official scroll of the Torah was kept in the archives of the Second Temple. The Mishnah, in listing the things that cannot be done during the intermediate days of Passover or Sukkot, notes:

---

20. The dots are attributed to Ezra in Avot de Rabbi Natan B, chapter 37. The first recension of this text, known as Avot de Rabbi Natan A, chapter 34, and Bamidbar Rabbah 3:13 echo this, but it is not clear whether they are ascribing the dots to Ezra only in Deuteronomy 29:28 or in all ten places in the Torah where they occur.

21. b. Megillah 3a.

> Books [of Scripture] or *tefillin* or *mezuzot* may not be written out during mid-festival, nor may a single letter be corrected, even in the scroll of the Temple court. (m. Mo'ed Qatan 3:4)[22]

Lieberman tells us that

> Although it appears from the earlier rabbinic sources that only one authoritative book was deposited in the [archives of] the Temple, it does not follow that other copies were not to be found there. It means only that this book was the standard copy par excellence, the book, as the Rabbis tell us, from which the scroll of the king was corrected under the supervision of the High Court.[23]

In the light of a passing reference in the Talmud, Lieberman further notes that

> a special college of book readers (מגיהי ספרים, *magihei sefarim*), who drew their fees from the Temple funds, checked the text of the book of the Temple. This was probably the only genuine text which was *legally* authorized for the public service.[24]

* * *

The final triumph of the written word over the oral came after Alexander the Great conquered the Near East (ca. 330 BCE) and disseminated the values of Greek culture, what we call Hellenism. Now a text was written not so much to be performed, but as something to be read in private by any individual with the competence to do so. Now we begin to see the formation of an educated class that read and wrote in ways that we today would recognize. Now the scribal class was not confined to the priests and the Levites in the Temple, who, as custodians of the Torah text, read or could read for the purposes designated by their sacerdotal functions; it extended also to those who specialized in textual matters as they pertained to the public reading of the Torah in the synagogue and, eventually, to those who studied and interpreted it in non-liturgical settings such as the academy. By the time of the destruction of the Second Temple in 70 CE, the scribal enterprise was devoted to producing versions of the Torah that were not only correct in

---

22. An interesting variant reading has "even in the scroll of Ezra."

23. Lieberman, *Hellenism in Jewish Palestine*, 22.

24. Lieberman, *Hellenism in Jewish Palestine*. Emphasis in original. The reference is to b. Ketubot 106a.

their consonantal composition, but also conformed to the usages of scribal tradition as that tradition had evolved over the preceding centuries.

The scribal tradition came to comprise a host of requirements and regulations about all aspects of the scribal craft as they pertained to the writing of a Torah scroll. These regulations specified, for example:

- what kind of writing material—parchment and ink—should be used;
- what kind of Hebrew script should be employed;
- how much space should be left between letters and words and between columns and books;
- how many columns there can be on each sheet of parchment;
- how large or small a Torah scroll can be;
- how one treats a Torah scroll and where one can and cannot place it;
- how to handle errors and erasures of the divine name and other words.

The last item has a direct bearing on the subject of the markings. Consider the plight of a *sofer* who was writing a scroll and came across a word or a letter that did not appear in the same verse in another scroll or scrolls from which he was copying, or which was written differently from it. Did the word or letter in question belong or not? The *sofer* would clearly be reluctant to tamper with the consonantal text that he believed was unalterable since it had emanated from God via Moses at Sinai. If he wanted to do anything at all with the text—correct or emend it, delete it, or emphasize it, or interpret it—scribes back then had no recourse to underlining or italics. The only thing this scribe could do without monkeying with the letters on the scroll was to mark them, again not with vowels that might indicate pronunciation or interpretation, but in special ways that were acceptable. What these ways were depended on what it was the scribe wanted to do with or say about the letters or words or verses he needed to mark, as we shall see in the following chapters. By the late Second Temple period these devices were clearly defined by the emerging rabbinic tradition.[25]

The scribal rules eventually were compiled in a collection called *Massekhet* [Tractate] *Sefer Torah*. Interestingly, this tractate was not included in the Mishnah, the compendium of Jewish teaching that appeared in its

---

25. This is not to say that rabbis had invented them; similar markings, presumably with similar functions, can be found among the Dead Sea Scrolls. See Tov, *Textual Criticism*, 48 (and elsewhere in the book).

final form around 200 CE. We can only speculate why. Perhaps its contents did not concern the mass of Jews but only those who were professional *sofrim*, an elite literate class.[26] Or perhaps this tractate was not formed until after the Mishnah had been redacted.

3. THE SCRIBES OF THE EARLY MIDDLE AGES

As the Middle Ages dawned, the role and function of the professional custodians of the text changed—again. The Torah text was now firmly established, and the scribes' mission now was to safeguard its integrity and preserve the associated traditions.[27] By now, of course, these traditions governed the preparation not only of the scroll but also of the codex.

For those unfamiliar with the difference between the two, an explanation is in order. Scrolls are sheets of parchment, usually written on one side only, sewn together—in the case of Jewish sacred texts with the sinews of kosher animals—and then rolled up. Codices were made by stitching together a group of separate sheets of parchment or papyrus, normally written on both sides, in the form we know today as a book.

Because of the greater convenience (you can put markers in more than one place) and more efficient use of expensive materials (you can write on both sides), the codex format steadily displaced the scroll as the normal format for lengthy written documents. After the Talmudic period it was the codex and not the scroll that became the standard format for the study of sacred texts among the Jews, although the scroll continued to be the format—in traditional environments the only permitted format to this day—for the public reading of the Torah. The codex format had been in use by other groups, especially the Christians, for several centuries by the

26. See b. Berakhot 45b.
27. On the integrity of the proto-Masoretic text, Tov explains,
> The principal component of [the Masoretic text] is that of the letters, evidenced fragmentarily in antiquity in the Judean Desert texts, and to this text all other elements were added during the early Middle Ages. Therefore, although the medieval form of [the Masoretic text] is relatively late, its consonantal framework reflects an ancient tradition that was in existence more than a thousand years earlier in many sources, among them many Judean Desert texts from places other than Qumran, copied in the period between 50 BCE and 115 CE.... Accordingly, scholars usually designate the consonantal base of [the Masoretic text] (evidenced in the Second Temple period) as *proto-Masoretic* although sometimes, anachronistically, also as the Masoretic text (*Textual Criticism of the Hebrew Bible*, 25).

time the Jews had begun to avail themselves of it. Lieberman suggests that the reason Jews resisted the codex for use in the synagogue was precisely to differentiate themselves from the Christians.[28]

At some point in the post-Talmudic geonic period (ca. 700–1000 CE), the rules and regulations that had appeared in Tractate Sefer Torah were collected into a new and larger work, *Massekhet Sofrim*, Tractate Sofrim. This is a compendium of all things scribal and more. The first five chapters repeat and expand on what is in Tractate Sefer Torah; the remaining sixteen chapters cover a host of related matters concerning the writing of Torah scrolls, such as how scribes should handle textual variants and pronunciation, and then they go on to detail the procedures for the public reading of the Torah and haftorahs on Shabbat and various holidays. Tractate Sofrim is also a source for what we are concerned with here. Chapter six lists those passages in the Torah that must be marked in special ways and describes how they should be marked, whether with dots or reversed *nun*s. Chapter nine notes which letters in certain verses are to be written large or small.

As we get into the Middle Ages, we no longer speak of the scholars who specialized in the transmission of Torah text as *sofrim*. That nomenclature was never officially dropped, but now such people are better known as *baʿale masorah* ("masters of the tradition") or Masoretes. The Masoretic project evolved from the work of the *sofrim* as a consolidation of their achievement; this meant systematizing and standardizing once and for all and *in writing* all the details involved in preparing and reading the Torah text: spelling, pronunciation,[29] and so forth. These details had been handed down orally for centuries and at some point were written as brief notes on the margins of scrolls. What the Masoretes did was first and foremost to collect, preserve, and organize these scribal traditions, and this has led many to conclude, not incorrectly, that the word *masoret* or *masorah*

---

28. Lieberman, *Hellenism in Jewish Palestine*, 203–8.

29. An example may help to demonstrate the complexity of this undertaking. The Hebrew root *d-b-r* (דבר) can be formed into a great many words. As a noun, *davar* can mean "word," "thing," or "matter"; with different vowels, the word *devar* means "the word/thing/matter of" and must be associated with a second noun to complete the phrase. As a verb, again with different vowel combinations, the root can mean "lead" or (more usually) "speak." Finally, as though to make things even harder, a linguistically different root consisting of the same letters but pronounced *dever* means "plague," and designated one of the Ten Plagues in the story of Passover. Without written vowels, those who read and interpreted the text simply had to know the correct form for each appearance of a word derived from this root.

derives from the Hebrew verb stem *m-s-r* (מסר), which means "hand over," "pass down," or "transmit."³⁰

There was a lot to preserve and transmit. Yeivin summarizes the Masoretic enterprise in the early Middle Ages:

> Since it was forbidden to add any sort of sign to Torah scrolls, it can be assumed that the notes of the Masorah were at first transmitted orally.... Eventually, however, the Masoretes, who received the masoretic tradition from their teachers, or who possessed various lists of masoretic [scribal] notes, began to write the notes of the Masorah ... in the margins of their codices. As a general rule ... a scribe would write the letters of the biblical text, while a Masorete would add the vowel and accent signs [i.e., point the consonants and place the cantillation signs over or under the syllable to be accented] and the masoretic notes ... The Masorete was also responsible for the correctness of the textual tradition. If the scribe had copied a certain word in one form, and the Masorete found from his notes that the word should be written in another form, he would erase and correct it.³¹

> The Masoretes transmitted their tradition one to another, each generation adding to the material it had received from the last, until the margins of the text were filled with notes on a large number of words in which errors of spelling might easily be made. They worked with reverent devotion to analyze and record all significant details of the textual tradition so as to fix the traditional form of the text, and maintain it unchanged. However, they did not all reach the same conclusion on all points, so that, in the course of time, "schools" which held different opinions were formed. We do not, however, know the reason for the differences between these schools. Presumably, they received their traditions from different sources, or used different compilations of masoretic lists, etc. In any case it seems probably [*sic*] that there never was a single uniform Masorah at any period.³²

Some Masoretic notes were written in the side margins next to the biblical verse to which they referred; others were written in the bottom margin. The Masoretic annotations that appear in the margins at the side

---

30. In Israel today, the Conservative movement calls itself "*masorti*," precisely to identify itself as rooted in *masoret*, the transmitted tradition.

31. Variants were recorded and preserved. In regard to how the Masoretes treated variants of irregularly written letters, see Schnitzer, "'Otiyot Gedolot," 257–65.

32. Yeivin, *Introduction to the Tiberian Masorah*, 123.

of the text comprise the Little Masorah (*masorah qetanah*), those in the top and bottom margins comprise the Big Masorah (*masorah gedolah*).[33]

The dominant Tiberian school of Masoretes was in many ways a family affair. It centered around two families: the Ben Asher family and the Ben Naftali family. We don't know much about the latter; not many of the manuscripts its scribes produced have survived. However, the notes that issued from the Ben Asher scribes at Tiberias and the codices that were based on them became the "gold standard" for fixing the biblical text. So authoritative were these notes that they came to be known as "the Masorah" and the biblical text written in accordance with them came to be known as "the Masoretic text" (often abbreviated as MT). MT was—and is today—regarded as the one that replicates most closely and accurately the original texts, insofar as we can speak of original texts, of the books that comprise the Tanakh.

Scholars on the Masoretes, and on the Ben Ashers in particular, debate a fascinating question: what was it that impelled them to focus so unrelentingly on the minutiae of the Bible's text? After all, it was the Talmud and its exegesis that were the main concern of rabbinic literati at that time. This question has led some scholars to speculate that the Ben Asher family, if not all Masoretes, were Karaites, followers of a Jewish sect that held only the Written Torah was revealed and sacred, while the Rabbanites regarded the Oral (rabbinically derived) Torah as no less divine and authoritative. Arguments have gone back and forth over this question, and the consensus seems to be that Aaron ben Asher was probably not a Karaite; otherwise, why would Maimonides,[34] the quintessential Rabbanite Jew, have endorsed his work as authoritative?[35]

An alternative explanation for the Masoretes' preoccupation with fixing the biblical text is the challenge posed by the other monotheistic religions of the time. As the Christian interpretive tradition was developing,

---

33. These annotations come with a whole apparatus of signs and abbreviations and are not so much read as deciphered, and then only by experts. There is one other kind of Masoretic list that appears at the end of biblical books. It provides all sorts of information about the book; e.g., number of verses, etc. These lists were compiled later than the other two Masorahs and are known collectively as the "Masorah of the conclusion." For further details, see above, p. 5.

34. For more on the Masoretes, the Ben Asher family, and Maimonides, see below, pp. 27–28.

35. We could, of course, also draw the conclusion that the lines dividing the Rabbanites from the Karaites were not as impermeable as we think.

it is possible that a need arose to make sure that the Hebrew text was as authentic and as accurate as possible so as to protect against the danger that Christian theologians would take liberties with it in their interpretations. Islam, for its part, was itself a strongly scripture-based religion; the name of the Karaite sect and the Arabic word *qur'an* are linguistic first cousins. When Muslim experts were busy establishing an authoritative text of their holy book, how could the Jews not do the same?

Aaron Ben Asher is considered the last of the Masoretes. After him masoretic notes on the biblical text began to be written not so much on the margins of codices but collected into separate masoretic handbooks and treatises. There were many of these in the centuries that followed, and they varied in the quantity and the quality of the information they presented. The most comprehensive of these handbooks is a compendium dating from the ninth or tenth centuries entitled *Sefer Okhlah ve-Okhlah*. This is a book of some 400 lists compiled from many of the notes in the Big Masorah that enumerates a vast number of textual details in the Tanakh. I will have more to say about it (including an explanation of its title) when we look at the large and small letters in the Torah. Another important later work that must be mentioned is Eliahu Levita's *Masoret ha-Masoret* ("The Handing Down of the Tradition," 1538).[36]

The title of Levita's work shows us the evolution of the term *masorah*. It had now come to mean

> the whole "philology of the Hebrew Bible," including all the varied activities which go into the transmission of the text (transcription with all its special features, pointing, and the Masora in the narrow sense) [i.e. the marginal notes].[37]

This endeavor has continued down into modernity and proceeds unabated in our time; it has now been enriched by increasingly sophisticated analytical methodologies and by computer technology. Today the study of how the Bible was written and transmitted has been subsumed under the general rubric of textual criticism. In the multi-disciplinary field that contemporary biblical scholarship has become, textual criticism now is but one

---

36. *Sefer Okhlah ve-Okhlah* was edited by Solomon Frensdorf and published in 1864. A facsimile edition was issued by KTAV Publishing House (New York, 1972). *Masoret ha-Masoret* was translated into English by Christian D. Ginsburg and published in 1866 (also by KTAV [New York, 1968]).

37. Würthwein, *Text of the Old Testament*, 10n2.

branch. But it is an important one. Levita's description and prognostication, written nearly five centuries ago, still stands:

> There were hundreds and thousands of Massorites [sic], and they continued generation after generation for many years. No one knows the time when they commenced, nor when they will end in future.[38]

The *sofrim* and the Masoretes were devoted to the production and transmission of the sacred texts upon which Judaism and, in the view of many, the Jews predicated their existence. In the ultimate scheme of things what they did was no less crucial in enabling Judaism and the Jews to negotiate their passage through time and place than what the *kohanim* or the prophets or the rabbis accomplished.

* * *

These are the historical and cultural contexts in which we can consider the unusual markings in the Torah. As we proceed to do so, let me recapitulate:

- The words of the Torah, or at least some of them, were first committed to writing by the early scribes who inscribed them on papyrus or parchment as a script for oral declamation.
- In writing the words down, those scribes marked the text in certain places with a variety of non-lexical signs.
- Those signs were placed in or over or around certain words or verses in order to encode some pre-understood meaning in them or about them.
- These meanings were never recorded, probably because in an oral culture there was neither the need nor the means to do so.
- Later, when the biblical text was written to be read by individual readers, the scribes of those times faithfully made sure that the received textual markings were preserved.
- Later generations of readers, who saw the signs in the written text and did not know what they signified, exercised their interpretive energies and ingenuity to try to uncover the secret meanings.

---

38. Ginsburg, *Masoret ha-Masoret*, 137.

The Scribal Tradition in Israel

And here we are today, the latest generation to receive the written text of the Torah and to ask: what are the stories behind the different kinds of markings in it?

In the next chapter I will tell them.

APPENDIX

One product of the Ben Asher school became pre-eminent, and its story is worth relating here. Around the year 930 CE the venerable scribe Shlomo ben Buya'a wrote out a consonantal text of the entire Tanakh on 491 sheets of parchment. This text was then pointed by the last of the great Tiberian Masoretes, Aaron ben Asher (though a few scholars dispute this), and bound into a codex. At some point this codex was taken to Jerusalem, where it became the model from which other codices and Torah scrolls were proofed and corrected. In the latter half of the twelfth century, Moses Maimonides (1138–1204) saw the codex in Egypt, where it had apparently been taken after the Crusades, and he pronounced it as the definitive version of how a Tanakh should be written and laid out. In fact, when he wrote his grand code of Jewish law, the *Mishneh Torah*, he based his formulation of the laws of the Sefer Torah on it (see below, n. 39). By the end of the fourteenth century the codex was in Aleppo in northern Syria, and it remained there, closely guarded by the Jewish community, until 1947. In that year riots broke out in Aleppo in the wake of the United Nations resolution to create the State of Israel, and the synagogue in which the codex was housed was set on fire. Somehow the codex was rescued, but it was not intact. Of its 491 pages, only 295 survived. It is not known whether the remaining 196 pages, about 40 percent of the total, had been burned, destroyed, looted, or were otherwise missing. This is most regrettable since these pages include most of the five books of Moses. The codex was then hidden in an unknown place and in 1958 was brought to Israel. It is known today as the Aleppo Codex, and it resides now in a parchment-friendly environment in the recesses of the Shrine of the Book at the Israel Museum in Jerusalem. Modern textological analyses and comparisons of it against the oldest available manuscripts of the Tanakh have confirmed Maimonides' assessment of the codex. Yeivin describes it as "superior to any other MS [manuscript] in spelling, in the writing of the songs of the Bible, and in its Masorah [i.e., its marginal notations]. Not only this, but [the Aleppo Codex] is the only one of these [manuscripts] in which the presentation of these features is almost everywhere flawless."[39]

---

39. Yeivin, *Introduction to the Tiberian Masorah*, 16–17. Maimonides refers to what we are now quite certain was the Aleppo Codex in the *Mishneh Torah, Sefer Ahavah, Hilkhot Sefer Torah* 8:4. The Ben-Zvi Institute in Jerusalem maintains an excellent website that provides a detailed account of all aspects of the Aleppo Codex and the Masoretic project. See www.aleppocodex.org. In recent years, two fragments from the missing parts of the Codex have come to light. A family originally from Aleppo now living in New York City discovered that it possessed one page and gave it to the National Library of Israel. And another ex-Aleppian living in the United States somehow came to realize that the small piece of an ancient page that he kept in his wallet as a lucky charm was actually a tiny fragment of the book of Exodus from the Codex! For a full account of the history of the Aleppo Codex, see Tawil and Schneider, *Crown of Aleppo: The Mystery of the Oldest Hebrew Bible*. For a literary memoir of life in the Aleppo Jewish community, while the Codex still resided there, see Sabato, *Aleppo Tales*.

CHAPTER II

The Extraordinary Texts in the Torah

1. CONNECTING THE DOTS

There are ten places in the Torah where we see dots over certain letters and words. The ten places are listed in the accompanying table. Scholars call them *puncta extraordinaria*, or extraordinary points. In Hebrew they are referred to as *nekudot*. They are not to be confused with Hebrew vowel signs; those dots are also called *nekudot* but are not written in Torah scrolls. These dots are written in.

I would imagine that most of the time when we read from a Humash these little dots are not extraordinary at all; we probably don't even notice them. If and when they do happen to attract our attention, we are likely to assume they are the result of some miscue in the production of the printed text of the Humash we are using. Those kinds of things sometimes happen. But if you look at the words or passages in question on a Torah scroll, every letter of which was painstakingly hand-inscribed by a qualified *sofer*, you see that the dots are there as well. And if they are there, it is because they must be part of the text. If they weren't, the scribe would not have included them.

This chapter will explore the possible reasons why they were included and what it is they are doing in or to the text.

We know now that these dots have been there for a long time, possibly for as long as the Torah has been written on scrolls. How far back that goes we can't say for sure, but it could be as early as the First Temple period, before the Babylonian exile that began in 586 BCE.

The truth is that in spite of the fact that our understanding of the biblical period has increased exponentially and impressively in the past century, there is still a lot about the 24-book anthology that is the Bible that we do not know. Such basic questions as how, when, and why many of its books were created are still matters of conjecture. We are talking about a period that spans over a thousand years, from about 1200 BCE, when the entity called Israel begins to appear in Canaan, to about 165 BCE, when the latest parts of the book of Daniel were written. Scholars arrive at that late dating because they believe that those verses in Daniel refer to the Maccabean revolt against the Seleucid kingdom that held sway over Judea at that time.

> ## The Ten Dotted Passages in the Torah (in canonical order)
>
> 1. Genesis 16:5
>
> וַתֹּאמֶר שָׂרַי אֶל־אַבְרָם חֲמָסִי עָלֶיךָ אָנֹכִי נָתַתִּי שִׁפְחָתִי בְּחֵיקֶךָ וַתֵּרֶא כִּי הָרָתָה וָאֵקַל בְּעֵינֶיהָ יִשְׁפֹּט יְהוָה בֵּינִי וּבֵינֶיךָ׃
>
> *And Sarai said to Abram, "The wrong done me is your fault! I myself put my maid in your bosom; now that she sees that she is pregnant, I am lowered in her esteem. The LORD decide between me and you!"*
>
> 2. Genesis 18:9
>
> וַיֹּאמְרוּ אֵלָיו אַיֵּה שָׂרָה אִשְׁתֶּךָ וַיֹּאמֶר הִנֵּה בָאֹהֶל׃
>
> *They said to him, "Where is your wife Sarah?" And he replied, "There, in the tent."*
>
> 3. Genesis 19:33
>
> וַתַּשְׁקֶיןָ אֶת־אֲבִיהֶן יַיִן בַּלַּיְלָה הוּא וַתָּבֹא הַבְּכִירָה וַתִּשְׁכַּב אֶת־אָבִיהָ וְלֹא־יָדַע בְּשִׁכְבָהּ וּבְקוּמָהּ׃
>
> *That night they made their father drink wine, and the older one went in and lay with her father; he did not know when she lay down or when she rose.*

The Extraordinary Texts in the Torah

4. Genesis 33:4

וַיָּ֨רָץ עֵשָׂ֤ו לִקְרָאתוֹ֙ וַֽיְחַבְּקֵ֔הוּ וַיִּפֹּ֥ל עַל־צַוָּארָ֖ו וַׄיִּׄשָּׁׄקֵ֑ׄהׄוּׄ וַיִּבְכּֽוּ׃

And Esau ran to greet him. He embraced him and, falling on his neck, *he kissed him;* and they wept.

5. Genesis 37:12

וַיֵּלְכ֖וּ אֶחָ֑יו לִרְע֛וֹת אֶׄתׄ־צֹ֥אן אֲבִיהֶ֖ם בִּשְׁכֶֽם׃

One time, when his brothers had gone to pasture their father's flock at Shechem,

6. Numbers 3:39

כָּל־פְּקוּדֵ֨י הַלְוִיִּ֜ם אֲשֶׁר֩ פָּקַ֨ד מֹשֶׁ֧ה וְׄאַׄהֲׄרֹ֛ׄןׄ עַל־פִּ֥י יְהוָ֖ה לְמִשְׁפְּחֹתָ֑ם כָּל־זָכָ֗ר מִבֶּן־חֹ֨דֶשׁ֙ וָמַ֔עְלָה שְׁנַ֥יִם וְעֶשְׂרִ֖ים אָֽלֶף׃

All the Levites who were recorded, whom at the LORD's command Moses and *Aaron* recorded by their clans, all the males from the age of one month up, came to 22,000.

7. Numbers 9:10

דַּבֵּ֛ר אֶל־בְּנֵ֥י יִשְׂרָאֵ֖ל לֵאמֹ֑ר אִ֣ישׁ אִ֣ישׁ כִּי־יִהְיֶֽה־טָמֵ֣א ׀ לָנֶ֡פֶשׁ אוֹ֩ בְדֶ֨רֶךְ רְחֹקָ֜הׄ לָכֶ֗ם א֚וֹ לְדֹרֹ֣תֵיכֶ֔ם וְעָ֥שָׂה פֶ֖סַח לַיהוָֽה׃

Speak to the Israelite people saying, When any of you or of your posterity who are defiled by a corpse or are on a *long* journey would offer a Passover sacrifice to the LORD.

8. Numbers 21:30

וַנִּירָ֛ם אָבַ֥ד חֶשְׁבּ֖וֹן עַד־דִּיבֹ֑ן וַנַּשִּׁ֣ים עַד־נֹ֔פַח אֲׄשֶׁ֖ׄרׄ עַד־מֵֽידְבָֽא׃

Yet we have cast them down utterly, Heshbon along with Dibon;
we have wrought desolation at Nophah, *which is* hard by Medeba.

9. Numbers 29:15

וְעִשָּׂר֤וֹן עִשָּׂרוֹן֙ לַכֶּ֣בֶשׂ הָֽאֶחָ֔ד לְאַרְבָּעָ֥ה עָשָׂ֖ר כְּבָשִֽׂים׃

And one-tenth for each of the fourteen lambs . . .

10. Deuteronomy 29:28

הַֽנִּסְתָּרֹ֔ת לַיהוָ֖ה אֱלֹהֵ֑ינוּ וְהַנִּגְלֹ֞ת לָ֤ׄנׄוּׄ וּׄלְׄבָׄנֵ֙ׄיׄנׄוּׄ֙ עַד־עוֹלָ֔ם לַעֲשׂ֕וֹת אֶת־כָּל־דִּבְרֵ֖י הַתּוֹרָ֥ה הַזֹּֽאת׃

Concealed acts concern the LORD our God; but with overt acts, it is for *us and our children* ever to apply all the provisions of this Teaching.

What complicates matters is that at some point during the biblical period ancient Israel underwent the transition from being a culture where information was communicated orally to one of writing and reading.[1] What that transition means regarding the text of the Torah, the five books of Moses, is hard to pin down; as I noted in the introduction, this question has become an important focus for contemporary biblical scholarship.

The uncertainty becomes consequential when we consider the origin of the supralinear dots. Scholars have pretty much established that they are an integral part of the written text of the Torah. *Sofrim* today, those who write Torah scrolls, are careful to make sure they are included. Over the years, two different schools of thought have emerged about the origin and the purpose or meaning of the dots: a text-critical one and a midrashic one.

A text-critical approach to the dots seeks after their historical origin. It assumes that if that origin can be determined, then we will know what the true purpose of the dots is. The scholarship that reflects this approach—it has been going on since the Middle Ages—spends a lot of time and energy trying to find out when and where the dots first show up in the Torah's text. Textual critics do this by comparing the different versions of the Pentateuch that existed in antiquity. They want to see whether the same passages are dotted in all versions, and, if they are, whether the dots appear over exactly the same words and letters. They check the Hebrew version of the Tanakh most respected by Jews then and now, the Masoretic Text (MT), against the Samaritan Pentateuch, the Septuagint (the Greek translation produced by the Jews of Alexandria, c. 250 BCE), the Aramaic and Syriac translations, and against the copies of the biblical books which were found among the Dead Sea Scrolls (written, we believe, between about 250 BCE and 135 CE).[2]

A lot of what this minute analysis has yielded need not concern us here. It is numbingly technical. What is of note is the consensus that the textual critics have pretty much reached about why the dots were put in: they were devised by scribes in the post-biblical Hellenistic period (c. after 300 BCE), centuries after the Torah had become a written text, as a way to indicate erasure,[3] that is, to signal to the reader that the letter or words dotted are *not* part of the text and should not be read or interpreted with it.

---

1. For recent scholarship on the subject, see footnote 5 of chapter 1.
2. [We use the term "Dead Sea Scrolls" here very broadly, to include not only the texts found at Qumran, but also at Masada and in the Bar Kokhba caves (Naḥal Ḥever, Wadi Muraʿabbat, etc.).—eds.]
3. [Or in a few cases, a textual variant.—eds.]

The Extraordinary Texts in the Torah

Figure 1: A portion of the Great Isaiah Scroll (1QIsa^a), cols. 34–37, containing Isaiah 40:28—44:23, found amongst the Dead Sea Scrolls, written c. 100 BCE, as an indication of the ancient Jewish scribal tradition.
[Photo © The Israel Museum, Jerusalem, by Ardon Bar-Hama.]

This conclusion is anchored in the actualities of writing a text on a scroll. Suppose a scribe in antiquity is copying the text of the Torah from a master scroll onto fresh clean parchment. As he works, he sees a problem: some words or letters in the scroll from which he is copying are different from other scrolls or codices he has on hand, or, even more disquieting, those words or letters aren't even in those other scrolls. Are the words or letters in question part of the "official" or "authentic" text of the Torah or not? Since it is the Torah he is writing and not some business document, he is in a bind. He can't not write the questionable words or letters, because if they really do belong in the text of the Torah, they are not subject to his editorial discretion; they are verbal sparks from the divine anvil and cannot be excluded from the sacred text. If the words or letters in question are, in fact, spurious, then they really shouldn't be copied and the error perpetuated.

What would he do? He would write the debatable letters or words, but mark them in such a way that the reader would know that those letters or words are contested. He would put dots over them. Why dots and not dashes or asterisks or some other sign? Because in the scribal training that he received he was taught that that is how letters and words that possibly require deletion are marked.

Somewhat more than a century ago, a scholar named Father Romain Butin helped establish this understanding of the dots. Butin was a French Roman Catholic priest who had come to America in 1890 and wrote his doctoral dissertation (in English) on the whole history of the dots.[4] His work, published in 1906, reads even today as an impressive display of Judaic and classical scholarship. Butin examined the full range of sources in the Talmud and the Midrash and other parts of the corpus of rabbinic literature that discuss the Pentateuchal dots. His analysis led him to reject the idea, put forth by other scholars of his time and before, that the dots had been put in for exegetical reasons. He concludes that they could only have been inserted for one reason: to signal the cancellation or the deletion of textual material that was of questionable provenance. For if they carried interpretive implication:

> We do not see why our present dotted elements should have been selected in preference to so many others. . . .
>
> [T]here were many other places [in the Pentateuch] apparently more important and more likely to attract the attention of the Rabbis.[5]

As for why dots were used to denote deletion and not other signs, Butin believes that this was the device employed for this purpose in the great scribal schools of Alexandria, where the classics of Greek literature were copied and commented on. Jewish scribes in Alexandria and in Eretz-Israel, he says, were much influenced by these schools and their practices. We are talking about the period after 332 BCE when all things Greek permeated the cultures of the Near East in the wake of Alexander the Great's conquests.

Over against this text-critical approach is one that Butin rejects. It holds that the dots are there for midrashic or exegetical reasons. This view is less concerned with determining the precise historical explanation for the dots, though at the same time it is open to the possibility that Jewish scribal traditions go back much earlier than Hellenistic Alexandria. Rabbinic sources tell us that *sofrim* were already writing the Torah in the Persian period (538–333 BCE), i.e., before Alexander the Great. The exegetical or midrashic approach holds that attributing the use of dots in the Torah strictly to signal erasure, as Butin and mainline textual criticism do, overlooks the fact that scribal understandings of some of the dotted passages in the Torah are rooted in very early times, when the Torah was primarily transmitted orally. According to this view, the dots, or some such visual symbol, were put into written versions of that text to remind the scribes or

---

4. Butin, *Ten Nequdoth of the Torah*.
5. Butin, *Ten Nequdoth of the Torah*, 38.

bards who declaimed from it that the words over which they occur required special vocal emphasis because they carried some special meaning. Those words were marked for such emphasis or interpretation much as a musical score is marked with crescendos or slurs or, most appositely, staccato notations. A few centuries later, when a culture of writing had taken hold among the Jews, the dots continued to be written in those places, and the interpretation of what they signaled proliferated beyond the original one, if that original one was even remembered. The dots became a stimulus to apply the energy of the poetic imagination to the text to which they were attached. Such is the conjecture.

I have presented these two approaches as if they were mutually exclusive; the dots are there either to denote deletion or to signal a significant exegetical moment. As we shall see when we look at each of the ten instances of their occurrence in the Torah, this is sometimes the case. But there are places where the opposite is true, and the two approaches are, if anything, mutually inclusive. We will see some dotted passages where the implication of erasure leads directly to the development of a whole range of midrashic possibilities inherent in the text in question. The master antiquarian of the past generation, Saul Lieberman, observes that while the rabbinic *sofrim* of the Hellenistic period did appropriate some scribal practices of their Greek counterparts in the libraries of Alexandria—and he concludes that dots over particular words in the Torah certainly did denote erasure—they did so only in some instances; in others the dots indicated that interpretation was called for. He writes:

> A closer examination of the rabbinic source [sic] will show that the Rabbis did not always treat these dots as a mark of a doubtful reading ... The Rabbis also interpreted the dots not as a sign of spuriousness, but as a mark of an unusual allusion in the passage.[6]

To make this point Lieberman cites various midrashic comments on the passage that describes the enigmatic kiss of Esau in Genesis 33:4. I will look at that passage and those comments in detail later in this chapter. Lieberman adds importantly that "It is in exactly the same spirit that the rabbis interpreted the dots in many other instances ... [as] signs calling for special interpretation."[7]

---

6. Lieberman, *Hellenism in Jewish Palestine*, 45.
7. Lieberman, *Hellenism in Jewish Palestine*, 45–46.

The versions of various biblical books that were found among the Dead Sea Scrolls confirm Lieberman's opinion. While no scrolls have been found that contain any of the ten Pentateuchal passages where we could look for, and maybe expect to find, the scribal dots, many others, such as some scrolls of the Nevi'im (Prophets) and Ketuvim (Writings), do show them. It is clear that they are employed there for a variety of purposes, including to signal deletion.[8]

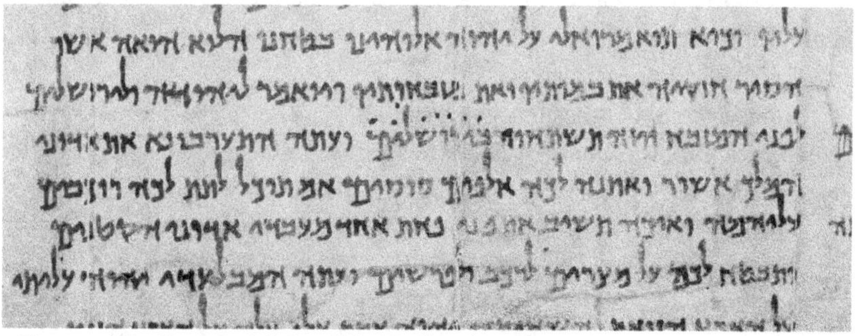

Figure 2: The Great Isaiah Scroll (1QIsaª), col. 29, written c. 100 BCE, with line 10 (the third line in this image), including the dots above the word בירושלים in Isaiah 36:7. The word is missing in the later Masoretic text, as adumbrated here by the dotted letters, indicating that the word was written in error and should be deleted.
[Photo © The Israel Museum, Jerusalem, by Ardon Bar-Hama]

All this having been noted, can we say which one of the two approaches to the dots, the critical-historical and the midrashic-exegetical, is more correct, more accurately accounts for and more truly comprehends them? A lot of important issues are tied up in this question and they are very much worth exploring; that exploration appears in the epilogue to this book.[9] But now we are ready to look at the ten dotted passages in detail and learn the specific story each one tells. In my treatment of them I will pitch the discussion in two very different keys and give both approaches their due.

8. See Talmon, "Prolegomenon," xviii–xxv.
9. [Alas, the epilogue never was written.—eds.].

The Extraordinary Texts in the Torah

* * *

The ten dotted words and passages occur at various places in the Torah. Another glance at the list will show that a full five of these instances are in Genesis, four are in Numbers, and one is in Deuteronomy. There are none in Exodus or Leviticus.[10] Sometimes the dots range over several words in a verse, sometimes over just one word, and sometimes over just one letter. In Genesis they occur in narrative verses; in Numbers they occur in narrative, law, poetry, and a list of sacrificial details, as befits the potpourri of textual genres that we find in that book. The lone Deuteronomy occurrence is in a provocative verse that seems to be a stand-alone statement among the utterances of Moses.

The ten dotted sites also vary widely in their interpretive possibilities. Some invite, and in some cases require, close textual analysis so as to clarify their plain sense, while some are quite straightforward in their meaning. Some have attracted a lot of midrashic attention over the centuries, some have not. In his commentary on the Torah, Rashi remarks on six of the ten cases.[11] Evidently he concluded that not all of them were deserving of elucidation or interpretive elaboration. I would agree with him on this, though my choice of the six would be different.

In the succeeding pages I will treat all ten dotted passages, but I have placed them in two groups. The first group consists of six sites, each of which in my view offers a rich field of midrash and implication. I separate the remaining four sites because, compared to the other six, to my mind they are rather pedestrian in their dotted content. They involve nothing more than fussing over technical particularities of Hebrew grammar and syntax or quibbling over other trifling details. I include them for the reader who can read Hebrew and who has some appetite for linguistic pedantry (both will be necessary). The reader who does not, or who lacks the inclination, may wish to skip them.

For the first group I will:

---

10. Could this fact have any bearing on the scribal transmission of the individual books of the Pentateuch? [We believe that Rabbi Diamond had the following in mind: could one scribal tradition (which countenanced the dotted letters) be responsible for Genesis and Numbers, and another scribal tradition (which did not recognize this technique) be responsible for Exodus and Leviticus—with Deuteronomy representing the midpoint in some way?—eds.]

11. See Rashi on Genesis 18:9; 19:33; 33:4; 37:12; Numbers 9:10; and Deuteronomy 29:28. Rashi, an acronym for Rabbi Shelomo Yitzhaqi (1040–1105), was the dominant commentator on Bible and Talmud in the Middle Ages.

1. set the context in which it occurs;
2. note how textual criticism understands it;
3. look at what the midrash and other rabbinic sources do with it;
4. suggest the particular issue or issues which I think that verse or passage raises from a contemporary perspective.

For the second group only the first three steps are possible. I invite the reader so inclined to propose a fourth step for any of them.

In the Hebrew citation of the passages, the dot or dots are shown exactly where the Masoretic text says they should be placed. (For an image with one example, see Figure 3 on Deuteronomy 29:28.) As I will repeatedly note, there are several cases of non-Masoretic textual traditions where the dots fall over different words and letters from what the Masoretic text shows. In the English renderings, I have used a different typeface to represent the dotted Hebrew word or phrase. I would advise the reader of this book to have handy the full text in both Hebrew and English as it appears in a modern edition of the Pentateuch.

1. Genesis 16:5 — A Marital Quarrel

וַתֹּאמֶר שָׂרַי אֶל־אַבְרָם חֲמָסִי עָלֶיךָ אָנֹכִי נָתַתִּי שִׁפְחָתִי בְּחֵיקֶךָ וַתֵּרֶא כִּי
הָרָתָה וָאֵקַל בְּעֵינֶיהָ יִשְׁפֹּט יְהוָה בֵּינִי וּבֵינֶיךָ׃

And Sarai said to Abram, "The wrong done me is your fault! I myself put my maid in your bosom; now that she sees that she is pregnant, I am lowered in her esteem. The LORD decide between *me* and *you!"*

The Context: We are here in the midst of a domestic quarrel. Sarai (she is not yet Sarah) and Abram (he is not yet Abraham) are living with the tension of unfulfilled expectations. They have been in the Promised Land for ten years, and the promised heirs who will inherit that land have not materialized. Sarai's childlessness weighs heavily on her. Fearing that her infertility is her fault, Sarai proposes that Abram take her maid Hagar as a surrogate mother so the divine promise can be realized through her. Abram promptly obliges and, presto, Hagar is pregnant (from their very first sexual encounter, as Rashi, citing a midrashic tradition, observes).

Fertility was a status symbol for women in those days, as it still is in some non-western societies, and Hagar flaunts her newly attained motherhood before Sarai. The power balance between the two women has shifted, and Sarai is hurt. Now feeling victimized, she goes to her husband and vents her anger at him. "This is all your fault," she says, and appeals in this verse to God to adjudicate her claim.

Textual Criticism: Practitioners of this kind of biblical scholarship note that not all ancient sources are agreed about the dotting in the last word of the verse. Some sources point the whole word with dots, thus וּבֵינֶיךָ; some the first *yod*, thus וּבֵינֶיךָ; and some the last two letters, i.e., the second *yod* and the final *kof*, thus וּבֵינֶיךָ. (Such comparative analysis is a staple in the scholarly treatment of all ten dotted passages or words.)

The consensus is that the Masoretic text that we have is correct and that only one dot should appear over the second *yod*. The dot is there to tell us that the *yod* beneath it should be deleted, and the last word of the verse should read וּבֵינְךָ (*u-venkha*), and not וּבֵינֶיךָ (*u-venekha*).

What's the difference? It's a matter of correct Hebrew form. The word set בֵּינִי וּבֵינְךָ (*beni u-venkha*) means "between me and you," with "you" in the singular: just between me and you. If, however, the second word is spelled וּבֵינֶיךָ (*u-venekha*) as the Masoretic text has it, this implies that the "you" is plural, i.e., "between me and you" plural. Grammatically this would be incorrect, for if the plural were truly to be indicated, the word form would be וּבֵינֵיכֶם (*u-venekhem*) So the dot in וּבֵינֶיךָ is there to tell us to delete that second *yod* and go ahead and read וּבֵינְךָ (*u-venkha*, "between me and you"), singular.

Why? What meaning could be achieved by this orthographical alteration?

We can propose a literary meaning, one that reads the verse as reflecting the stylistics of biblical Hebrew poetry. The essence of such style is a parallelism between the constituent parts of the verse. Deleting the *yod* from וּבֵינֶיךָ to read וּבֵינְךָ would produce a visual parallelism between the four words in the verse that end with a second-person suffix:

ותאמר שרי אל אברם חמסי עליך אנכי נתתי שפחתי בחיקך
ותרא כי הרתה ואקל בעיניה ישפט יהוה ביני וביניך

This visual parallelism would complement the assonantal parallelism.[12]

Midrashic Perspectives: The midrashic compilation Sifre Bamidbar[13] advances an explanation rooted in the dynamics of a marital squabble.

---

12. This was suggested to me by Herbert Levine.

13. Sifre Bamidbar section 69, on Numbers 9:10. This source lists and succinctly tries to explicate all ten dotted passages. All references to Sifre are from here. I recognize, of

Sarai here is demanding that God judge whose fault it is that Hagar is demeaning her former mistress. Is it Abram's or her own (Sarai's)? Dropping the second *yod* suggests that Sarai wants God to judge only on the single issue of Hagar and not with reference to other women or to other factors that may have precipitated this strife between her and her husband, such as the two wife-sister episodes (Gen 12:10–20; 20). Those events would surely have left a residue of resentment in Sarai's mind over the way her husband, acting purely in his own self-interest, had put her at risk.

Another Midrash[14] elaborates on what Sifre states. It supposes that the heated exchange between Sarai and Abram goes something like this:

> Sarai: Since she's now lording it over me, let Hagar revert to her former maidservant status.
>
> Abram: No. We can't. Now that we've made Hagar a co-wife with you, to diminish her status would be disgraceful. It would be a *ḥillul ha-Shem* (a desecration of God's name).
>
> Sarai: So let HaShem[15] decide!

And HaShem decides, or seems to decide. Just as later, when God says, "whatever Sarah tells you, do what she says" (Gen 21:12), it is in reference to Hagar, so, too, here it is in reference to Hagar.

And so in the very next verse Abram tells this to Sarai: "Your maid is in your hands. Deal with her as you think right" (Gen 16:6). Case closed. Sarai very quickly comes down hard on Hagar, and Hagar leaves.

What Can We Make of This? It is painful to watch a married couple argue. In his commentary on Genesis, Robert Alter observes that Sarai's words to Abram comprise her "first reported speech [and it] is a complaint about her childlessness."[16] This enables us to catch early on the tension that simmers beneath the idealized surface of this iconic marriage. It will boil up later (Gen 18:10–15) when Sarah laughs to herself—scoffs is what she really does—at the notion that her husband could impregnate her in their dotage. The divine messenger, cognizant of Sarah's unarticulated cynicism, then asks Abraham why Sarah laughed. We do not know whom Sarah

---

course, that there is also Sifre Devarim (Deuteronomy), which I have not had occasion to cite in this book.

14. Midrash Mishle (on the book of Proverbs) 26:24.

15. [That is, God, using a Hebrew circumlocution, which literally means "the Name."—eds.]

16. Alter, *Five Books of Moses*, 77.

answers—Abraham or the messenger—but whoever it is, she is not straight with him; she denies that she even laughed, and the messenger calls her on this. Then, still later (Gen 21:9–14), when Isaac is born, there is more strain in the household. Sarah insists that Abraham throw out Hagar and Ishmael. Abraham acquiesces.

I should think that polygamous marriage is intrinsically suffused with sexual tension and competitiveness between the wives. But monogamous couples, too, sometimes have to deal with "the other woman" or "the other man." The dots in this verse raise the question whether, when husband and wife are at odds with each other over fidelity, this is the only issue between them or whether there other deeper problems involved. Perhaps we may say that in any major marital argument there are dots over what lies "between me and you."

2. Genesis 18:9—The Hidden Question

וַיֹּאמְר֤וּ אֵלָיו֙ אַיֵּ֖ה שָׂרָ֣ה אִשְׁתֶּ֑ךָ וַיֹּ֖אמֶר הִנֵּ֥ה בָאֹֽהֶל׃

They said to him, "Where is your wife Sarah?" And he replied, "There, in the tent."

The Context: Abraham, his name now enlarged literally and figuratively, is sitting at the entrance to his tent at the heat of the day, when three visitors appear before him. The scorching noonday Negev desert sun beats down. Graciously, Abraham invites them to sit down in the shade of a tree and refresh themselves with water and some food. They wait as he runs into the tent to instruct Sarah, her name also now changed, to throw together a quick meal for the guests. This is done speedily, and lunch is served. The three guests dine while Abraham hovers over them in the manner of a solicitous waiter who will inevitably ask, "Is everything ok?" Except that the visitors pre-empt him and put to their host the question the verse records. Abraham gives them the answer.

Textual Criticism: The Masoretic text has it that three of the four letters in the word אֵלָיו have dots above them: the *'aleph*, the *yod*, and the *vav*. But other versions and sources vary widely in where they say the dots should be placed. Some have them over all four letters, some over two of the four, and some present still other possibilities. If the dots indicate erasure, the permutations of possible words that emerge from the letters that remain are many. They need not concern us. Let's just go with the Masoretic text and say that the three dotted letters here should be deleted and the remaining *lamed* should disappear along with them for good measure.[17] The whole word אליו should thus be cancelled, and the verse, now more compact, retains the same meaning. Or we could take the vestigial *lamed* and hook it up with the final *vav* of ויאמרו, "and they said," to read ויאמר לו, "and he said to him."[18] Again, the meaning of the verse would not be changed; the only difference would be the shift from plural speakers to a single speaker. Instead of "they," the three angelic visitors inquiring of Abraham where Sarah is, it is "he," the main angel who asks, as is the case in the very next verse.

Midrashic Perspectives: The Midrash Bereshit Rabbah offers a pragmatic way to proceed when we are confronted, as we are here, with a word in which only some of its letters are dotted. Rabbi Shim'on ben Elazar says that when the number of dotted letters exceeds the number of those that are not dotted, we first delete the undotted letter(s) and then make sense of the letters that remain by unscrambling them into a word. Conversely, when the undotted letters outnumber the dotted ones, we delete the dotted letters and construe something out of the undotted ones. By this reckoning, in the verse we are concerned with here, the former situation obtains; there are more dotted letters than undotted ones. Accordingly, we delete the undotted *lamed* and what's left, namely the *'aleph*, the *yod*, and the *vav*, can be combined to produce the word איו (*'ayyo*), which means "where is he?"[19]

What the dots, then, ultimately come to tell us is that there was an additional question the visitors put to Abraham besides the one about Sarah's whereabouts (איה שרה אשתך, "where is your wife Sarah?"). The second question, here only hinted at, was addressed to Sarah about Abraham's whereabouts: איו (*'ayyo*, "where is he?"). That is what the Midrash suggests the dots here tell us.

Now if these visitors are really angels traveling incognito as human beings, these questions are puzzling. Unlike people, angels don't ask silly questions. Why would they ask Abraham where Sarah is? Being angels, wouldn't they know where she is? And why would they ask Sarah where Abraham is? After all, he was right there talking to them, was he not? The rabbis suggest two possibilities:

---

17. [Presumably the *lamed* does not have the dot above it because this single letter in the Hebrew alphabet has a height to it, with its upper portion extending above the line.—eds.]

18. So Butin, *Ten Nequdoth of the Torah*, 64.

19. Bereshit Rabbah 48:15; and Rashi on Genesis 18:9.

The Extraordinary Texts in the Torah

1. The angels knew where Sarah was, but they asked about her anyway as a matter of etiquette, for a polite guest always should ask about his hostess. And about his host, too, for they inquired of Sarah about Abraham for the same reason.

2. The angels knew where Sarah was but they asked about her anyway, so that Abraham, in telling them where she was, would realize again and appreciate anew his wife's modesty in not making a public spectacle of herself.[20]

The Zohar pitches this whole exchange in another key entirely. It reads this incident, as it does all the narratives in Genesis, as a re-enactment on the human level of the dynamics of events in the supernal realm of the *sefirot*, the nodal points that embody the various attributes that emanate from the unknowable God.[21]

The Zohar follows the Midrash in seeing not one but two questions here, one explicit, one only implicit. But it hears them differently. The question suggested by the dots, איו (*'ayyo*, "where is he?") does not refer to Abraham at all. Rather, the supralinear "dotted letters איו [are] a symbol alluding to that which lies above, alluding to the blessed Holy One."[22] The angels are not asking where Abraham is—presumably they know that—but where is God, where is holiness, in this house. More precisely, "since איו (*alef, yod, vav*) is dotted, why is it followed by איה (*'ayyeh*), *where*? Because of [the] union of male and female as one."[23] In his commentary on the Zohar, Daniel Matt explains:

> The final letter of איה (*ayyeh*) "*where*," is ה (*he*), often a feminine marker, so the two questions allude to the divine couple, *Tif'eret* and *Shekhinah*, whose union constitutes the mystery of faith.[24]

And so, when Abraham answers the visitors by saying הנה באהל (*hinneh ba-' ohel*, "there, in the tent"),

---

20. Rashi on Genesis 18:9, and b. Bava Meṣiʻa' 87a.

21. [The Zohar (thirteenth century CE) is the most important text of the Kabbalah, or Jewish mysticism. In essence, it is a running commentary on the entire Torah. The term *sefirot* refers to the emanations from God, according to the mystical tradition.—eds.]

22. Zohar 1:101b . Translation by Matt, *Zohar*, 125.

23. Matt, *Zohar*, 125.

24. Matt, *Zohar*, 125n71.

he is really telling them that the tent, the home that he and Sarah have built, is the "all-encompassing nexus."[25] It embodies the fullness of the sefirotic energy system as the Zohar conceives of it, the flow of the masculine *Tif'eret* into the feminine *Shekhinah*. And the Zohar inter-textually links the tent here with the tent referred to in Isaiah 33:20:

> *When you gaze upon Zion, our city of assembly,*
> *Your eyes shall behold Jerusalem*
> *As a secure homestead,*
> *A tent not to be transported,*
> *Whose pegs shall never be pulled up,*
> *And none of whose ropes shall break.*

This reading is in line with the Kabbalistic idea that this human reality, the "lower world," is integrally connected to the supernal "upper world" of the divine emanations. What we do here not only reflects what is done there; it influences it.

What Can We Make of This? It is not readily apparent why or how the word אליו here got dots in the first place. The issues emanating from the text-critical approach to this dotted word seem trivial. Similarly, the midrashic take on this yields only the banality that guests should inquire into the welfare of both host and hostess.

The Zohar's reading is more interesting. "Where is He?" is a nice question to put to couples by a rabbi at a pre-marital interview. But it would hardly be appropriate for anyone else to ask it of a couple or to ask it in any other context.

3. Genesis 19:33—What Went On in the Cave

וַתַּשְׁקֶיןָ אֶת־אֲבִיהֶן יַיִן בַּלַּיְלָה הוּא וַתָּבֹא הַבְּכִירָה וַתִּשְׁכַּב אֶת־אָבִיהָ וְלֹא־יָדַע בְּשִׁכְבָהּ וּבְקוּמָהּ:

That night they made their father drink wine, and the older one went in and lay with her father; he did not know when she lay down or when she rose.

The Context: Sodom and Gomorrah and the other cities of the plain have been totally destroyed. Lot and his two daughters wander alone in a silent, smoldering landscape. It is as if the world has ended. They become cave-dwellers. Thinking they are the last humans on earth, the daughters

---

25. Matt, *Zohar*, 125.

conclude that the only way to perpetuate the race is to have their father inseminate them. But how to get him to do that? They concoct a plan: ply their father with wine, lie with him, and let nature take its course. The women indeed supply the wine and, as the verse tells us, the older one goes first.

Textual Criticism: Most sources indicate that there is one dot in the last word of the verse and that it is placed over the second *vav* in the word thus: וּבְקוּמָהּ (*u-v-qumah*, "when she arose"). Sifre has it that all the letters in the word וּבְקוּמָהּ should be dotted.

Now if erasure is the issue here, what exactly is to be erased? If the dots are over all the letters (though according to some views even if they are over just one letter), then the whole word is, as scholars put it, to be "condemned" or "annulled." If the dot is only over the second *vav*, then it is that *vav* that should be erased and the word would be written without it thus: ובקמה, instead of ובקומה. The difference, as can be seen, is over which vowel point should be used to represent the /oo/ sound. This spelling does not change the meaning of the word or its pronunciation and is common enough in Hebrew usage. Scholars call the shorter version *defectiva* (חסר, literally "missing," in Hebrew) and the former version *plene* (מלא, literally "full," in Hebrew). Writing the word "defective" in our verse (v. 33) would make its appearance parallel with how the same word is written in the verse about the second daughter (v. 35).

What different meanings accrue from these possible erasures? If we drop the word ובקומה in its entirety, the verse would say that Lot was too drunk that night to know that his first daughter lay down with him. It would say nothing about her getting up in the morning or Lot's awareness of that. If, however, we read the verse with the whole word ובקומה retained, it would be explicit that Lot was oblivious at both times: he did not know when she came to bed with him or when she got up.

We are clearly dealing with linguistic minutiae here, yet they are not trivial. They make all the difference in how we are to understand what Lot knew about what went on between him and his two daughters and when he knew it. As we ponder the verse as we have it in the Masoretic text with its one dotted letter, we wonder: Where do text-critical considerations stop and midrashic interpretations begin? It is hard to tell. Text-criticism does not address the human issues, here or anywhere for that matter. It is concerned only with variant readings, possible erasure, and how the dots play out syntactically and grammatically.

Midrashic Perspectives: We would expect that midrashic reading would go further and explore the larger import of the dot or dots in this verse. The classical midrashim here disappoint. Sifre, which, as we have noted, sees dots over all the letters of the word ובקומה, explains them with one laconic comment: The dots serve to tell us that Lot did not know when his eldest daughter lay down, but he did know when she got up.[26] And it leaves it at that. One wants to hear more about this qualification of what the verse is saying. Did Lot at some point during the night sober up? What is the implication of this shift in his awareness, his not knowing what transpired when his daughter got into bed with him but his awareness of her leaving in the morning? How does this shift in his awareness of what happened on the first night with the elder daughter relate to what took place on the very next night with her younger sister?

The Talmud supplies an answer by developing Sifre's interpretation. If the dot is there to suggest that Lot knew when his elder daughter left in the morning, then he would or should have realized what had transpired. He should have taken instruction from it and been wary when the next night the daughters convened another "happy hour" and the drinking started again.[27] But he didn't, and the same thing happened with the younger one. The dot in its wider import serves, then, to confirm Lot's moral deficiency and leads to the upshot of the whole story: the moral depravity of the ancestors of the Moabites and the Ammonites, Israel's neighbors.

There is another current of opinion that takes a more sympathetic and positive view of what on the surface looks like a sordid tale. Midrash Śekhel Ṭov, a late (twelfth century) collection, expands on the Talmud's spin on the dot and combines it with an idea in Bereshit Rabbah to offer a wholly different construction of the consequences of Lot's knowledge of when the elder daughter arose. According to this interpretation the daughters hatched the plan to have sex with their father out of laudable motives: they wanted to re-populate the world. But being virgins, they had to make sure they would each conceive from the very first penetration. And so they perforated their hymens. On the first night Lot, who was on automatic pilot at the initiation of coitus, came to consciousness upon ejaculation. It was at that point that he saw what had happened as his daughter got up from under him.[28] And

---

26. Likewise Bereshit Rabbah and Bamidbar Rabbah, though they indicate that only the *vav* is dotted.

27. b. Nazir 23a.

28. Buber, *Midrash Śekhel Ṭov*, 40. See also Bereshit Rabbah 51:9.

yet, as the Talmud has it, he failed to stay away from the next night's "cocktail hour" and the ensuing activities. These copulations, though incestuous, were *le-shem shamayim*, "for the sake of Heaven." The two boys who issued from them were the eponymous ancestors of Moab and Ammon, both of whom eventually produce the Messiah. For the book of Ruth informs us that the Davidic line—and by extension according to later Jewish tradition the Messiah—stems from the union between Ruth the Moabitess and Boaz (Ruth 4:13–22), while the book of Kings informs us that Solomon's son and successor Rehoboam was born unto Na'amah, an Ammonite woman (1 Kgs 14:21). Hence, the conception of Moab and Ammon, as recorded in the book of Genesis, was, in the total scheme of things, a salutary event.

The Zohar echoes this interpretation with an even more redemptive reading of the dotted *vav* in ובקומה. The *vav* is

> dotted above, [to signify] supernal assistance attending that act, from which King Messiah was destined to issue, so here *vav* is included. Concerning the other [the younger daughter], it is written ובקמה (*uvqumah*) *or her rising* (v. 35)—lacking *vav* since from her a share of the blessed Holy One did not issue, like the other [the elder]. So concerning the other, older one, it is written ובקומה (*uvqumah*), *or her rising*, with a *vav* dotted above.[29]

Matt, elaborating on this dispossession of Lot's younger daughter, writes that the second *vav* in the word ובקומה is a:

> letter of the divine name ... [and] is dotted ... [to] imply divine assistance. God approved and encouraged this apparently sinful act, since the Davidic Messiah is destined to descend from Ruth the Moabite[30]
>
> According to one view, the Messiah is descended not from Na'amah and Solomon's son Rehoboam but from a different son of David.[31]

What Can We Make of This? Read in one context, this is a nasty story designed to impugn the character of two neighboring peoples whose

---

29. Zohar 1:110b, for which see Matt, *Zohar*, 160.

30. Matt, *Zohar*, 160n339.

31. Matt, *Zohar*, 160n340. [One wonders if such a statement does not constitute an anti-Christian polemic, since the better known of the two genealogies of Jesus in the New Testament specifically mentions Solomon and Rehoboam as ancestors of Jesus (Matt 1:7). The alternative tradition recorded in Luke 3:31, interestingly, lists David's son Nathan and his son Mattatha as the ancestors of Jesus.—eds.]

cultural practices were a constant temptation and a threat to Israel's religious integrity. It could evoke a wry smile in some contemporary readers. But what else can we find in it? A statement about incest? Perhaps. But there's another issue in the story that resonates even more strongly in our society, and that is the connection between intoxication and sex. The culture of the one-night stand and the drunken hook-up invites us to explore this connection and the issues it raises.

As it is told, this story of sex between Lot and his daughters foregrounds the matter of knowledge. The daughters have to get their father drunk in order to have him copulate with them. He has to not know who they are if he is going to do the deed. And so the text stresses that his cognitive faculties were impaired, and that they were impaired by alcohol. It is interesting that the verb for knowing that is used here ידע (*yada'*) is the same verb the Bible uses for the sexual act, as in:

וְהָאָדָם יָדַע אֶת־חַוָּה אִשְׁתּוֹ וַתַּהַר וַתֵּלֶד אֶת־קַיִן

> *Now the man knew his wife Eve, and she conceived and bore Cain.* (Gen 4:1)

Alter, ever attentive to the nuances of the text, writes that:

> the Hebrew verb suggests intimate knowledge and hence sexual possession. Amos Funkenstein notes that it is the one term for sexual intercourse associated with legitimate possession—and in a few antithetical instances, with perverse violation of legitimate possession.[32]

Equally instructive is Nahum Sarna's comment that "the verb is never employed for animal copulation . . . 'Knowing' in the Bible is not essentially intellectual activity . . . Rather, it is experiential, emotional, and, above all, relational."[33]

The sexual intercourse between Lot and his daughters was not animal copulation. But it might as well have been, for there was no knowledge of the kind Sarna and Alter describe in their comments.

This biblical perspective on the relationship between sexual activity and unclouded perception should be seen in contrast to the Dionysian element in Greek culture. Dionysus, in later Roman mythology Bacchus,

---

32. Alter, *Five Books of Moses*, 29. As an example of the latter, consider Genesis 9:24, וַיִּיקֶץ נֹחַ מִיֵּינוֹ וַיֵּדַע אֵת אֲשֶׁר־עָשָׂה־לוֹ בְּנוֹ הַקָּטָן, "And Noah woke up from his wine and learned [lit. "knew"] what his youngest son had done to him."

33. Sarna, *Genesis*, 31.

embodies a divinity that privileges ecstasy as the fundamental human experience and the combination of wine and sex as the catalysts for it. This in contrast to Apollo, the god of light and clarity. Nineteenth-century classical scholarship saw the forces embodied by these two figures in binary opposition. Judaism seeks to harmonize them. The traditional Jewish Shabbat experience seems to acknowledge and make room for the Dionysian. We are bidden to drink wine at the evening meal, following which married couples are enjoined to engage in conjugal sex. But I would opine that on the whole Judaism is more Apollonian in its approach to sex and alcohol.

4. Genesis 33:4—A Kiss Is Still a Kiss

וַיָּרָץ עֵשָׂו לִקְרָאתוֹ וַיְחַבְּקֵהוּ וַיִּפֹּל עַל־צַוָּארָו וַיִּשָּׁקֵהוּ וַיִּבְכּוּ׃

And Esau ran to greet him. He embraced him and, falling on his neck, he kissed him; and they wept.

The Context: I have outlined the context of this verse in the introduction. We are at the tense climax of the confrontation between Jacob and Esau, who are meeting up after having been separated from each other for twenty years. The dots over the word וַיִּשָּׁקֵהוּ (*vayyishaqehu*, "and he kissed him") call attention to the kiss and invite us to ponder it.

Textual Criticism: The obvious critical view would be to regard the dots, which here are over all the six letters of the word וַיִּשָּׁקֵהוּ (*vayyishaqehu*), as indicating that the entire word is to be deleted. This is plausible, the logic being that it is possible to say that the verb is out of sequence in the verse and really belongs immediately after וַיְחַבְּקֵהוּ (*vayehabeqehu*, "and he embraced him")—an embrace and a kiss. But if we do not or cannot emend the verse by re-locating the problematical word, then deletion is in order: there simply was no kiss. Esau embraced Jacob, fell on his neck, and the two estranged brothers, now re-united, wept. Not an unreasonable reading.

But all early translations preserve the pointed word and the kiss that it narrates, which would argue for the integrity of the Masoretic text.[34] Which means that in this verse the word in its entirety belongs, and the dots here probably do not signify deletion but are there strictly for exegetical reasons. The issue, then, is not to dismiss the kiss as implausible in the context in which it is told, but to accept it and try to understand it.

---

34. Talmon, "Prolegomenon," xii.

Midrashic Perspectives: The Rabbis take on this task with gusto and, as we might expect, offer a host of interpretations. The basic question for them is not whether Esau kissed his brother, but whether the kiss was sincere. Those who say that it was not see the dots as coming to indicate just that. In other words, the dots are there to signal to the reader not to read what is being told at face value. Rabbi Yannai, in Midrash Bereshit Rabbah, goes further: the kiss was not a kiss but a bite, or an attempt to bite. He notes the linguistic affinity in Hebrew between the verbal stem נ-שׁ-ק (*n-sh-q*, "kiss") and the similar sounding verbal root נ-שׁ-ך (*n-sh-k*, "bite"). This implicitly suggests that the word וַיִּשָּׁקֵהוּ (*vayyishaqehu*, "and he kissed him") is dotted to hint that what is really meant is וַיִּשָּׁכֵהוּ (*vayyishakkehu*, "and he bit him").[35] But, he says, Esau didn't succeed. Jacob's neck miraculously turned to ivory, and Esau broke his teeth. And *that* is why each one was crying: they were both in pain—one over his teeth, one over his neck![36]

Then there are those who argue the reverse. In the words of R. Shimon bar Yohai in Sifre, "it is known that Esau hated Jacob, but at that particular moment compassion overcame him and he kissed him with all his heart." The kiss is dotted to show precisely that this climactic encounter was a transformational one, both for Esau and for Jacob. A grudge of twenty years evaporated in that instant.

What Can We Make of This? R. Shimon's reading is remarkable in two respects. It goes against the general way Esau is constructed in rabbinic literature, and in so doing it offers a refreshingly encouraging view of what human beings can achieve.

The rabbis were not inclined to see good in Esau. They develop what Genesis gives us of him—a macho deerhunter of a man ruled by his emotions and appetites—into the prototype of the Gentile (whereas in Jacob they see the quintessential Jew: bookish and shrewd, a student in the Yeshiva of Shem and Ever, who lived by his wits). Esau was the progenitor of the neighboring tribe of Edom, and Edom in rabbinic mythology becomes the progenitor of Rome and, by historical extension, the Christian West. It is clear that in reading the fateful meeting of the two brothers, they are projecting onto it their own psychological, historical, and cultural sensibilities and sensitivities.

---

35. There is no indication that *ketiv-qere*, where a word is to be written with one spelling and read with the other, applies here, especially since it is indicated two words later for the word צוארו.

36. Bereshit Rabbah 78:9. See also Ba'al HaTurim on Genesis 33:4.

But Esau as Genesis presents him is hardly so malevolent. True, he was angry at Jacob after the latter had filched the birthright from him—who could blame him?—but it's not at all clear that he's out for blood here. One could read Esau's proactive running toward Jacob and initiating the embrace not as an attack, but as the culmination of a long-standing desire on Esau's part to let bygones be bygones and to reconcile with his brother. That is how the medieval commentator Abraham ibn Ezra, very much in line with R. Shimon bar Yohai, sees it. He dismisses R. Yannai's interpretation of the dots as infantile ("fit for those just weaned from the breast") and insists that we simply read what's written. He takes the last word of the verse ויבכו (*wayivku*, "and they wept") at face value and connects it to another situation where brothers overcame past enmity and wept on each other's neck—when Joseph revealed himself. Why, ibn Ezra suggests, is this weeping any less sincere than that one?[37]

I find in R. Shimon's interpretation of Esau's kiss something even more intriguing: the idea that it was transformational. Let's examine what made it so. Assume that as he headed toward the meeting, Esau was not really sure of what he would do or what he wanted to do. We can well appreciate that he would have had some ambivalence. Could he, would he overcome years of resentment? Was he ready to do that? It was a serious emotional dilemma, for what you think and how you feel about someone predisposes you to how you will act toward them. The thought is the father of the deed, intention the mother of action.

Not necessarily. Not always. Sometimes what we do prefigures what we think, and a specific deed can influence how we feel. R. Shimon bar Yohai uncovers the emotional dynamics that underlay Esau's kiss. He is suggesting that in acting against the ambivalence in his heart and mind, Esau precipitated a revolution in his own consciousness. The kiss transformed him, and Jacob, too, and that is why, if you look closely at the verse you will see that the verb "and he kissed him" is in the singular. Esau kissed Jacob, Jacob did not reciprocate—and yet the verb "and they wept" is in the plural.[38] Notice also, then, that the verbs in the verse are in exactly the right sequence. The brothers, who moments before were tense and conflicted, wind up crying on each other's neck.

---

37. Ibn Ezra on Genesis 33:4. He is referring to Genesis 45:14–15: "With that he embraced his brother Benjamin around the neck and wept, and Benjamin wept on his neck. He kissed all his brothers and wept upon them."

38. This is pointed out by Hakohen, *'Al HaTorah*, 108.

Read this way, this is one of the great moments in the Bible. It shows us that not only can relationships be repaired, but that in all of life what we do is ultimately more decisive than what we think or how we feel. Judaism, with its burden of *mitzvot ma'asiyot,* specific things we are commanded to *do,* rests upon this insight. Actions, what we actually do, are the catalyst for the capacity Judaism imputes to us to change what is in our hearts and minds.

5. Numbers 9:10—How Far is Far?

דַּבֵּר אֶל־בְּנֵי יִשְׂרָאֵל לֵאמֹר
אִישׁ אִישׁ כִּי־יִהְיֶה־טָמֵא ׀ לָנֶפֶשׁ אוֹ בְדֶרֶךְ רְחֹקָה לָכֶם
אוֹ לְדֹרֹתֵיכֶם וְעָשָׂה פֶסַח לַיהוָה׃

Speak to the Israelite people saying,
When any of you or of your posterity who are defiled by a corpse or
are on a long journey would offer a Passover sacrifice to the LORD.

The Context: The Israelites' march into the desert is about to begin, but one important matter must be attended to: the observance of the Passover. It had been celebrated the year before in Egypt, on the night of the Exodus, but then it was, for the one and only time, an actuality. Now for the first time, the Israelites had to do what the Jews have been doing ever since: commemorate the historical event by re-enacting the Passover sacrifice. A question arises: what about those who had come into contact with a corpse and were thus in a state of ritual impurity? Could they partake in and of the Passover sacrifice or did their impure status disqualify them from participating in the observance? Moses is stumped and says that on this matter he has to consult God. (Remember: only Moses had that kind of access.)

The word comes down: those who are impure or are away from home on a journey must sit this Passover out and observe it one month later. We should note that the problem in the wilderness that provoked the promulgation of the law of the second Passover in the first place was ritual impurity. The incident as it is told in vv. 6–7 says nothing about being away on a long journey. That stipulation comes only in the law when it is handed down, as expressed in our verse. Jacob Milgrom notes that the law "applies to [later] conditions in the settled land (v. 10)."[39]

---

39. Milgrom, *Numbers,* 68.

The Extraordinary Texts in the Torah

Textual Criticism: The majority of rabbinic texts reflect the Masoretic text with the dot over the last letter of the word רחקה (*reḥoqa*, "long," i.e., "distant"); hence, they would read it as רחק (*raḥoq*). Other sources either dot all the letters in the word, or place the dot over other letters in the word, or simply delete the dot.[40] But clearly, the Masoretic text is widely accepted.

Midrashic Perspectives: So if we read the text as בדרך רחק, "on a long journey" (or "far away"), does this change the meaning of the verse? Not at all. The specific word in the Masoretic text, whether it takes the form רחק or רחקה, remains an adjective meaning "far, distant"—the only difference between the two forms is simply one of gender. The shorter form רחק, without the *he*, is the masculine form; the longer form רחקה, with the letter *he*, is the feminine form. The salient question for the midrashist is: what noun does רחק modify? There are two possibilities:

1. It could modify the noun that immediately precedes it, דרך (*derek*, "journey" or "way"). Either form (רחקה or רחק) would work because this noun, unlike most in Hebrew, can have either gender.[41] Erasing the *he* would have no effect on the meaning of the verse; it would still mean what it means in the translation given: *When any of you or of your posterity who are defiled by a corpse or are on a distant journey.*

2. Alternately, if we drop the *he* and read רחק, the masculine form of the adjective, it could conceivably modify the masculine noun איש, literally "man" or "person," which as רחקה it could not. The text would now mean something like: *When any of you or of your posterity are distant [or at a distance], having been defiled by a corpse, or [are] on a journey, [and] would offer a Passover sacrifice to the LORD . . .*

The issue here is what does "distant" (רחק) mean or imply? Milgrom writes that:

> this passage presumes that the paschal sacrifice must be offered at the one authorized sanctuary: the Tabernacle or, once Israel is settled in its land, its legitimate successor. Only this assumption renders plausible the contingency that someone on a journey is not able to offer the sacrifice (vv. 10, 13). For if multiplicity of altars were assumed, then the journeyer would simply turn to the closest altar in order to fulfill the requirement of the paschal sacrifice.[42]

---

40. For details, see Butin, *Ten Nequdoth of the Torah*, 84.
41. For the masculine, see Deuteronomy 17:16; for the feminine, see Exodus 18:20.
42. Milgrom, *Numbers*, 372.

And so "distant," as Milgrom explains it, seems to mean distant from the Temple. The question then is: to be distant from the Temple, how far away geographically from Jerusalem did one have to be on the 14th day of Nisan, when the Passover fell and the obligation to offer the sacrifice took hold? Or perhaps being "distant" is a function not of space *per se* but of the person, in which case the question becomes: what state was the man in that prevented or disqualified him from offering up the Passover sacrifice on the 15th of Nisan?

There is a debate about this in m. Pesaḥim 9:2. Rabbi Akiva says "distant" is spatial. The word רחק in our verse means how far a person who was not in Jerusalem could walk and still get to the Temple during the hours when the Passover sacrifice was being offered. Those hours were from midday until sunset, so assuming people normally traveled during the daylight hours, the maximum distance needed to be traversed would be a half day's walk. In the Mishnah Rabbi Akiva formulates this as the distance from Jerusalem to the village of Modi'in (about 28 kilometers or 16.8 miles) in any direction.

Rabbi Eliezer, however, holds that "distant" has nothing specifically to do with space. To him it means that anyone who was beyond the threshold of the Temple *for whatever reason* at the time the Paschal sacrifice was offered up would have to do the offering a month later. A person, for example, who was in a state of impurity for whatever reason, whether from defilement by a corpse or anything else, would be disqualified even if he were situated on the Temple's very doorstep because he could not enter into its precincts. In Rabbi Eliezer's scheme of things distance has to do with the person, not with physical propinquity to or remoteness from the Temple. And the *he* in רחקה is dotted to make just that point, says Rabbi Yosi. Sifre concurs: "although the distance be short, if the man is defiled he should not offer the Passover with the others." In other words, as Butin explains, "If he is [ritually] defiled the distance matters little, for he himself is morally remote, and cannot celebrate the Passover."[43]

Jewish law, however, upholds Rabbi Akiva's opinion. The phrase בדרך רחקה, "on a long journey," is understood as being a half-day's walk from Jerusalem.[44]

---

43. Butin, *Ten Nequdoth of the Torah*, 86.

44. [The matter is discussed further in b. Pesaḥim 93b. For additional material, see Lieberman, *Tosefta ki-Fshuṭah*, 619; and Maimonides, *Mishneh Torah, Sefer Qorbanot, Hilkhot Qorban Pesaḥ*, 5:8.—eds.]

What Can We Make of This? The issues that this biblical verse and the ensuing Mishnaic debate present are relevant not only for our understanding of the Jewish past but also for our ongoing attempt to comprehend the realities of the Jewish present. Consider the whole notion of there being a second Passover. In the Torah the Passover sacrifice is the only holiday ritual that, if it cannot be celebrated at its proper time, can be made up—indeed, must be made up. If an Israelite, and later on a Jew, cannot celebrate Shabbat, Yom Kippur, Sukkot, or Shavu'ot—well, that's regrettable, but the opportunity once lost is gone forever. But with Passover the Torah mandates a second chance, indeed requires it. Here contingencies are taken into consideration, such as being impure or far away at the time of the sacrifice. For Passover is the covenantal holiday, the moment a Jew affirms his or her essential belonging to the people redeemed from Egypt.

The issues of belonging and being far away from Jewish life and its institutions are very much with us in our time, especially in view of the extreme mobility of our society and the processes of suburbanization and exurbanization. Like the rabbis, we too struggle with how spatial distance affects belonging to the Jewish community and its institutions and participating in the key moments of Jewish time. The question of how we define distance is as immediate now as it was then. Is distance a physical matter determined by how far one lives from a synagogue or from areas where the Jewish community is concentrated? Or is distance a function of the subjective state of the individual in question, a matter measured not by the odometer but by the intensity of feelings of alienation or connection?

In the Mishnah the *halakha* falls on the side of Rabbi Akiva, and distance is defined in spatial terms. This has some resonance today, for we know that the further one lives from the Jewish community and its institutions, the more attenuated one's Jewish identity can become. The language of Judaism expresses itself in the first person plural—consider Jewish liturgy—and to try to speak it only in the first person singular will produce a strange discourse. Yet this is not the whole story. I know a family in the South which lived, for professional reasons, an hour and a half from Atlanta. For years they drove their three children to Sunday school and Shabbat and holiday services there. Now grown, all three children live substantial Jewish lives and are active leaders in their Jewish communities. And I also know families and individuals who live a block from a synagogue or close to a Jewish community center and have never once gone in to check out what might be going on there.

Scribal Secrets

For this reason I think that both understandings of distance that the Mishnah preserves are there for us to consider—that distance can be either objectively geographical or subjectively attitudinal. Both have a claim on our concern as we look out at the many Jews who for whatever reason are far away from Jews and Judaism. The dot in the word רחקה asks us to be mindful that when it comes to belonging and involvement in Jewish life, distance is not an absolute term but *relative* and *contingent*. When opportunities for connection are missed for whatever reason, the first time around is not the only opportunity.

6. Deuteronomy 29:28—The Revealed and the Hidden

הַנִּסְתָּרֹת לַיהוָה אֱלֹהֵינוּ וְהַנִּגְלֹת לָנוּ וּלְבָנֵינוּ עַד־עוֹלָם לַעֲשׂוֹת אֶת־כָּל־דִּבְרֵי הַתּוֹרָה הַזֹּאת׃

Concealed acts concern the LORD our God; but with overt acts, it is for us and our children ever to apply all the provisions of this Teaching.[45]

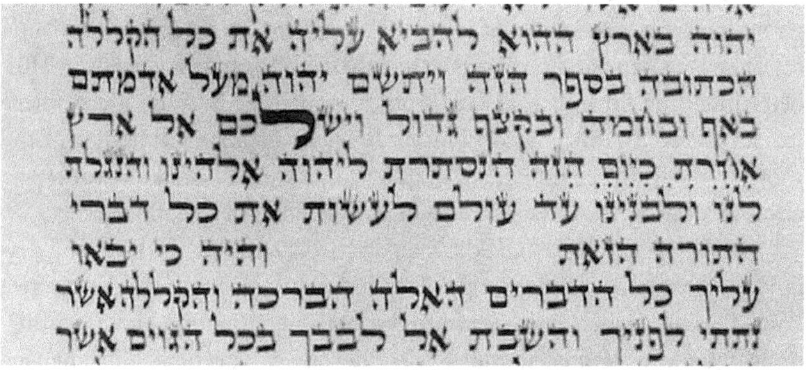

Figure 3: Deuteronomy 29:28 as represented in a contemporary Torah scroll. Note the dots above the letters לנו ולבנינו and above the following ע. This image also appears later, as Figure 10, regarding the large letter *lamed* in the preceding verse.
[Torah scroll by scribe Rabbi Gustavo Surazski.
Scroll image courtesy of Temple Aliyah, Needham, Mass.]

45. [In the discussion which follows, the author reflects the consensus of modern Jewish editions of the Torah with eleven dotted letters in this verse, as seen previously: over each of the letters in the two words לנו ולבנינו and then, somewhat oddly, over the *ayin* of the next word עַד. In the two great medieval codices (Aleppo and St. Petersburg [Leningrad]), however, only the ten letters of the two main words bear the supralinear dots.—eds.]

The Extraordinary Texts in the Torah

The Context: This verse's context is not easily established. Moses is in the middle of his third and last farewell speech, preparing the people for a ceremony in which they will be initiated into the covenant (a ceremony that never gets narrated). This verse, the last in the chapter, seems discontinuous with what has come before and with the rest of the speech (chapter 31).

W. Gunther Plaut thinks that the verse "is not connected to the preceding and appears to be a later insertion."[46] He notes that in the verses that come immediately before this one Moses speaks of the Israelites in the third person ("The LORD uprooted them from their soil" [v. 27]), but here he talks to them in the first person plural ("It is for us and our children to apply"). This would suggest that this is a stand-alone verse.[47] Robert Alter felicitously calls it a "gnomic declaration."[48]

Textual Criticism: The verse is a crux. It is not only its context that is problematical; its plain sense, its *peshat*, is too. To what do הַנִּסְתָּרֹת (*ha-nistarot*) and הַנִּגְלֹת (*ha-niglot*) refer? The NJV translation given previously renders them respectively as "concealed acts" and "revealed acts," but there is nothing in these words that suggests that they necessarily refer to acts. Alter translates them as "things hidden" and "things revealed," which gives the verse a rather different range of implication. Until we establish the *peshat* and the context in which it is said, we cannot even begin to consider the purpose of the eleven dots—regardless of whatever meaning we assign to the verse.

If we read the verse in the context of what Moses tells the people back in verse 17 ("Perchance there is among you some man or woman, or some clan or tribe, whose heart is even now turning away from the LORD our God),″ we see that the issue of secret apostasy is being raised. And so our verse (v. 28), in which Moses again addresses the people in the first person plural, harks back to the earlier one and adds to it. In his commentary on Deuteronomy, Jeffrey Tigay understands it this way:

> Apparently Moses is here [in v. 28] assuring the people, who have heard how the private schemes of one man (vv. 17–20) may lead to the destruction of the entire land (vv. 20–27), that this does not mean that they will be held collectively responsible for sins

---

46. Plaut, *Torah*, 1375.

47. Butin, *Ten Nequdoth of the Torah*, 100, remarks that whether these words are an interpolation or not, "the verse was accepted as genuine when the *Nequdoth* [dots] were placed." Otherwise there would be dots over the whole verse.

48. Alter, *Five Books of Moses*, 1026.

committed by individuals in secret. God will punish those and will hold the people responsible only if they fail to punish sins of whose commission they are aware.[49]

Read thus the verse looks like a statement of the one of the obligations entailed by the covenant into which the people are about to enter.

But then, what about the dots? How do they impinge on this reading? Tigay writes:

> Ancient scribes commonly used such dots to indicate corrections, usually to delete the words thus marked, but there is nothing obviously questionable about the dotted words in this verse.[50]

Be that as it may, there is in fact something questionable about some of the other words in Deuteronomy 29:28. This can be clarified by reviewing the various attempts at a midrashic approach to this enigmatic verse.

Midrashic Perspectives: The Talmud's discussion (b. Sanhedrin 43b) of the verse is terse to the point of being unclear. I will try to flesh it out. The rabbis assume that the verse is talking about *sins* committed by Israel both covertly (הנסתרות, *ha-nistarot*) and publicly (הנגלות, *ha-niglot*). They understand the verse in its plain sense to be saying that the responsibility for punishing covert or "hidden" sins is God's; overt or "revealed" sins are the responsibility of the whole community ("for us and our children"—the words with the dots above the letters), for which they are culpable. How the dots modify this meaning is debated. R. Yehuda holds that the dots come to qualify how and when secret transgressions are punished. Before the Israelites crossed the Jordan such offences were the domain of God. After all, God, being God, would know of them even if no one else did, and He would deal with the offenders. But after the people had crossed the Jordan and the covenant ceremony presumably would have occurred, the responsibilities incumbent on a nation living in its land would be assumed, and private sins would be punished by the community (along with those committed publicly). That is what the dots teach.

R. Nehemiah agrees that sins committed covertly are the province of God, but he understands the verse to be saying that this was and is true at all times, before and after the crossing of the Jordan. In his view the dots pertain not to private but to public sins. What they serve to qualify is when the people are held responsible for them. Before the crossing of the Jordan

---

49. Tigay, *Deuteronomy*, 283.
50. Tigay, *Deuteronomy*, 283.

they were not, just as they were not culpable for sins done in secret; after the crossing public sins were their responsibility. That is the force of the dots.

The problem with these interpretations is that neither of their proponents explains exactly how the dots serve to produce them. It is left to the major commentators to try to work this out. Both R. Yehuda and R. Nehemiah seem to agree that since the dots over עַד וּלְבָנֵינוּ לָנוּ ("for us and our children") extend only up to the first letter of the word עַד ("until"), an exegetical point can be ferreted out: the dots delimit the point at which communal exemption from punishment for sins committed in private ended and the whole people became liable for them (R. Yehuda) or the point at which communal exemption from punishment for public sins ended and the whole people became liable for them (R. Nehemiah). That point was when the Israelites crossed the Jordan and came into the Promised Land. Were these respective exemptions permanent the dots would have continued over both words עַד עוֹלָם ("until forever").

R. Yehuda's view seems to imply that the extent of God's jurisdiction over *nistarot*, that is, hidden sins, is being modified. Accordingly, the dots should really fall over the words ליהוה אלהינו ("concerning the Lord our God"). But, the major commentators suggest, it is not appropriate to dot words that refer to God. Instead, the dots intended for these words were displaced onto the words עַד וּלְבָנֵינוּ לָנוּ ("for us and our children"—with one additional letter), where they serve to modify the time frame: the community is first exempt from liability for the *nistarot* and then becomes liable for them. We can prove that there is such displacement from the number of dots—eleven—and from the curious way they stop in the middle of the word עַד. This is exactly the number of letters in the words ליהוה אלהינו.[51]

In contrast to this labored reading of the exegetical force of the dots is the rather straightforward one of Sifre. Sifre reads the verse as referring not to sins covert or public and their punishment, but to what Moses is foregrounding as he addresses the people: the *mitzvot*, the commandments that Israel must fulfill as its part of the covenant. To Sifre the *nistarot* are "the hidden things" and *niglot* are "the things revealed" to the people. The plain sense of the verse thus is that though the hidden things are God's province, it is for Israel לעשות את כל דברי התורה הזאת, "to apply all the provisions/words of this [revealed] Teaching." The dots qualify this assertion

---

51. So Tosafot's accounting for how the dots work according to R. Yehuda's interpretation, b. Sanhedrin 43b, s.v. *melammed*. On the Tosafot, see below, n. 55.

by turning it into a stipulation of what will accrue to the people of Israel when they fulfill the Torah:

> God is saying to them [in this verse]: when you will have fulfilled the things that are revealed, then I will also make known to you the things that are concealed.

This strikes me as a perfectly appropriate midrashic move. The dots assist the rabbis in parsing an extremely opaque verse.[52]

Butin, however, in his late nineteenth century positivistic fervor, cannot countenance any interpretation that accords any exegetical function to the dots. He states that the Sifre passage, "I will also make known to you things that are concealed,"

> clearly indicates that the הנסתרות [ha-nistarot] as well as the הנגלות [ha-niglot] will belong to us and our children. If so, we should refer הנסתרות to לנו ולבנינו "for us and our children" and leave out the two divine names ליהוה אלהינו "the Lord our God".[53]

With this erasure the verse should properly read:

הנסתרות והנגלות לנו ולבנינו עד עולם לעשות את כל דברי התורה הזאת

Concealed acts and overt acts are for us and our children to apply forever all the provisions of this Teaching.

Such a reading, he acknowledges, would be unthinkable. How could a scribe erase, or even consider erasing, words that denote the Deity? On no account would a scribe remove them from the Torah text. Instead he would put dots over them. "The words ליהוה אלהינו are virtually non-existent and the Points stigmatize them."[54] But even that would be problematical, for, as the Tosafot observed,[55] how could words relating to God be stigmatized? Butin then adduces Tosafot's explanation of the displacement of the eleven dots onto the words לנו ולבנינו עד as the true reason for the pointing of the

---

52. Avot de Rabbi Natan, recension B (known as ARN B), seems to read the verse in a wider context. "The *niglot* refer to what we know in this world, the *nistarot*, known now only to God, will become known to us in the world to come." How this meaning is derived from the dots in unclear because the text itself is unclear.

53. Butin, *Ten Nequdoth of the Torah*, 102.

54. Butin, *Ten Nequdoth of the Torah*, 103.

55. [The Tosafot, "Supplements," are a compilation of further commentary on the Talmudic text produced by Rashi's disciples and descendants in twelfth-century France.—eds.]

The Extraordinary Texts in the Torah

'ayin ("alone") in עד.⁵⁶ An exegetical explanation for the dots in this difficult verse is thus conscripted by Butin to serve his *idée fixe* that supralinear dots are placed for one reason and one reason only: to signal the "condemnation" or "cancellation" or "annulment" of words or letters that really don't belong in the text.⁵⁷

The key issue from which all these interpretations flow is the fundamental indeterminacy of the verse's plain sense. Although they never say so, the rabbis were as puzzled by it as we are. We can hear this perplexity in an encounter they imagine between Ezra, whom they regarded as the most authoritative of the scribes, and the prophet Elijah, who, in rabbinic literature, always seems to show up for important conversations. In the rabbinic mind it was Ezra who wrote this verse and inserted the dots in it. Why he did so is explained in the following colloquy:

> Ezra reasoned thus: If the prophet Elijah were to come and ask me, "Why have you written them [these letters and words]?" I will reply, "That is why I put dots over them." And if he says to me, "You have done well to write them," then I shall erase the dots over them.⁵⁸

This hypothetical dialogue, I think, bespeaks something more than a confusion over the exegetical import of the dotted words. It suggests—masks—an uneasiness about the possibility that some words in this verse don't belong and need to be excised from the text. The rabbis do not have Elijah asking Ezra, "Why have you put dots over these letters and words?" They have him asking, "Why have you written those letters and words in the first place?" And if Elijah agrees that those letters and words do indeed belong, then it is the dots that are erased. We can debate what the letters and words in question are—whether they are the ones that the Masoretes

---

56. Butin, *Ten Nequdoth of the Torah*, 103. Butin lamely adds that "The reason that לנו ולבנינו has been chosen to replace ליהוה אלהינו, is probably due to the fact that, as לנו ולבנינו is to take the place of ליהוה אלהינו in interpretation, they should also be substituted for them in receiving the points."

57. Amongst classical Jewish sources, the only composition that explicitly speaks of erasure is Midrash Leqaḥ Ṭov, a late collection (late eleventh to early twelfth centuries). It follows the reading of the verse of b. Sanhedrin 43b and says that the words "לנו ולבנינו are dotted as if they do not exist" (cited in Butin, *Ten Nequdoth of the Torah*, 104 and 130; see also Talmon, "Prolegomenon," xvii).

58. Bamidbar Rabbah 3:13 and repeated in Avot de Rabbi Natan, recension A (ARN A), chapter 34. The parallel passage in the second recension (ARN B) seems to ascribe all the dotted letters and words in the Torah to Ezra.

say should be dotted, לנו ולבנינו ע, or whether they are, as Butin claims, the ones over which the eleven dots really belong: ליהוה אלהינו. This dialogue suggests that the issue that concerned the rabbis was not the one the various midrashic sources address—the exegetical import of the dots—but the issue of erasure and all that might imply both for the meaning of the verse and the very nature of the Torah's text. Butin's tendentiousness in manipulating Sifre's statement notwithstanding, erasure may well be what the dots here are indicating.

What Can We Make of This? In what context can we read this verse today? Determining this is no less a challenge for us than it was for the rabbis. They placed the verse in the covenantal moment the Israelites were approaching as they were about to cross the Jordan, and it was in that context that they explicated the *nistarot* and the *niglot*.

I think that if we are to read the verse within its biblical context, we do better when we see it as a distillation of the general outlook of the book of Deuteronomy, in which, after all, it occurs. Deuteronomy highlights the Torah and its written text as the *raison d'être* and the ground of Israelite existence. The Deuteronomist, in an artful act of textual ventriloquism, has Moses repeatedly emphasizing the concrete, operational nature of the teaching he has brought to his people. This is clearly articulated when, towards the end of his summarizing speeches, he says:

> Surely this Instruction which I enjoin upon you this day is not too baffling for you, nor is it beyond reach. It is not in the heavens, that you should say, "Who among us can go up to heaven and get it for us and impart it to us, that we may observe it?" Neither is it beyond the sea, that you should say, "Who among us can cross to the other side of the sea and get it for us and impart it to us, that we may observe it?" No, the thing is very close to you, in your mouth and in your heart, to observe it. (Deut 30:11–14)

Torah here is something accessible, lived out in the here-and-now. It is not something arcane or esoteric. Our verse is an earlier part of that same speech and deserves to be read within its conceptual framework. Accordingly, the *nistarot*, "hidden things," do not really need to be defined. Whatever they may be, they are not of human concern; they are irrelevant. What is of human concern are the *niglot*, the revealed particulars of the Torah. It is these that need concern us, that are primary in our lives and the lives of our children. That is why the words והנגלת לנו ולבנינו עד עולם are dotted: *it is* for us and our children *ever to apply all the provisions of this Teaching.*

The epigrammatic nature of our verse, its integrity as a stand-alone statement, invites us to ponder it and its dotted words in a wider context. The verse can be read as a statement about human knowledge—its limits and its possibilities. The plain sense is that the *nistarot* are what God knows, the *niglot* what humans can know. These appear to be two separate cognitive realms. The question is whether they really are separate. As the millennia pass and human intelligence operates on and with what it knows, and science progresses, do the boundaries between the two realms get rolled back? Does what was once known only to the divine mind become part of acquired human knowledge? Do the things hidden from us now, the *nistarot*, become over time the *niglot*, the things human intelligence has made known?

The dots and their placement and displacement suggest that this is exactly what happens. Because there are eleven of them, it seems clear that the dots really were placed over the words ליהוה אלהינו ("the Lord our God."). They were there to emphasize that the hidden things belong to God. But when displaced onto the human side of the binary that underlies the verse, they sit over the words לנו ולבנינו עד and thereby indicate that what was once the province of God is now known to humans.

Is God, so to speak, erased from the verse? Does human endeavor gradually encroach upon and ultimately usurp the divine realm? The question is open and will be until Elijah comes and tells us where the dots belong.

* * *

The following four passages, as noted previously (p. 38), are limited in their interpretive possibilities and range of implication.

7. Genesis 37:12—Grammar Matters

וַיֵּלְכוּ אֶחָיו לִרְעוֹת אֶת־צֹאן אֲבִיהֶם בִּשְׁכֶם׃

One time, when his brothers had gone to pasture [OBJECT MARKER][59] *their father's flock at Shechem.*

The Context: This verse comes early in the story of Joseph and his brothers. The brothers are already jealous of Joseph, for their father has

---

59. [A grammatical object marker appears here in the Hebrew text; see the ensuing discussion.—eds.]

made no secret of his favoritism. The two dreams that Joseph has told them have only served to feed their resentment. Now the brothers have departed with the family sheep to Shechem—without their younger brother.

Textual Criticism: Unlike some of the other dotted words and passages, where there is disagreement over where exactly the dots should be placed, here there is consensus among the sources that the dots fall only over the word את (*'et*). How this would affect our understanding of the verse entails a little excursion into some fine points of Hebrew grammar.

Much as I would like to, I cannot translate the word את. If you know Hebrew, you know that this word—or better, this grammatical particle[60]— has no equivalent in English. It is a usage that occurs only in Hebrew and some related Semitic languages. It carries no meaning and functions only in conjunction with a word that is in the accusative, i.e., the direct object of a verb. More specifically, in Hebrew, it functions when the direct object is definite, for example, it is preceded by the definite article ה- (*ha-*, "the"). Hence, when you see את, you know that the word which immediately follows is the object of whatever verb has preceded it. But here's the problem: at times in Hebrew the particle את is simply omitted, especially in poetry, but even in prose texts occasionally.

Now, in the text as we see it, "their father's flock" is the direct object of the verb "to pasture." If dots come to indicate erasure, and the את disappears, what does this do to the meaning of the verse? Is צאן אביהם (*ṣo'n 'avihem*, "their father's flock") no longer the direct object of the verb לרעות (*lirʿot*, "to pasture")?

So we would think. But not necessarily. Apparently there were some early versions of Genesis that somehow omitted the את (see the previous comment regarding the occasional non-use of this particle), and later scribes concluded that its legitimacy in the text was questionable. Hence it was retained but dotted. Talmon writes that "although the word was handed down in the text, it should not be pronounced in the official reading of the Law."[61] To my knowledge it is nowhere noted in handbooks for Torah readers that this or any other dotted word in the Torah is not to be read in the public reading. I therefore understand Talmon's words as a suggestion made out of scholarly responsibility.

---

60. Thus the technical term for את (*'et*). Hebraists frequently use the Latin term *nota accusativi* to describe it more specifically.

61. Talmon, "Prolegomenon," xiv.

But still, the question of the meaning of the verse *without* the את remains. We could read it as if the את were still there and continue to see "their father's flock" as the object of the verb "to pasture." This would be jarring to an ear attuned to normal Hebrew usage (though again, see prior comment), but are there not bigger problems to deal with in our imperfect world? On the other hand, the deletion of the את or the presence of dots over it could arouse our exegetical impulses. Irregular usages or unusual textual features do that, or, at least, they did for the rabbis.

Midrashic Perspectives: Sifre has what seems like a strange explanation for the dotted אֹת: it is there to tell us that the brothers did not go to Shechem to pasture, i.e., feed, the family sheep, but rather to feed themselves. All the other midrashic collections repeat this or say virtually the same thing. What prompts them to say that?

The dotted word אֹת raises their eyebrows. If it weren't dotted, they would read the verse like most other verses in the Torah: in its normal, grammatical sense. If the את weren't there at all, they would read the verse likewise and gloss over the irregular Hebrew usage. But a dotted אֹת calls attention to itself. It raises the possibility that the word is dubious, and this, in turn, opens up the possibility for a completely different way to construe the verse and what it is telling us. If the את is to be deleted, then צאן אביהם is not the direct object of the verb לרעות. That verb now can be construed as *intransitive*, i.e., it has no object, and a whole new configuration of the verse comes into view (putting the English comma to good use here):

וילכו אחיו לרעות, צאן אביהם בשכם

The brother went to feed, their father's sheep being in Shechem.

The verb לרעות can mean both "to pasture" or "to feed" (transitive, such as to pasture one's sheep) or "to graze" (intransitive), generally used in reference to sheep or livestock.[62] In reading the verse this way the brothers are implicitly compared to animals. If we were to render it colloquially we might say that "the brothers went to feed their faces." This is the self-indulgent situation in which Joseph will find them, and it is not hard to imagine why, when he does appear, the stage is set for their sinful conduct.

In any case we now can see how the rabbis get to the explanation they give for the dotted word את. Presumably they are not too concerned about

---

62. See, for example, Genesis 41:18, where the seven healthy cows וַתִּרְעֶינָה בָּאָחוּ ("grazed in the reed grass").

the way the re-configuration of the verse relegates the latter clause "their father's sheep being in Shechem" to irrelevance.

Midrash Sekhel Tov obviates this problem by reading the verse in an altogether different way. It sees את not as a particle but as a preposition, the equivalent of the Hebrew word עם ("with"). This is not as arbitrary as it might sound, for indeed את can bear this meaning. In fact, earlier in our chapter, at Genesis 37:2, את is used in precisely this way:

יוֹסֵף בֶּן־שְׁבַע־עֶשְׂרֵה שָׁנָה הָיָה רֹעֶה אֶת־אֶחָיו בַּצֹּאן

At seventeen years of age, Joseph tended the flocks with his brothers.

We may note that both these midrashic sources are directed at finding a *peshat*, a sense of the plain meaning of the verse, and not at advancing a homiletical interpretation of it. To that end I will propose one.

The verb לרעות (*lir'ot*) alliterates with, or suggests an echo of, the Hebrew word for evil, רע (*ra'*, "evil"). On this basis we could translate the re-configured verse not as "the brothers went to feed," but rather "the brothers went to conspire to do evil." Such a play on words is quite in the spirit of the narrator of this story.

8. Numbers 3:39—Count Aaron Out

כָּל־פְּקוּדֵי הַלְוִיִּם אֲשֶׁר פָּקַד מֹשֶׁה וְאַהֲרֹן עַל־פִּי יְהוָה לְמִשְׁפְּחֹתָם כָּל־זָכָר
מִבֶּן־חֹדֶשׁ וָמַעְלָה שְׁנַיִם וְעֶשְׂרִים אָלֶף׃

All the Levites who were recorded, whom at the LORD's command Moses and Aaron recorded by their clans, all the males from the age of one month up, came to 22,000.

The Context: The Mishkan (the portable Tabernacle) having been built, the Israelites are encamped in the wilderness, awaiting the order to begin the march to the Promised Land. A census of the twelve tribes has been taken and their arrangement in the procession set. Now comes a census of the Levites and a delineation of their duties.

Textual Criticism: The dots over Aaron's name tell us that the word is, apparently, spurious, and Jacob Milgrom notes that it is "missing in some Hebrew manuscripts and in the Samaritan and the Peshitta."[63]

---

63. Milgrom, *Numbers*, 22. The Peshitta is a Syriac (Christian dialect of Aramaic) translation of the Tanakh done likely some time in the second to fourth centuries CE.

It merits deletion presumably because it was Moses, not Aaron, who was originally commanded to take the census of the Levites and who did so, as we learned at Numbers 3:14–17. Milgrom writes further, "That Aaron's name may have been originally omitted is . . . supported by the singular verb *paqad* ["recorded"] and by Aaron's absence . . . in verses 14 and 16 [of chapter 3]."[64] The question is how Aaron got into this verse in the first place. Butin surmises that "it may be an echo of some former tradition according to which [Aaron's name] אהרן would have been introduced on the strength of 4:34,"[65] where, at the end of the census of the Levites, the text informs us that "*Moses, Aaron, and the chieftains of the community recorded the Kohathites by the clans of their ancestral house*" (the Kohathites being one of the three sub-groups or clans of the Levitical tribe).

Midrashic Perspectives: Sifre and other Midrashic collections explain the dots in just this way. Aaron was not one of the numberers; only Moses implemented the census of the Levites, as God had commanded him. The Talmud (b. Bekhorot 4a), however, says that the import of the dots here is that Aaron was not included among those *numbered*, an explanation that Rashi repeats in his commentary on this verse.

The supercommentary on Rashi, Sifte Hakhamim, tries to reconcile the contradiction by suggesting that what Rashi means is that the force of the dots is to tell us that Aaron was neither among the numberers nor among the numbered.

9. Numbers 21:30—How Far Did They Go?

וַנִּירָם אָבַד חֶשְׁבּוֹן עַד־דִּיבוֹן וַנַּשִּׁים עַד־נֹפַח אֲשֶׁר עַד־מֵידְבָא׃

Yet we have cast them down utterly, Heshbon along with Dibon;
We have wrought desolation at Nophah, which is hard by Medeba.

The Context: The Israelites are now well on their way to the Promised Land, traversing Transjordan between the Sea of Galilee in the north and the Dead Sea to the south. This is the land of Moab, which, as we will learn later (Deut 2:9), the Israelites were commanded not to conquer, it being the possession of Abraham's nephew Lot. But just before this verse we are told:

---

64. Milgrom, *Numbers*, 22.
65. Butin, *Ten Nequdoth of the Torah*, 83.

> *Heshbon was the city of Sihon, king of the Amorites, who had fought against a former king of Moab and taken all his land from him.* (Num 21:26)

We see from this that when the Israelites were in the vicinity, Moab was in the hands of the Amorites. Thus when Moses asked permission from Sihon to let the Israelites pass though his territory peaceably and Sihon refused and went out to oppose them militarily, it was permissible for the Israelites to engage the Amorites in battle. The result was a resounding Israelite victory.

The verse we are considering, and the two preceding it, are probably a snippet from a poem. Milgrom suggests that the passage, often called "the Song of Heshbon" by scholars, could be "the work of an Amorite poet celebrating the victory of his people over Moab."[66] It is one of three brief quotations from ancient lost poems or collections of poems that somehow were interpolated into this chapter of the book of Numbers. (The other two are a fragment from "the Book of the Wars of the Lord" [vv. 14–15] and a passage from "the Song of the Well" [vv. 17–18].) The author or redactor of Numbers presumably inserted this fragment into the narrative here in order to show that in occupying what had once been Moabite land, the Israelites conquered it not from the Moabites but from the Amorites.

Textual Criticism: Before we can try to discover what the purpose and meaning of the dot over the word אשׁר might be, we need some clarity about what the verse itself means. This is easier said than done. Milgrom writes, "The verse is an insoluble crux. It may not even belong to the song but may be part of the itinerary."[67]

In order to see how problematic it is, let us cite the passage in its entirety as rendered from the Hebrew by the New Jewish Publication Society translation (NJPSV). Verse 30 contains the dotted word:

> [26] *Now Heshbon was the city of Sihon, king of the Amorites, who had fought against a former king of Moab and taken all his land from him as far as the Arnon [river.]*
> [27] *Therefore the bards would recite:*
> *Come to Heshbon; firmly built*
> *And well founded is Sihon's city.*
> [28] *For fire went forth from Heshbon,*
> *Flame from Sihon's city,*
> *Consuming Ar of Moab,*
> *The lords of Bamoth by the Arnon.*

---

66. Milgrom, *Numbers*, 462.
67. Milgrom, *Numbers*, 182.

²⁹ *Woe to you, O Moab,*
You are undone, people of Chemosh!
His sons are rendered fugitive
And his daughters captive
By an Amorite king, Sihon.
³⁰ *Yet we have cast them down utterly,*
Heshbon along with Dibon;
We have wrought desolation at Nophah,
Which is hard by Medeba.

Without going into the details of just how and why the translators arrived at this particular rendering, we should note that it is the end result of a struggle over almost every word. Consider how Robert Alter in his translation chose to solve the problems which the vocabulary and the syntax of the Hebrew original present:

²⁶ *For Heshbon is the city of Sihon king of the Amorites, and he had done battle with the first king of Moab and he took all his land from his hand as far as the Arnon.*
²⁷ *Therefore do the rhapsodes say:*
Come to Heshbon, let it stand built,
may the city of Sihon be unshaken.
²⁸ *For fire has come out of Heshbon,*
flame from the town of Sihon.
It consumed Ar of Moab,
the notables of Arnon's high places.
²⁹ *Woe to you, Moab,*
You are lost, O people of Chemosh.
His sons he has turned into fugitives,
and his daughters to captive state
to the Amorite king Sihon.
³⁰ *And their mastery is lost,*
From Heshbon to Dibon.
We wrought havoc up to Nophah,
*which is all the way to Medeba.*⁶⁸

A comparison of these two estimable renderings shows that there is general agreement between them about how verses 26–29 should be handled, but verse 30 was more challenging to them. As a third example, here is Richard Elliot Friedman's version of that verse:

And their fiefdom perished,
Heshbon to Dibon,

---

68. Alter, *Five Books of Moses*, 793–94.

Scribal Secrets

*and we devastated up to Nophah
which reaches to Medeba.*[69]

Now the dot is over the third letter in the word אשׁר̇, correctly translated in all three versions as "which." In the Hebrew the word serves, as it does in the English, to introduce the final clause in the verse that explains the location of the town or city of Nophah, or possibly defines its extent. If we proceed on the assumption that the dot over the *resh* in אשׁר̇ indicates erasure, the word becomes אשׁ, the Hebrew word for "fire." That is how the Samaritan Pentateuch and the Septuagint apparently read the verse, and the Talmud (b. Bava Batra 78b–79a) seems to have done so too. In an "adjusted" or "modified" NJPS version the verse would then read:

וַנִּירָם אבד
חשבון עד דיבן
ונשים עד נפח
אש עד מידבא

*Yet we have cast them down utterly,
Heshbon along with Dibon;
We have wrought desolation at Nophah,
Fire at Medeba.*

Or with Alter:

*And their mastery is lost,
From Heshbon to Dibon.
We wrought havoc up to Nophah,
Fire up to Medeba.*

Such a reading makes sense poetically, for "fire" in this last verse would nicely bracket the fire mentioned near the opening of the passage (v. 28).

Other rabbinic sources suggest that the dot or dots are placed elsewhere in verse 30. There are many views, but they need not detain us here. They tell us only that the rabbis, too, struggled over what this verse is saying.

Midrashic Perspectives: Though they did not bring to the Torah text the historical-critical perspective of moderns, the rabbinic midrashists and the medieval commentaries understood that the poetic fragment we are discussing was an importation from a non-Israelite source. They attribute these lines to the prophet Balaam and his father.[70]

---

69. Friedman, *Commentary on the Torah*, 501.

70. See Bamidbar Rabbah 19:30, Rashi on Numbers 21:27, and Naḥmanides on Num 21:29.

The midrashic sources which accept the Masoretic placement of the one dot over the *resh* in אֲשֶׁר all focus on what this means with respect to the final clause of the verse. Sifre cryptically says that the dot is there to tell us that "even further on from these [places] it was also thus." That is to say, the bard in the ancient poem is bragging that the conquest of Nophah in Moab by the Amorites extended as far as the Moabite city of Medeba. The dot indicates that the final clause "which is hard by Medeba" is not adjectival, modifying Nophah, as we might think, but adverbial. In other words, the conquest was not (only) up to Nophah, a place that is near Medeba, but went beyond it, extending all the way to Medeba. Butin suggests that in explaining the dot this way, Sifre is implicitly suggesting that the *resh* be dropped from אשר, thus yielding the clause אש עד מידבא, "fire as far as Medeba."[71]

[On this particular form, see the Editorial Addition by Gary A. Rendsburg at the end of this section, pp. 74–75.]

10. Numbers 29:15—Much Ado About Little

וְעִשָּׂרוֹן֙ עִשָּׂר֔וֹן לַכֶּ֖בֶשׂ הָאֶחָ֑ד לְאַרְבָּעָ֥ה עָשָׂ֖ר כְּבָשִֽׂים׃

And one-tenth for each of the fourteen lambs . . .

The Context: Chapters 28 and 29 of Numbers comprise a master catalog of the various sacrifices that were to be offered throughout the year. Listed are the required ingredients for the daily offerings and for those brought on Sabbath, New Moon, the seven days of Passover, Shavuʿot, Rosh Hashanah, Yom Kippur, the seven days of Sukkot, and the Shemini ʿAtzeret festival. The above verse is part of the passage that outlines the sacrificial protocol for the seven days of Sukkot. On each of those days fourteen lambs had to be offered, in addition to a specified number of other animals. The verse is referring to the amount of fine flour that had to be included with the lamb sacrifices. "One-tenth" here means one-tenth of an ephah, a unit of dry measure in biblical times that equaled about 20 dry quarts.[72]

---

71. Butin, *Ten Nequdoth of the Torah*, 90. Avot de Rabbi Natan, recension A (ARN A), has a completely different approach to dropping the *resh* in אשר. Its view is that the dot "comes to teach that [in the conquest] they destroyed the peoples but not the provinces." Butin offers a strained attempt to explicate this interpretation (*Ten Nequdoth of the Torah*, 91).

72. See Numbers 28:5 and www.convert-me.com/en/convert/volume/bibephah.html. One-tenth of an ephah, accordingly, would equal two quarts dry measure.

Textual Criticism: The amount of confusion about almost all aspects of this short verse is amazing. There is no consensus in the sources about whether the word עשרון (*'iśśaron*, "one-tenth") should occur here once or twice; whether the first one should have a *vav* in front of it; whether the word itself should be written עשרון (that is, *plene*, "full") or עשרן (that is, *defectiva*, with one less letter); whether there should be dots above it, and, if so, whether they should fall over all the letters or over just one; and if so, over which letter.

Part of the problem is that as the sacrifices are itemized in the course of the two chapters, the word עשרון occurs differently. In four verses it is doubled, though with different spellings, and with variation on the presence or absence of the initial *vav*; while on one occasion it is written only once, though with the numeral "one" following. To which we add the verse with the supralienal dot. Hence we find the following:

ועשרן עשרון	(Num 28:13)
עשרון עשרון	(Num 28:21)
עשרון עשרון	(Num 28:29)
ועשרון אחד	(Num 29:4)
עשרון עשרון	(Num 29:10)
ועשרון עשרון	(Num 29:15)

In our verse the key word is doubled, but the dot over the *vav* in the first one might indicate that the whole word should be excised, in which case 29:15 would be like 29:4, with the word עשרון occurring only once (though note the presence of the numeral אחד ["one"] there). If this is true, we would have something parallel to what we saw previously in Genesis 19:33, ובקומה, where the dot comes over the second *vav* so as to indicate erasure of the entire word. (In both cases, were it placed over the first *vav*, which serves as the conjunction "and," we might think it comes only to indicate erasure of that particular letter.)

Midrashic Perspectives: Sifre explains the dot as indicating that "there was but one *'iśśaron*," and most other sources echo this. This sounds as if Sifre is simply noting that the dot cancels one of the two *'iśśaron* measurements. From what we've been seeing about the purpose of the dots, that would make perfect sense. In actuality, though, Sifre is saying something even more narrow and technical. It concerns the number of measuring cups there were in the Temple for the flour that accompanied the lamb sacrifice.

The dot in the first וְעִשָּׂרוֹן is there not to cancel it from the text—both וְעִשָּׂרוֹן and עִשָּׂרוֹן belong—but rather to highlight this doubling in order to tell us the following less-than-uplifting fact: that in the Temple there were (only) two sizes of such measuring cups, one an *'iśśaron*, i.e., a one-tenth of an ephah, and one a half- *'iśśaron*, or one-twentieth of an ephah.

* * *

The foregoing discussion makes it clear that the insertion of dots over the letters and words of the ten verses in the Torah that we have examined was done for any one of the following reasons:

1) to indicate deletion of the letters or words over which they sit;

2) to indicate that those letters or words are spurious or superfluous;

3) to flag—originally for the declaimer and, later, for the reader—that there is some interpretive issue in the verse that needs to be noted. What that issue is will vary, from important and even profound to banal and even trivial.

These reasons are not mutually exclusive. They may in some cases be mutually inclusive. A text-critical approach to the dots does not always stand on its own but sometimes leads to—indeed necessitates—a more imaginative midrashic way of ferreting out their import.

Ultimately, though, the most salient thing about these curious dots is that they are there. They stand as visual testimony to the existence of (about) two millennia of a scribal tradition, one that faithfully labored to preserve and maintain the accuracy and integrity of every single detail of the Torah's text. The original purpose and meaning of these dots may not always have been apparent to the scribes who copied them, but there they are in the text, for us to recover their meanings and extend them into the present.

An Editorial Addition, by Gary A. Rendsburg

In a recent article entitled, "What We Can Learn about Other Northwest Semitic Dialects from Reading the Bible,"[73] I surveyed evidence for the various Canaanite and Aramaic dialects as reflected in the Bible. §14 of said article was devoted to Ammonite, with a focus on

---

73. Rendsburg, "What We Can Learn."

Scribal Secrets

Numbers 21:30 in sub-section §14.1, as follows (with some slight stylistic editing):[74]

14.0. Ammonite

1. Relative pronoun אש֗:

וַנִּירָם אָבַד חֶשְׁבּוֹן עַד־דִּיבוֹן וַנַּשִּׁים עַד־נֹפַח אֲשֶׁ֗ר עַד־מֵידְבָא׃

(Num 21:30)

We know slightly more about Ammonite than we do about Edomite. One grammatical feature known, via Heshbon Ostracon 4.6, is the relative pronoun אש ("that, which"[75]). It is rather striking, accordingly, that in the difficult verse that we are citing—quoting from the (ancient? Trans-Jordanian?) הַמֹּשְׁלִים, "the balladeers" (see v. 27)—the relative marker אֲשֶׁ֗ר appears with supralinear dot above the *resh*, one of the ten times in the Torah that such a diacritic appears. Even more remarkable is the fact that this verse appears within the account of the Israelites' passage through Trans-Jordan (see v. 24 for specific reference to Ammon), and indeed mentions Heshbon explicitly (see also v. 27)! We should conclude, accordingly, that the "original" text read אש, which a later Hebrew scribe changed to אשר—even as the Masoretic tradition remained aware of this alteration, hence the *punctum extraordinarium*.[76]

This explanation, propounded by Nahum Slouschz more than 70 years ago based on Phoenician evidence (see n. 76), and renewed now here on the basis of Ammonite documentation, speaks to "The Context" and "Textual Criticism" sections of Rabbi Diamond's treatment—though naturally the "Midrashic Perspectives" section stands independently.

2. LETTERS GREAT AND SMALL

Writing a Torah scroll is unlike any other kind of writing. It is more than the mere inscription of letters and words on a writing surface, in this case parchment prepared from the skin of a kosher mammal. It is more than the

---

74. Rendsburg, "What We Can Learn," 173–74.

75. Cross, "Ammonite Ostraca," 1–20, esp. 2 and 5; Israel, "The Language of the Ammonites," 143–59, esp. 146; and Garr, *Dialect Geography of Syria-Palestine*, 85.

76. This point was noted long ago by Slouschz, *Thesaurus of Phoenician Inscriptions*, 10, though with reference to the Phoenician relative pronoun אש. Obviously, this was before the discovery of the same morpheme in Ammonite, which makes the case even stronger. Note that the Samaritan Pentateuch reads אש, which is understood as "fire" in the Samaritan tradition. See also LXX pŭr, indicative of a Hebrew *Vorlage* reading אש.

The Extraordinary Texts in the Torah

mechanical copying of one text from another, even as great care is taken to ensure that nothing has been left out or added. Writing a Torah scroll is a sacred act in which the scribe's intentionality must inform every stroke of the quill as letter is added to letter and word to word. In his great code of Jewish law, Moses Maimonides states that when a scribe writes a Sefer Torah (a Torah scroll of the five books of Moses):

> he should be careful about [writing] the large letters and the small letters, the dotted letters and the irregularly shaped letters.[77]

And so when we find at various places in a Torah scroll certain letters that are written larger or smaller than the others, we should not conclude that a mistake was made and the scroll is defective. Rather, we should recognize that in fact those letters had to be written in just that way, larger or smaller as the case may be. Like the dots we have considered, these unusually sized letters are part and parcel of scribal tradition. Scholars call the large letters majuscules and the diminutive ones minuscules. Forbidding (or maybe imposing) as these terms may sound, I will use them here for brevity's sake.

How did it this curious textual phenomenon come about? What purpose(s), if any, do these unusually sized letters serve? And why *these* letters? These are the questions we shall explore in this chapter.

This is not a simple matter. Unlike the dotted words, the number of which in the Torah is fixed at ten, there is no consensus at all in the sources on how many letters in the Torah (and in the rest of the Tanakh, too, but these will not concern us here) have to be written irregularly. This is because there is no agreement on exactly which letters need to be written large and which small. The implications of the wide range of opinion and practice on this matter are significant and we will get to them in the course of this discussion. But our first order of business is to try to pin down just what letters we are talking about.

Origins

The Talmudim, both Babylonian and Palestinian, have little to say about majuscules and minuscules. They seem to know about them, at least a few

---

77. Moses Maimonides, *Mishneh Torah, Sefer Ahavah, Hilkhot Sefer Torah* 7:8. He regards these as "best practices" and not rigid requirements. In the next statement (7:9), he says that if a Torah scroll is found to lack these scribal features, it is still kosher. See also the laws of Torah scrolls in the *Tur, Yoreh De'ah* 275.

of them, but don't make too much of them.[78] The first source that speaks substantially about them is Tractate Sofrim, a post-Talmudic collection of teachings about scribal and related matters that was compiled early in the post-Talmudic period, at some time in the seventh century. This is what Sofrim (chapter 9) says about majuscules and miniscules:

9:1 On the *bet* of *be-reshit* [Gen 1:1] there must be four crownlets, and the letter(s)[79] of the word must be extended above all the other letters, because by its means the world came into existence.

9:2 The *vav* of *gaḥon* [Lev 11:42] must be enlarged, because it is the middle letter of the Torah. . . .

9:3 *Vayyishḥaṭ* [Lev 8:15 or 8:23] must be enlarged because it is half of the verses of the Torah.

9:4 *Shemaʿ yiśraʾel* [Deut 6:4] must be written at the beginning of a line, and all its letters are to be enlarged, while *ʾeḥad* must come at the end of [the same] line.

9:5 The *lamed* of *vayyashlikhem* [Deut 29:27] must be long.

9:6 The *he* of *ha-la-yhwh* [Deut 32:6] must be longer than any other *he*, because it is a word on its own.

9:7 The *yod* of *teshi* [Deut 32:18] must be smaller than any other *yod* in the Scriptures. The *yod* of *yigdal* [Num 14:17] must be bigger than any other *yod* in the Torah. *Yisraʾel* at the end of the Torah [Deut 34:12] must be enlarged, while the *lamed* in it must be higher than any other *lamed*.

It is not clear on just which sources Tractate Sofrim bases these instructions. Sofrim, let us remember, is a compilation of earlier teachings. We must assume that in articulating them, it is not inventing these instructions but rather is reflecting, and possibly elaborating upon, traditions and understandings that were in place already in the early stages of Israel's scribal history, including the few Talmudic ones I have just cited. We can only speculate.

---

78. See, for example, y. Megillah 1:8 (71c) regarding the letter *he*, serving as the interrogative particle, at the beginning of Deuteronomy 32:6. [To be honest, however, it is not clear whether the Talmud Yerushalmi recognizes this letter as written large or whether it simply notes that the letter is written alone (the only such case in the Bible), that is, detached and hence not prefixed to the word. See also b. Megillah 11b on the same form, and b. Qiddushin 66b on the broken *vav* in Numbers 25:12 (discussed below).—eds.]

79. Many editions read "letter" in the singular, referring to the first letter of the first word, that is, *bet*.

The Extraordinary Texts in the Torah

Here follow the full texts of the ten verses included in Sofrim and their translation. These passages would have appeared in Torah scrolls—and still do—without the full *niqqud* (vowels) and *te'amim* (accent marks) presented here, but we include them to allow for easier reading.

בְּרֵאשִׁית בָּרָא אֱלֹהִים אֵת הַשָּׁמַיִם וְאֵת הָאָרֶץ׃

When God began to create the heaven and earth . . . (Gen 1:1)

וַיִּשְׁחָט וַיִּקַּח מֹשֶׁה אֶת־הַדָּם

And it was slaughtered, and Moses took the blood. (Lev 8:15)

or

וַיִּשְׁחָט ׀ וַיִּקַּח מֹשֶׁה מִדָּמוֹ

And it was slaughtered, and Moses took its blood. (Lev 8:23)

כֹּל הוֹלֵךְ עַל־גָּחוֹן . . . לֹא תֹאכְלוּם

Anything that crawls on its belly . . . you shall not eat. (Lev 11:42)

וְעַתָּה יִגְדַּל־נָא כֹּחַ אֲדֹנָי כַּאֲשֶׁר דִּבַּרְתָּ לֵאמֹר׃

Therefore, I pray, let my Lord's forbearance be great, as you have declared, saying . . . (Num 14:17)

שְׁמַע יִשְׂרָאֵל יְהוָה אֱלֹהֵינוּ יְהוָה ׀ אֶחָד׃

Hear O Israel! The LORD is our God, the LORD alone. (Deut 6:4)

וַיִּתְּשֵׁם יְהוָה מֵעַל אַדְמָתָם בְּאַף וּבְחֵמָה וּבְקֶצֶף גָּדוֹל וַיַּשְׁלִכֵם אֶל־אֶרֶץ אַחֶרֶת כַּיּוֹם הַזֶּה׃

The LORD uprooted them from their soil in anger, fury, and great wrath, and cast them unto another land, as is still the case. (Deut 29:27)

הֲ־לַיהוָה תִּגְמְלוּ־זֹאת עַם נָבָל וְלֹא חָכָם

Do you thus requite the LORD, O dull and witless people? . . . (Deut 32:6)

צוּר יְלָדְךָ תֶּשִׁי וַתִּשְׁכַּח אֵל מְחֹלְלֶךָ׃

You neglected the Rock that begot you,
forgot the God who brought you forth. (Deut 32:18)

וּלְכֹל הַיָּד הַחֲזָקָה וּלְכֹל הַמּוֹרָא הַגָּדוֹל אֲשֶׁר עָשָׂה מֹשֶׁה לְעֵינֵי כָּל־יִשְׂרָאֵל׃

> and for all the great might and awesome power that Moses displayed before all Israel. (Deut 34:12)

Reasons

Yeivin, who has studied the history of transmission of the Tanakh's text from its obscure beginnings in the early Second Temple period (i.e., after 515 BCE) through to the advent of printing in the mid-fifteenth century, theorizes that majuscules were devised for any one of three possible reasons:

1. [to mark] the beginning of a book or ... a new section ...
2. [to draw] attention to some significant point, as גָּחוֹן (Lev 11:42) ... which mark[s] the half-way point in the Torah in letters ... or הֲ־לַיהוה (Deut 32:6) where the *he* is written as a separate word.
3. [as] a warning that reading must be precise, as in שְׁמַע יִשְׂרָאֵל ה׳ אֱלֹהֵינוּ ה׳ אֶחָד (Deut 6:4).[80]

These are plausible conjectures from the text-critical perspective in which Yeivin's work is grounded. But they leave a lot unaccounted for and do not explain all the textual phenomena we are examining here, as we shall see below when we look more closely at some of them. Yeivin does qualify his generalizations when he says that "in most cases ... there is no obvious reason for the large letter."[81] But like most textual critics, Yeivin seems to overlook the possibility that some of these unusual letters serve not as technical textual markers but to encode some midrashic interpretation, as may be the case with וישלכם in Deuteronomy 29:27 or even the Shema' (Deut 6:4), where there may be more involved than pronouncing the words correctly. And what about the minuscule in תשי in Deuteronomy 32:18 and others?

As for the minuscules, all Yeivin says is that they "are less common than large letters."[82] Samuel David Luzzatto (1800–1865) explains that they occur whenever a word begins with the identical last letter of the word that immediately precedes it. He theorizes that it was the practice of ancient scribes to omit one of the two identical letters, and when later scribes sought to reinsert the missing letter, they had to write it in miniature because there was no space for a full-sized one. This notion has some basis

---

80. Yeivin, *Introduction to the Tiberian Masorah*, 47–48.
81. Yeivin, *Introduction to the Tiberian Masorah*, 48.
82. Yeivin, *Introduction to the Tiberian Masorah*, 48.

in fact because, as Luzzatto does not say, in ancient manuscripts there was no space between words; one ran into the next. It could account for such minuscules as קצת in Genesis 27:46 or ויקרא in Leviticus 1:1, but not for those where identical letters do not follow one another in that way (e.g., Gen 2:4, בהבראם; Lev 6:2, מוקדה; or Deut 32:18, תשי).[83]

Alternatively, Page Kelley and colleagues write:

> it has been suggested that ... the small letters may have served one of two purposes: 1) the letters hint at an alternative textual tradition, or 2) the letters were intended as corrections but their meaning was forgotten.[84]

What that alternative textual tradition or that forgotten meaning was or might have been, can only be conjectured.

It is clear, then, that no one explanation suffices to account for every majuscule or every minuscule. Some explanations work for some, but none apply to all. Like the dotted words, some are best understood in a historical-critical context—that is, within the framework of scribal tradition and practice as they developed over time—and some by the application of a midrashic or homiletical interpretive procedure, of which there are several. Some are amenable to both approaches, and some can be rendered meaningful only within the interpretive canons of Kabbalah. And then there are some that are best described by Abraham Maimonides (1186–1237), son of the illustrious Moses Maimonides: "They are among the things handed down to us by the tradition. Their secrets are indiscernible to us, nor do we know their true explanations."[85]

Proliferation and Variation

In any case, wherever they came from, the ten letters noted in Tractate Sofrim were never regarded as a definitive or official list. We do not see them at all in the few fragments of biblical text that we have in the Dead Sea Scrolls, which are much earlier than Sofrim. They are completely absent in versions of biblical texts found (so far) in the Cairo Geniza.[86] Furthermore, the scrolls and

---

83. Cited from Luzzatto's commentary on Genesis 27:46 in Ron, *Sefer Qaṭan ve-Gadol*, 62.

84. Kelley et al., *Masorah of Biblia Hebraica Stuttgartensia*, 36.

85. Responsum no. 16, cited in Ron, *Sefer Qaṭan ve-Gadol*, 8.

86. Schnitzer, "'Otiyot Gedolot," especially 256, where the author states: "An examination of Geniza fragments shows a complete absence of majuscules and minuscules

codices of the Tanakh produced by the Ben Asher family of Masoretes, which flourished in Tiberias from the eighth through the tenth centuries—versions that came to be regarded as the "gold standard" for accurate and authoritative editions of the biblical text—show a distinct disregard for or disinclination to follow the rabbinic prescriptions regarding unusual letters listed in Tractate Sofrim. This includes the Aleppo Codex written c. 920 CE and the Leningrad Codex written in 1009 CE. The latter shows *only four majuscules* (all in the Torah) and *three minuscules* (one each in Isaiah, Jeremiah, and Proverbs, which books are outside the scope of this discussion).[87] The four majuscules include the two words in the Shema' listed in Tractate Sofrim (Deut 6:4, noted previously) and the following two "new" ones:

וַיַּקְרֵב מֹשֶׁה אֶת־מִשְׁפָּטָן לִפְנֵי יְהוָה׃

Moses brought their case before the LORD. (Num 27:5)

מַמְרִים הֱיִיתֶם עִם־יְהוָה מִיּוֹם דַּעְתִּי אֶתְכֶם׃

As long as I have known you, you have been defiant toward the LORD.[88] (Deut 9:24)

Here the plot of the story behind these unusual letters thickens. For alongside this tendency to disregard the tradition of writing the Torah text with particular majuscules and minuscules or to minimize their occurrence, we see an opposing one whereby their number proliferates.

An early example of this tendency is a list found in a Genizah fragment in the Bodleian Library at Oxford that reckons a total of 29 majuscules and 37 minuscules in the whole Tanakh (see Figure 4).[89] A list of this vintage is particularly valuable because it incorporates information about the biblical

---

both in manuscripts with Babylonian pointing and in those with Palestinian pointing." See p. 81 for a different finding in a Genizah fragment that Jose Faur has examined.

87. Schnitzer, "'Otiyot Gedolot," 254–55.

88. Schnitzer, "'Otiyot Gedolot," 254; Yeivin, *Introduction to the Tiberian Masorah*, 48, makes no mention of this verse as written with this majuscule in the Leningrad Codex. According to him, Leningrad has only three majuscules: one in Numbers 27:5 and the two in Deuteronomy 6:4. [An inspection of the manuscript, however, reveals that the first *mem* in Deuteronomy 9:24 is slightly larger than the second *mem* and the other neighboring letters. Space considerations appear to have prevented the scribe from writing this *mem* even larger; this factor presumably led Yeivin to the conclusion that the verse as presented in the Leningrad Codex does not include a large letter.—G.A.R.]

89. Faur, "Reshima," 1–10. Faur dates this fragment to the latter half of the fifth century, making it a very early source in this context. [Though we believe that this dating is too early, by several centuries, if not half a millennium.—eds.]

text that until this fragment came to light was known only from masoretic notes written on the margins of biblical manuscripts.

Some scholars speculate that early on there was the notion that in the entire text of the Tanakh each one of the 22 letters of the Hebrew alphabet appears—or should appear—both in majuscule and in minuscule. The Large Masorah contains three such lists, two lists of majuscules (in the top margins at Genesis 1:1 and at 1 Chronicles 1:1, though the two lists do not agree in every respect) and one list of minuscules (at Leviticus 1:1).

Similar enumerations are given in various biblical "Books of Lists" that began to appear around the ninth century and later, around the same time as Tractate Sofrim was compiled. Scholars call these collections Masoretic handbooks. We do not know—so much in this field is not known—who made them or edited them, but they testify to a large corpus of material that noted and recorded all sorts of details about the text of the Tanakh.

The largest independent masoretic compilation is that known as *Okhlah ve-Okhlah*, and this was the only such compilation known before the discovery of the Genizah. This compilation contains some 400 masoretic lists, long or short, mostly from the collative MM [= *Masorah Magna*, a collection of lists which appears at the end of many Bible manuscripts].[90]

The lists in *Okhlah ve-Okhlah* are numbing in their quantity, nature, and detail. They are clearly the result of centuries of microscopic examination and analysis of the biblical text. The lists enumerate a wide range of textual phenomena, such as the frequency and location of certain words, word pairs, prefixes, suffixes, spellings, vocalizations, pointings, and other matters that have a definite capability to send any reader, even the seasoned Biblicist, well into the realm of biblical arcana.

---

90. Yeivin, *Introduction to the Tiberian Masorah*, 128. He writes: "The first of these lists is an alphabetic list of pairs of unique words, of which one has [a] prefixed *waw* while the second does not. The first of the pairs in this list provides the title [of the book]: *Okhlah ve-Okhlah*."

SCRIBAL SECRETS

Figure 4: Cairo Geniza document listing the large and small letters in the entire Bible (not just the Torah). MS Bodl. Heb. d. 66, fol. 134a/134b.
[Used with kind permission of the Bodleian Libraries, University of Oxford. Photo © Bodleian Libraries, University of Oxford.]

The Extraordinary Texts in the Torah

Three lists in *Okhlah ve-Okhlah,* numbers 82, 83, and 84, concern majuscules and minuscules.[91] They itemize a total of 42 majuscules (27 of which are in the Torah alone) and 25 minuscules in the whole Tanakh. Likewise, the Leningrad Codex: though its text shows only four majuscules and three minuscules, as noted, its Masoretic notes collected at the end reckon 30 majuscules and 38 minuscules in the Tanakh.[92]

With this proliferation in number comes, as we might expect, variation in scribal practice. Scholars who have inspected scrolls and codices written in the Middle Ages have found many divergences from what Tractate Sofrim prescribed. For example:

- In writing Genesis 1:1, it became standard practice to enlarge only the first *bet*: בראשית.

- The enlarged word וישחט in Leviticus 8:15 (or 8:23) was never accepted as being in the middle verse, probably because many medieval scholars questioned the accuracy of Tractate Sofrim's verse count (as they did not question its letter count). Even if the large *vav* in the word גחון in Leviticus 11:42 is not the middle letter, as we shall see, yet writing it large is standard in all masoretic texts. And to compound the confusion, the Talmud (b. Qiddushin 30a) names Leviticus 13:33 as the middle verse.

- The majuscule *mem* in Deuteronomy 9:24, ממרים, becomes for some reason a minuscule ממרים in later manuscripts and printed editions of the Pentateuch. This is in line with Schnitzer's important finding that "a letter that is minuscule in one list appears as a majuscule in another."[93]

One rarely if ever sees the last word of the Torah enlarged as ישראל or the *lamed* made even larger, as mandated by Tractate Sofrim.

How do we explain such proliferation and variation? One would have expected that in their attempt to ensure the accuracy and the integrity of the biblical text the Masoretes would have taken pains to be very precise about which words and letters required majuscules and minuscules and how they should be written. Such is not the case. The various notes the Masoretes appended to the margins of scrolls and codices are surprisingly

---

91. Frensdorf, *Sefer Okhlah ve-Okhlah*, 88–89.
92. Schnitzer, "Otiyot Gedolot," 252.
93. Schnitzer, "Otiyot Gedolot," 253; See footnote 88 [p. 80]

unclear about this. The annotations are sometimes unintelligibly terse, and all too often they do not identify the exact verse they are referring to, since the word they are naming as requiring special treatment often occurs many times in a given book. (It may help here to remember that the numbering of verses has no basis in Jewish textual tradition and was instituted only in the late Middle Ages—by Christians—after the masoretic notes were formulated.) The result is that the lists of letters large and small derived from the marginal notes of the Masoretes, which are compiled in later masoretic handbooks, vary greatly and are not authoritative catalogs.[94]

Add to this the fact that, as they did their work, the Masoretes did not erase or correct majuscules and minuscules they found in places where scribal tradition did not mandate them. Subsequently, scribes would faithfully copy all such letters regardless of who mandated them or wrote them. We should, therefore, not be surprised that Schnitzer, after examining a wide variety of biblical manuscripts from the thirteenth and fourteenth centuries, found many majuscules and minuscules in places where there was no masoretic note indicating that they should be so written there.[95]

Then add to this the rise of Kabbalistic interpretation in the late Middle Ages, which generated even more such letters and enabled scribes inclined to this kind of reading to write them in. The Kabbalists drew on a long tradition of according mystical significance to the letters of the Hebrew alphabet. Rabbinic midrash is replete with attempts to ferret meaning out of the shape and numerical value (*gematria*) of the individual letters.

Thus did the designation and number of unusual letters gradually multiply until the whole thing fairly got out of hand.

Zvi Ron, after reviewing virtually all the relevant lists and handbooks, finds an aggregate of 56 majuscules named by one source or another in the Tanakh (31 in the Pentateuch) and 54 minuscules (11 in the Pentateuch) encompassing all the letters of the *aleph-bet*.[96]

The proliferation we see in the manuscripts and codices was perpetuated in the first printed Bibles. We can appreciate the struggles of the students of the Masorah of the early modern period to bring order out of this textual chaos. Notable here is the work of Yedidiah Shlomo Norzi, whose masoretic commentary *Minḥat Shai* (1626) is an important attempt to adjudicate the claims of conflicting authorities and manuscripts that theirs

---

94. Schnitzer, "'Otiyot Gedolot," 254–55.
95. Schnitzer, "'Otiyot Gedolot," 257–64.
96. Ron, *Sefer Qaṭan ve-Gadol*, 3–6.

was the correct and indisputable reading or spelling or vocalization or accentuation. Norzi was ultimately unsuccessful in his efforts to stabilize the biblical text, and so even today printed Bibles are far from standard in how they show the unusual letters and other such details.[97] There is a clear preference to privilege the Leningrad Codex version because of its antiquity, its connection with the Ben Asher school, and the fact that, unlike the older and even more venerable Aleppo Codex, it contains the complete Tanakh. Had not the Aleppo Codex lost so much of the Pentateuch in that disastrous riot or fire in 1948, it would surely hold pride of place.

We see from the foregoing that there never was one list of majuscule and minuscule letters that was universally accepted as binding on all scribes. Nor is there one today. But some—11 majuscules and 6 or 7 minuscules—are more firmly established in scribal tradition than others. Table 1 shows them.

In the pages that follow I will discuss individually each of the 19 letters shown in Table 1, proceeding book by book from Genesis to Deuteronomy. In each case my treatment will reprise the sequence followed in the previous chapter. First I will review the text-critical view of that particular letter such as it may be, and then present a selection of midrashic material that has accumulated around that letter.[98] Then, where appropriate and when so inclined, I will offer my own midrashic take and some reflection on the existential and theological implications of the ideas that have been put into play. All this in line with the multi-dimensional approach to the text that I outlined in the introduction, and the fact that the five books of Moses are not only the Pentateuch but also the Torah. As the Pentateuch, it is the object of our critical scrutiny; as Torah, it is our dialogical partner.

---

97. Schnitzer, "Oriyot Gedolot," 264–65.
98. The full compendium of such material for each letter is Ron, *Sefer Qaṭan ve-Gadol*.

Table 1: Letters Large and Small in the Torah

A) Large Letters (Majuscules):

1. Gen 1:1 — בראשית
2. Exod 34:7 — נצר
3. Exod 34:14 — אחר
4. Lev 11:42 — גחון
5. Lev 13:33 — והתגלח
6. Num 14:17 — יגדל נא
7. Num 27:5 — משפטן
8. Deut 6:4 — שמע
9. Deut 6:4 — אחד
10. Deut 29:27 — וישלכם
11. Deut 32:6 — ה ליהוה

B) Small letters (Minuscules):

1. Gen 2:4 — בהבראם
2. Gen 23:2 — ולבכתה
3. Gen 27:46 — קצתי
4. Lev 1:1 — ויקרא
5. Lev 6:2 — מוקדה
6. Deut 9:24 — ממרים
7. Deut 32:18 — תשי

C) Broken Letter

1. Num 25:12 — שלום

N.B. On the use of the strikethrough in the *vav* to represent this single broken letter in the Torah, see pp. 124–26.

In the pages that follow, we present these 19 items in canonical order (whether they be large, small, or broken), though in some cases we have elected to group two items in a single section.

Genesis 1:1

בראשית ברא אלהים את השמים ואת הארץ

When God began to create the heaven and earth . . .

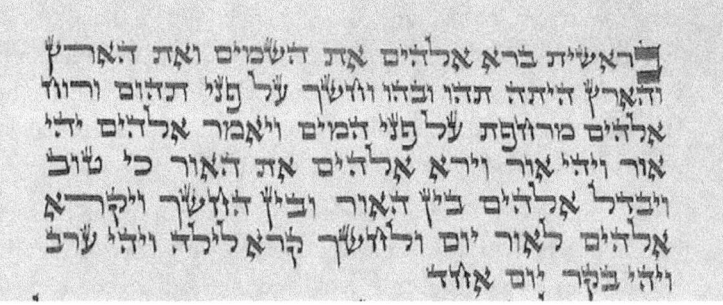

Figure 5: Genesis 1:1 as represented in a contemporary Torah scroll. Note the large *bet* which commences the verse and indeed the Torah. [Torah scroll by scribe Rabbi Gustavo Surazski. Scroll image courtesy of Temple Aliyah, Needham, Mass.]

One reason for majuscules that has been put forth by Yeivin is that they were used to mark the opening of a book or a new section of a book.[99] Majuscules are found at the openings of Genesis, Proverbs, Song of Songs, and Chronicles. But what about all the other books and sections of the Bible where they are not? Is Yeivin referring to a practice that was in vogue for a while and was later discontinued?[100]

It is interesting that Tractate Sofrim, when it prescribed that all six letters of the Torah's first word be written large, did not further stipulate this for the first words (or letters) of the other four books of the Torah, or for any of the other books of the Tanakh. The reason Sofrim gives for the majuscular opening of Genesis is more poetic and mystical than the functional one that Yeivin advances: "the letter(s) of the word בראשית [*be-re'shit*] must be extended above all the other letters, because by its means the world came into existence."[101]

Sofrim is undoubtedly thinking of the series of interpretations of Genesis 1:1 in the first section of the midrashic collection Bereshit Rabbah.

---

99. Yeivin, *Introduction to the Tiberian Masorah*, 47.
100. See Schnitzer, "Otiyot Gedolot," 251.
101. Sofrim 9:1; see p.76.

That series starts off with several different parsings of the first word of the verse, and they all lead to the idea that Sofrim expresses—that the world was created with the letter *bet*. I cite some key statements and number them so we can better see the different ways in which the rabbis ruminated on the *bet*'s significance:

1. Rabbi Yonah said in the name of Rabbi Levi: "Why was the world created with a *bet*? Just as the *bet* is closed at the sides but open in front, so you are not permitted to investigate what is above, what is below, what was before, and what will come after, but rather from the day on which the world was created and following."[102]

2. Rabbi Yehudah ben Pazzi interpreted the Creation in the presence of Bar Kapparah: Why was the world created with a *bet*? To teach you that there are two worlds, this world and the world to come.[103]

3a. Another interpretation: Why with a *bet*? Because *bet* connotes blessing [ברכה, *berakah*]. And why not with an *'aleph*? Because *'aleph* connotes accursedness [ארירה, *'arirah*].

3b. Another interpretation: Why not with an *'aleph*? In order not to give non-believers an opening to challenge [by asking] "How can the world endure, seeing that it was created with the language of cursing [i.e., with an *'aleph*]? Thus the Holy One, blessed be He, said, "Therefore shall I create it with the language of blessing [i.e., with a *bet*], and would that it will endure!"

4. Another interpretation: Why with a *bet*? Just as a *bet* has two protrusions, one pointing upward and one, on the bottom, pointing backward, so, when we ask this *bet* "Who created you?" it will show [us] its upward point and say, "The one who is above created me." [And if we ask] "And what is his name?" it will show [us] its backward point, saying "Adonai" [אדני, with *'aleph*] is His name!"[104]

---

102. Bereshit Rabbah 1:10.

103. The Hebrew letter ב (*bet*), the second letter of the alphabet, carries the numerical value 2.

104. Bereshit Rabbah 1:10. "Thus the backward projection points back to the *alef*, standing for אדון (*'adon*, "lord"; Freedman and Simon, *Midrash Rabbah*, 10n1). The commentary by Baʻal HaṬurim (on Genesis 1:1) multiplies the possibilities to which the opening *bet* visually alludes: e.g., the two Torahs, Written and Oral, with/for which the world was created (ברא שתי = בראשית), and others. The first word also confirms that the world was created on Rosh Hashanah (א בתשרי = בראשית). [These latter interpretations are based on anagrams of the six Hebrew letters of the first word of the Bible.—eds.]

The Extraordinary Texts in the Torah

Notice what the rabbis are doing here. In contemplating the opening *bet*, at no point do they give any indication of how it is to be written on the Torah scroll. At no point in these midrashic riffs do the rabbis ask: "Why is the *bet* that begins the Torah written large?"

Rather, their single question, to which they give multiple answers, is: "Why was the world created with a *bet*?" Should we conclude from this that they did not know of the practice of writing the first letter or word of a book large? Or that they knew about it but it was no longer in vogue to do so? Or that doing so was only optional? Or that it was not a particularly important matter?

We cannot say. What we can say is why Tractate Sofrim justifies the large *bet* the way it does. For what we see here is how the tradition privileges value over fact, the philosophical or theological meaning and purpose of the opening letter over the mechanics of its inscription.

I want to spell this point out, for it can help us understand how we in our time should read midrash and use it in our own attempts to make meaning of our selves and our life in this world.

The midrash here is interesting on two counts. In the first place, it shows us how the rabbis made meaning from a single letter. They contemplated its shape, its numerical significance, its consonantal sound, even the wispy tips at its upper left and lower right corners. As we will see, they will do similar things with some of the other unusually written letters. But this midrash is important not only because of how it arrives at meaning, but also because of the meaning itself. Consider what the four statements cited previously suggest:

- That the world is not a random or chance occurrence but the intentional creation of a creator (no. 4).
- That this material world is not the only reality (no. 2).
- That this reality is not random or meaningless but intrinsically good, created as a blessing (no. 3).
- That our life in this world unfolds within the three sides of the *bet*, i.e., within the quotidian limitations of the human situation in the here and now (no. 1).

It is easy to dismiss these ideas and how they are discovered in the text. Many of us, I would think, would find the notion that this world is not the only reality debatable. The issue is not so much the rabbis' saying this—who knows for sure that this world *is* the only reality?—but the certainty with which it is expressed. It is a certainty that has not been earned by lived human experience, and that is the problem.

Or, to give another example, the rabbis see signals of transcendence in the *bet*'s two little protrusions. Some would say that in doing this they are over-reading: sometimes a *bet* is simply a *bet*.

So we do have the option to dismiss this midrash and others like it.

I don't, though. I neither dismiss them outright nor swallow them and the tradition they embody whole. I look upon these texts as a challenge. The challenge is to read them and the tradition—and I mean the tradition in its biblical, rabbinic, and medieval manifestations—to read them critically, against the grain, and, at the same time, to listen to them and have my ears cocked to hear the issues they raise.

For the issues they raise are not only theirs and of their time, but mine and of my—our—time. I read the four statements prompted by the opening *bet*, and, yes, I am at odds with some things I see in them. But my encounter with the text is not finished. For when I look at this midrashic riff on the enlarged *bet*, I (now) see that underlying them are some fundamental existential questions that trigger the whole series of statements:

- what is this world?
- how am I—how are we—to relate to it?
- why am I—why are we—here?
- what am I—what are we—doing here?

These questions, as I say, are not visible on the surface of the midrash, just as they are seldom articulated in our day-to-day life. They lie at the bottom of what the rabbis are saying here. They lie in the deeper regions of the self, only occasionally, in liminal situations, percolating up into our consciousness.

I once thought that these were questions only someone living amid the confusion and the absurdity of this modern or post-modern era would ask. But now, reading this midrash, I see that in their time the rabbis were alive to them, too. This enables me to understand and appreciate the insight in the celebrated statement of the nineteenth-century German historian Leopold von Ranke that "every generation is equidistant from God." The rabbis were not any closer in their time, and we are not any further in ours.

The Extraordinary Texts in the Torah

One way or another, every generation, and maybe every reflective person, confronts the same existential facts:

- that we are not in this world because we chose to be here;[105]
- that as a consequence of this we are each saddled with the task of figuring out how to relate to this reality into which we have been cast and determine what we are doing in it.

Once we see these issues, the questions that are submerged within us, the very ones the rabbis are asking in this midrash, however implicitly, become real.

Here a basic question has to be answered: Is the world chaos or cosmos?[106] The answer is not obvious. I think it comes down to two possibilities.

One can see the world as suffused with "benign indifference." That, in Albert Camus' novel *The Stranger*, is what Meurseault looked out on from the window of his death cell on the morning of his execution. In that scene Camus takes us to the last stop in the itinerary of modernity and its attendant secularism.[107]

Or one can take the approach that the rabbis took: that this world did not come into being by chance or a random sequence of interstellar events, but by the intention of a creator. To put it in alphabetical terms, the world as the rabbis invite us to see it is not the after-effect of an accident but of the bestowal of a blessing.

In the wake of this question a hard choice has to be made, for both approaches have implications and consequences. The first runs the risk of leading to despair, apathy, nihilism, and worse: the blunting of moral sensibility. The second runs the risk of fostering what Rogers and Hammerstein in *South Pacific* called a "cockeyed optimism," which could lead to an inability to see the suffering brought on by the frequent incoherence of the world and our life within it.

It is the virtue of both perspectives—and this is what makes each of them attractive—that they both are adamant that we not be distracted or

---

105 That is to say, our presence here is involuntary. The philosopher Martin Heidegger described it as the result of our having been "thrown down" into this world.

106. This binary opposition is posited by Mircea Eliade in his study of the origins of religion, *The Sacred and the Profane* (1957).

107. In this respect, Camus has over time proved to be much more interesting, original, and relevant to the human condition than his contemporary Sartre. This was not the case in the 1940s and 1950s when both men were at the height of their powers. Today Camus' stature continues to grow while Sartre's diminishes.

seduced into escaping from living and dealing with the harsh realities of life by spending our time and energy speculating on matters that are beyond the reach of the human mind, however powerful it may be. Camus refuses, as he puts it, to "feed on the roses of illusion."[108] So, in their way, do the rabbis. The open side of the *bet* shows us that there is only one way ahead: forward, into life, into the nitty-gritty realities of this unredeemed world.

So we have to choose how we want to look at this world. Which one shall it be? We cannot dance at both weddings.

Neither approach is intuitive or counter-intuitive; the world as it presents itself to us is profoundly indeterminate, sometimes incoherent and absurd, sometimes suffused with meaning and purpose. To his credit, Camus (who rejected Christianity and theism) saw the dangers involved in putting all his chips on the absurd as the touchstone of reality: it would lead to a nihilism that he refused to accept. In his own way he fashioned a philosophy of resistance to it, one that I think is intellectually and morally responsible.

Yet much as I admire Camus—and I commend his writing, both his fiction and his essays, to all who seek to come to terms with ultimate issues—I go with the rabbis. I go with them because in the long run they give me more than Camus. They give me not only or merely a fund of ideas and accrued wisdom, but something even more important and valuable: an agenda, an agenda for living in this world—one anchored in the history and memory of a community. For all his nobility of soul and seriousness of purpose, I do not find this in Camus.

But to make this point is not the purpose of this discussion. My purpose here has not been to offer a lecture on what I think is the meaning and purpose of Jewish existence. Rather my aim, in reflecting on the enlarged letter *bet*, has been to hold up midrash and show what it can do and how it can do it. Even more so, it is to provide an idea of what it means to think midrashically.

And so I will conclude by citing a latter-day example of midrashic thinking. It is a short take by the literary critic George Steiner, but it is exactly the kind of spin on the text that I have been talking about. In his "Preface to the Hebrew Bible," Steiner is discussing the rich allusiveness of biblical Hebrew. After giving several examples, he adds this one:

---

108. Camus, *Myth of Sisyphus*, 31.

The Extraordinary Texts in the Torah

The consonant beth [sic] in bereshit—the opening word of Genesis, the word that begins all beginning—also means "house" when it is vocalized. Creation builds a house for man.[109]

Steiner is correct. The three consonants of the letter *bet* can be vocalized as בית (*bayit*), the Hebrew word for "house." In saying that "Creation builds a house for man," Steiner is adding to what we've seen the rabbis do with the enlarged *bet*. He is implicitly engaging some of the most interesting and important questions we can ever ask: is man at home in this world? Is the function of religion to enable man to feel at home in this world? Or is its ultimate purpose precisely the opposite—to imbue the human being with the feeling that he or she is a stranger?[110] Or maybe a guest? These are questions that come from deep within the context of modernity. We would not find them in rabbinic midrash. Steiner seems to suggest answers, but each of us has to work them out on our own.

Genesis 2:4

אלה תולדות השמים והארץ בהבראם

This is the story of heaven and earth when they were created

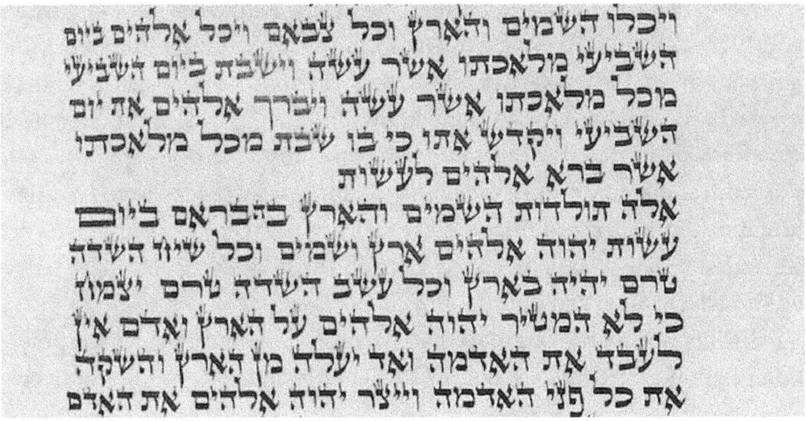

Figure 6: Genesis 2:4 as represented in a contemporary Torah scroll. Note the small letter *he* in the sixth line of text in this image.
[Torah scroll by scribe Rabbi Gustavo Surazski.
Scroll image courtesy of Temple Aliyah, Needham, Mass.]

---

109. Steiner, *No Passion Spent*, 59.
110. Rabbi David Hartman put this question to me in a conversation long ago.

Scribal Secrets

Although there is no necessary connection between the enlarged *bet* of Genesis 1:1 and the small *he* here, the linkage between them is easily made. Both are in verses that narrate The Beginning, and if we follow the source critics, these are the verses which, respectively, open the two Creation stories.[111]

We can't really say when or why this particular miniscule came to be. Emanuel Tov calls its occurrence "insignificant," though he doesn't explain why he says this.[112] This is surprising, since it is hard to imagine any detail of the biblical text being insignificant, even a letter. We could theorize that minuscules like this point to the existence of an alternate textual tradition that got left, so to speak, on the cutting room floor. Minuscules serve that purpose well. They signal by their small size that they might not really belong in the word, and the word should be read without them. If this is the case here, then the text could be read, or might once have been read, like this:[113]

בבראם אלהים אלה תולדות השמים והארץ

This is the story of heaven and earth when God created them.

Such a reading is plausible because the word בהבראם (*be-hibbar'am*, "when they were created," or more literally as a passive Niph'al infinitive, "in their being created") is awkward.

Removing the *he* to leave the five letters בבראם (*be-var'am*, "when [God] created them"), an active Qal infinitive, is smoother, though it requires a subject (אלהים God) to be added. We don't know if such a reading ever existed, and because we don't know, and because the minuscule here did establish itself in the Masoretic tradition—just when we cannot say—it was natural that midrash would come to supply what the received tradition forgot or did not record. It could even be argued that it was midrash that generated the *he* in its downsized form in the first place, and there never was an alternate textual tradition for this verse.

If this was so, the question then becomes: what midrashic interpretation might have led scribes to write the letter *he* in this verse diminutively?

---

111. Richard Elliot Friedman sees this first half of Genesis 2:4 as a suture which the Redactor inserted to bind the two Creation stories together. See his *Bible With Sources Revealed*, 35.

112. Tov, *Textual Criticism*, 54.

113. Kelley et al., *Masorah of Biblia Hebraica Stuttgartensia*, 36; and Biblia Hebraica Stuttgartensia (BHS), ad loc. Gen 2:4 (3).

Again, we can't say. The most plausible one is a midrash that senses that the word בהבראם is indeed awkward, and cleverly breaks the word in two to get around the problem, the text now reading בה בראם (*bah bera'am*). The midrash does not parse these words literally, because they make no sense, but instead reads them imaginatively as בראם ב-ה" (*be-he bera'am*, "with a *he* He created them"). In other words, the world, in this midrash, was created with the letter *he*. This is a different take on the Creation from the midrash on Genesis 1:1, in which the world was created with the letter *bet*. The two midrashim are not necessarily in conflict; they just make different points.

What might it mean to say that the world was created with a *he*? Here are some of the midrashic answers, based on the shape of the letter ה (*he*):

1. *he* is closed off on all its sides but open on the bottom to hint that the dead go down to Sheol, while the curlicue at the top [left corner] hints that they are destined to rise [again], and the window on the [left] side intimates [an opening for] those who turn in repentance [*ba'ale teshuvah*].[114]

2. Why was this world created with a *he*? Because it is [shaped] like a domed pavilion [open on the sides] so that whoever wishes to leave can leave. And why is its [left] leg suspended [with space between its top and the roof]? So that if one returns in repentance they can bring him back up [through it.]

   But let them bring him up through that [opening at the bottom, through which he left]?

   That will not happen . . . [because] if one comes to purify himself he is assisted, [and] if one comes to defile himself he is given an opening.[115]

3. [What does it mean to say that] with a *he* He created [the world? To tell us that] whereas all the other letters require the tongue [or the lips to be deployed], the *he* does not. Thus without effort or travail did God create His world . . .[116]

Here meaning or meanings are discovered not only in the shape of the letter, as in the case of the enlarged *bet* of Genesis 1:1, but also in its sound.

---

114. Bereshit Rabbah 12:10.
115. b. Menaḥot 29b.
116. Bereshit Rabbah 12:10.

And as in that verse, so here are the meanings in the service of ultimate questions. The three-sided *bet* was seen as a microcosm for this world as the proper arena for human endeavor. Now the three-sided *he* is interpreted as a visual metaphor that tells something about how man is to live in this world (points 1 and 2).

In truth, none of these various midrashic readings addresses the question of why the two letters *bet* and *he* are written large and small respectively. There are some later interpreters who do. The *Me'or Ha'Afelah*, a Yemenite compendium of midrash written by Rabbi Nathaniel ben Isaiah in 1328–29, suggests that the *he* is small to tell us that when measured by divine criteria, this world is infinitesimal. Rabbi Eliakim Gottschalk of Rothenburg, a seventeenth century commentator, explains it by developing the idea in point 2: the *he* is small to indicate the contraction of ego that is necessary for one who has fallen down from the right path to get back up through the narrow opening that is provided for him to return to it.[117]

Another current of midrashic interpretation handles the word בהבראם (*be-hibbar'am*) anagrammatically. Instead of breaking it up into two, it rearranges the letters to read באברהם (*be-'avraham*, "for Abraham").

This yields the idea that the world was created because of the merit(s) of Abraham.[118]

What those merits were the midrash doesn't say. But the Zohar does:

> Once Abraham was circumcised he ... entered the sacred covenant ... Then the world was created for his sake ... *These are the generations of heaven and earth* בהבראם [*be-hibbar'am*], *when they were created* (Gen 2:4): ב-ה" בראם [*be-he bera'am*] "with *he* He created them"; באברהם [*be-'avraham*] "through Abraham." All abides in a single mystery.[119]

In this reading, as Matt notes, "the two motifs [the creation of the world with a *he* and the creation of the world because of Abraham] are linked and constitute a single mystery."[120] The decisive event is Abram's circumcision, by which he entered the covenant and became Abraham, thus enlarging his identity. God had promised him: "I will make your name great" (Gen 12:2) and now, with the addition of the letter *he*, a letter of the

---

117. Rabbi Eliakim wrote this in his commentary on the Five Megillot, *Ge'ulat ha-Ger* (1618). Both sources noted here are cited in Ron, *Sefer Qaṭan ve-Gadol*, 39.

118. Bereshit Rabbah 12:9.

119. Zohar 1:91b (Matt, *Zohar*, 75). See also 1:93a (Matt, *Zohar*, 86–87).

120. Matt, *Zohar*, 75n579.

holy divine Name, YHWH, the promise is fulfilled. But Abraham receives it without a trace of hubris—"I am but dust and ashes," he will say to God in the bargaining over the fate of Sodom and Gomorrah (Gen 18:27)—and so the added *he* is written small. For such a one and his progeny is the world worth it.[121]

I don't know how appealing these anagrammatic constructions of meaning are to contemporary readers. They abound in the traditional sources, along with such interpretive staples as *gematria*, the ferreting out the import of the numerical value of the letter *he*, which is five. The world was created for the sake of "The Five" [books of Moses]. Abraham mastered the allurements of the five senses of sight, smell, hearing, taste, and touch. And so on. I often think these interpretations are too clever by half.

But the issues that the ruminations on the shape of the *he* identify seem more promising in their implications. They are of the same order as, and can be seen to complement, those on the shape of the opening *bet*: rabbinic reflections on man in the world. This blessed world may have been created for man, but there's more to it than that. Man was—is—created with free will. We are, apparently, autonomous beings. We may be living within the parameters of a *bet*, but the moral structure of the world is like a *he*. The natural attraction of the forbidden, like gravity, pulls us down to the nether regions of human behavior. Those regions are wide open to receive us, and it is easy to choose to go there. But that same ability to choose makes it possible for us to raise ourselves up again and overcome our failings. This is a harder trajectory. Going up requires more effort than going down, and we can't go back to who we were. We have been diminished, and need to grow again. We need a whole new route to a new place. We will also need the moral support of knowing that such a place exists and will be there for us when we seek it. That is the wisdom of the teaching that "if one comes to purify himself he is assisted, [and] if one comes to defile himself he is given an opening." In sum, our destiny is determined by our own choices. The world is a ה (*he*) with openings.

---

121. This interpretation is based on the Hasidic commentary on the Torah, *Ma'or va-Shemesh* by Kalonymus Kalman Epstein (1754–1823), cited in Ron, *Sefer Qaṭan ve-Gadol*, 41.

SCRIBAL SECRETS

Genesis 23:2

ותמת שרה בקרית ארבע הוא חברון בארץ כנען ויבא אברהם לספד
לשרה ולבכתה

*Sarah died in Kiriath-arba—now Hebron—in the land of Canaan;
and Abraham proceeded to mourn for Sarah and to bewail her.*

Our attention is drawn to the small letter *kaf* in the final word. There are many interpretive possibilities here. One is that the כ (*kaf*) is written small so as to distinguish it from the ב (*bet*) that precedes it. The two letters do look alike. By this reasoning, the *kaf* could just as well have been written large. And why the *kaf* and not the *bet* that got special treatment?

Another solution would be to regard the little *kaf* as spurious and to drop it. The word would now be ולבתה (*u-le-vittah*, "and for her daughter"), and the passage would read "and Abraham proceeded to mourn for Sarah and for her daughter."

Daughter? Abraham had a daughter?

Yes. Or maybe. There is an opinion recorded in the Talmud that in the next chapter, when we are told that "the LORD blessed Abraham in all things" (Gen 24:1), it means that Abraham, who had everything one could ever want, also had, in addition to his sons, a daughter by Sarah.[122] And so when Sarah died, Abraham mourned also for this daughter, who now would now grow up without her mother. Alternatively, the daughter died young, and as long as Sarah was alive her presence gave Abraham solace. But now that Sarah was gone, Abraham mourned the loss of both mother and daughter.[123]

This is imaginative, but it heaps speculation upon speculation. We cannot certify that the *kaf* does not belong here, and, on top of that, we cannot say that Abraham actually had a daughter.

Most interpreters read the text as it is and look for meaning in the way Abraham's weeping for Sarah is written. The small *kaf* is there to tell us something about that weeping. But what?

- The *kaf* is small to indicate that Abraham's mourning for Sarah was mitigated by the love he (soon? eventually?) found for another woman. This presumably was presumably Keturah, of whom we learn only later (Gen 25:1).

---

122. See the opinion of R. Yehudah in b. Bava Batra 16b.
123. See Ron, *Sefer Qaṭan ve-Gadol*, 50, 55.

- The *kaf* is small to teach us that even when they face the most shattering loss "real men don't cry."
- A variation of this is that Abraham wanted to preserve his dignity as a revered public figure and so displayed his grief in an understated way.
- Sarah's death is reported immediately after the trauma of the binding of Isaac (the Aqedah). Abraham did not—could not—weep for her, because his grief was neutralized by the relief and joy he felt when he saw that Isaac was spared.[124]

A very different approach is the one taken by the Ba'al HaTurim, Rabbi Jacob ben Asher (ca. 1269–1343). He finds that it is possible to conclude that Sarah brought about her own death! She had lashed out at Abraham over Hagar: "The wrong done me is your fault! I myself put my maid in your bosom; now that she sees that she is pregnant, I am lowered in her esteem. The LORD decide between me and you!" (Gen 16:5). In thus asking God to address the anger she felt at her husband, she became subject to a principle enunciated in the Talmud that "Whoever submits judgment of his fellow to Heaven is punished."[125] She did herself in, and she was, therefore, according to Ba'al HaTurim, tantamount to a suicide, for whom one does not mourn. *That* is why the *kaf* of the weeping is written small.

The diversity of these readings holds up for us an important aspect of midrash: its "hospitality to the very concept of multiple alternative narratives." In contrast to the plain meaning of the verse, its *peshat*, which conveys "the notion that knowledge of reality is singular, absolute, static, and eternal," midrashic versions fracture that meaning into a multiplicity of different and interesting possibilities and thus "convey a plural, contextual, constructed, and dynamic vision of reality."[126]

Genesis 27:46

ותאמר רבקה אל-יצחק קצתי בחיי מפני בנות חת אם לקח יעקב אשה
מבנות חת כאלה מבנות הארץ למה לי חיים

> Rebekah said to Isaac, "I am disgusted with my life because of the Hittite women. If Jacob marries a Hittite woman like these, from among the native women, what good will life be to me?"

---

124. Ron, *Sefer Qaṭan ve-Gadol*, 50–52.
125. See b. Bava Qamma 93a.
126. Zornberg, *Particulars of Rapture*, 4.

Earlier I noted Samuel David Luzzatto's explanation of the minuscule in this verse: to distinguish it from the regular *qof* at the end of the word that precedes it. Whether this is correct or not we cannot say, but in the absence of any other text-critical explanation we must perforce fall back on midrashic reasons for the small *qof* here.

The context is promising for this. Rebekah has just stage-managed the bestowal of the birthright by her aging, blind husband Isaac upon Jacob, and Esau immediately vows to take his revenge against his younger brother. On learning of this, Rebekah advises Jacob to flee for his life to her family back in Mesopotamian Haran. But Jacob's physical safety is not her only concern. Just prior to the story of the manipulation of the birthright blessing we are told: "When Esau was forty years old, he took to wife Judith, daughter of Beeri the Hittite, and Basemath, daughter of Elon the Hittite; and they were a source of bitterness to Isaac and Rebekah" (Gen 26:34–35). So now, having heard of Esau's murderous designs, she sees in them a pretext to address her and Isaac's anxiety about the kind of wife their younger son might marry, and it is this anxiety she lays before her husband in this verse.[127]

This disclosure of personal feelings is a rarity in biblical narrative. The storytellers in the Bible are good at relating what their characters do, their outer actions; they are quite laconic when it comes to telling us what they think or how they feel. We are a long way from the psychological realism of the modern novel. But Rebekah's words here are not perfunctory or formulaic; they spring from the depths of her being: "I am fed up," she is in effect saying, "not only with these Hittite women but with my whole life!" I don't think it is too much to say that in putting these words into Rebekah's mouth, the biblical writer is expressing what in modern narrative we would call the content of consciousness.

I think we could even surmise from this utterance that Rebekah is depressed. The verb she uses here, קצתי (*qaṣti*), derives from the root ק-ו-ץ (*q-w-ṣ*, "loathe"). To express loathing for one's life implies much more than the everyday dissatisfaction or unhappiness that accrue to most of us when our expectations are not met. I hear in Rebekah a deeper angst. This is not

---

127. Source critics see Genesis 27:46 and the verses we are looking at (26:34–35) as both reflecting the perspective of the priestly school (P), and the story of the manipulation of the birthright blessing that comes between them as the work of a different narrator (J). The apparent conflict between them can be resolved by this idea that "the distaste for Hittite women . . . becomes the pretext for [Rebekah's] saving her favorite son from his vindictive brother's rage." See Levenson, "Genesis," 53–54.

the first time she has talked this way. Early in her difficult pregnancy with the twin brothers, when she has felt them already striving with each other in her womb, she says, "If so, why do I exist?" (Gen 25:22).

Maurice Samuel, in his incisive interpretive portrait, little known today, of this mother of Israel catches the melancholy strain of her outburst:

> Is this Rebekah speaking? Rebekah, the self-assured, the valiant?
> It is the scream of a woman for whom the signals spell out contumely, ostracism, self-reproach, and the reproach of another. "Wherefore do I live?" What good am I? What has he done to me? Why was I brought into the world? . . .
> [I]t cannot be physical pain that has wrung such words from her. What we have just heard is the expression of a shattering physical disappointment. Wherefore do I live? What good am I to Isaac? What have I done to him? Why was I brought into his life? That is the meaning. She forefeels evil in the unnatural violence of the motions, and suspects that the nightmare has settled in her life for good.[128]

Samuel thus captures this profound sadness that pervades Rebekah's consciousness. He believes that it is rooted in her realization that the whole grand design of her life—to become the helpmate of Isaac and, in that capacity, "to guard [him] in the fulfillment of his destiny"[129]—is about to come to naught. It could be. But I think that her melancholy is even more personal than that. It flows from her sense of herself not only as a wife but as a mother. It has to do with the disquieting thought that in setting up the birthright blessing scenario and thereby tricking Esau, she may have precipitated the makings of a fratricide. She hints at this when, in advising Jacob to flee from Esau, she says "Let me not lose you both in one day!" (Gen 27:45).

There is a consensus among the traditionalist interpreters that in certain instances a minuscule letter in the Torah signifies some sort of lessening or contraction. What that lessening or contraction is can be discovered by pondering the letter that is written small. We shall see this when we examine some other verses with minuscules. Here it is a *qof* that is small, and this sets off a hunt for words that begin with that letter that would show what it is that has been diminished. Among those proposed is the word קצר (*qaṣar*, "short"). This prompts the sobering notion that the small *qof* is there

---

128. Samuel, *Certain People of the Book*, 154.
129. Samuel, *Certain People of the Book*, 184.

to indicate that the consequence of Rebekah's despondency was to shorten her years.¹³⁰ Actually, we do not even need to find a verbal connection to the letter *qof* to reach this hypothetical conclusion. We could simply let the diminution of the first letter of the first word of her anguished outburst (קצתי בחיי *qaṣti be-ḥayyay*, "I am disgusted with my life") serve as a subtle visual signifier of the diminution of self that Rebekah underwent watching her boys grow up.

This is admittedly a reading of Rebekah as a tragic figure. I wonder if it not supported by the fact that these despairing words that she utters to Isaac are the last we hear of her in the text. At this point Rebekah completely drops out of the story. Even the place and time of her death are omitted.¹³¹

Exodus 34:7

נצר חסד לאלפים נשא עון ופשע וחטאה

extending kindness to the thousandth generation, forgiving iniquity, transgression and sin.

Exodus 34:14

כי לא תשתחוה לאל אחר

For you must not worship any other god.

The two enlarged letters we shall now consider are not only near each other in the text, they are intrinsically linked in terms of what they tell us. That is why they deserve to be dealt with and understood in tandem.

This does not mean they cannot be discussed individually and separately. They certainly can. For each of them we can advance an explanation for their large size that is rooted in the actualities of writing Hebrew characters, in addition to an interpretation of their visual or phonetic or numeric meaning.

Let's take the second of these two majuscules first. In the introduction to this book I noted that in the last word of the Shemaʿ, אחד (*'eḥad*, "one" [Deut 6:4]), the last letter is written large: אחד.

---

130. Ron, *Sefer Qaṭan ve-Gadol*, 64.

131. Samuel, *Certain People of the Book*, 184; and Rendsburg, "Notes on Genesis XXXV," 364–65.

The Extraordinary Texts in the Torah

The reason for this is to avoid anyone mistaking the letter ד (*dalet*) for a ר (*resh*). There is not much difference between them: ד/ר.

It is really a matter of whether the scribe makes a tiny rightward extension of the top stroke or not. But the difference, however slight, is momentous. אחד (*'eḥad*) means "one"; אחר (*'aḥer*) means "another." In reciting the Shemaʿ, the quintessential statement of Jewish creed, one would not want to say that God is anything but one, i.e., unique and induplicable, the sole and exclusive deity in the totality of reality. To say anything else, that God is one among others, or that there even are any other gods, would be to say the exact opposite of what the Shemaʿ affirms. Similarly, with respect to אחר (*'aḥer*, "another") in Exodus 34:14, to read it as אחד (*'eḥad*, "one") and say "You shall not worship [lit. 'bow down' to] the one God" would completely controvert what the verse is saying. Hence in both cases the decisive letter is written large so the reader can't miss it.

The idea here is that words have power; language has consequences. The rabbis say that "if you make a *resh* like a *dalet* you can destroy a whole world!"[132]

The same situation may apply to the enlarged *nun* in Exodus 34:7, though this cannot be documented as clearly. The visual differential between the letter נ (*nun*) and the letter ו (*vav*) is not great: ו/נ.

If a *nun* is not written precisely, it could mean trouble. To write—and read—the verse with a *vav*—that is, וצר חסד לאלפים (*ve-ṣar ḥesed la-'alafim*, "and surpressing kindness to the thousandth generation")—instead of with a *nun*—that is, נצר חסד לאלפים (*noṣer ḥesed la-'alafim*, "extending kindness to the thousandth generation")—would subvert everything God is saying to Moses here.

These scribal issues and what they entail can certainly account for why the two letters in these two verses are written large. But we can also do this in a more midrashic way. Here, too, we take our cue from the Shemaʿ and the enlarged *ʿayin* and *dalet* it must display:

שמע ישראל יהוה אלהינו יהוה אחד

Hear, O Israel! The LORD is our God, the LORD alone.

The reader may recall from the introduction that the two majuscules form the word עד (*ʿed*, "witness"), and this yields the idea that to say the Shemaʿ is to bear witness to the reality of the One God of Israel. Now, in the two verses before us, the two enlarged letters, in their proximity in the text,

---

132. Vayyiqra' Rabbah 19:2.

invite the eye of the reader to take them in and the passage they bracket as a whole and to combine them to form the word נר (*ner*, "lamp, candle").

Lamp? Candle? What, we may ask, does a lamp or candle have to do with all this?

Answer: a lot. And to see why and how, let me walk you through some intricate midrashic steps that lead to a profound reading of this weighty passage.

1. We begin with an interpretive statement of Rabbi Shimon Bar Kappara (Eretz-Israel, late second—early third century). He holds up Psalm 18:29, where the psalmist says:

> It is You who light my lamp,
> the Lord, my God, lights up my darkness.

Bar Kappara comments: God says to man: "Your lamp is in my hands, and My lamp is in your hands. Your lamp is in my hands because 'The lamp of the Lord is the soul of man' (Prov 20:27). My lamp is in your hands [by virtue of the verse commanding the Eternal Light] 'Command the Israelite people to bring . . . clear oil of beaten olives for lighting, for kindling lamps regularly' (Lev 24:2). And so God says "If you light My lamp, I will kindle yours."

2. Rabbi Judah Moscato (Italy, ca. 1530–1590), one of the greats in the history of Jewish preaching, takes this mother lode of ideas and refines them into pure gold. He connects them to the lamp or candle [*ner*] that we see formed from the large *nun* and the large *resh* and to the respective contexts in which each of these letters occurs.[133]

The large *nun* in נצר חסד לאלפים (*noṣer ḥesed la-'alafim*, "extending kindness to the thousandth generation") is part of God's response to Moses after Moses had requested to "know" God's ways and to "behold" His presence.[134] It is a rare and crucial piece of self-disclosure to man by an unknowable, inscrutable God.

The large *resh* in כי לא תשתחוה לאל אחר (*ki lo' tishtaḥaveh le-'el 'aḥer*, "for you must not worship any other god") is a key—perhaps *the* key—element in the human side of the God/man equation.

3. Moscato sees the two verses as contingent on each other in the same way as the two lamps/candles are in Bar Kappara's little homily. Just as God

---

133. This is in Moscato's collection of sermons *Nefuṣot Yehudah* (1589), sermon no. 46. Cited in Ron, *Sefer Qaṭan ve-Gadol*, 77–78 and 84–85.

134. See Sarna, *Exodus*, 216.

says to man "you take care of My lamp/candle [i.e., the Eternal Light in the Mishkan and later, in the Temple, and still later, in the synagogue], and I'll take care of yours [i.e., the human soul, which is God's lamp/candle], so, by the same token, God says to man "worship no other but Me," and I will, as part of how I operate in the world, "extend kindness to the thousandth generation." The "lamp/candle" formed by the union of the two majuscular letters hints at the deeper relationship that underlies it. Just as the two letters need each other to complete their meaning, so do man and God need each other to complete themselves.

4. This idea that God needs man as much as man needs God is bold. It is at odds with much of the Greek philosophical tradition and with the medieval Jewish scholastics like Maimonides, who appropriated Aristotle in their religious thinking. To them God cannot have needs and is beyond any kind of emotion. It is the Jewish mystical tradition that holds up the notion that God has feelings and is affected by what people do, particularly by what Jews as individuals and as a people do. The Zohar, Lurianic Kabbalah, and Hasidism all develop in their own ways the implications and dynamics of the interdependence of God and man. In the latter decades of the twentieth century it was given currency in the writings of Abraham Joshua Heschel. Heschel locates the origin of the idea not in rabbinic midrash or in medieval Kabbalah, but in the Tanakh itself, specifically in the prophets. It is there, Heschel says, that the God of Israel is encountered as a Being who is not aloof or apathetic about man and man's actions, but One who is deeply interested in and affected by them. Heschel calls this fundamental attribute of God "divine pathos." His locution is not meant as an academic construct, but rather to convey that man is "relevant to God ... God is concerned about the world, [and] can actually suffer" when man fails to realize the expectations God had in creating him. This is well expressed in the rabbinic interpretation of the verse in Second Isaiah, "You are My witnesses, declares the Lord" (43:10), as follows:

> *If you [Israel] are My witnesses, then I am God; if you are not My witnesses, then I am, so to speak, not God!*[135]

So we have here two different ways of accounting for the two majuscules that occur so close together in this key passage of Exodus, two ways

---

135. Midrash Tehillim (on the book of Psalms) 123:2. See also Pesiqta de Rav Kahana 12:6, where this statement is reported in the name of Rabbi Shimon bar Yoḥai.

anchored in very different interpretive strategies. As we can see, these two strategies are not mutually exclusive.

Leviticus 1:1

ויקרא אל-משה וידבר יהוה אליו מאהל מועד לאמר

The Lord called to Moses and spoke to him from the Tent of Meeting, saying:

The small *'aleph* in this opening verse of Leviticus is, with the exception of the opening *bet* of Genesis, the most commented on of all the unusual letters. This could be due to its location at the very outset of a book; were it found in a word in the interior of a book it might have attracted less attention.[136]

The commentary that has accrued around this little *'aleph* is understandably midrashic in nature. No surprise there, for the letter *'aleph*, whatever its size, offers rich interpretive possibilities. Text-critical scholarship has little to say about it. There is Luzzatto's view of how minuscules came to be that can possibly be applied here: when two identical letters end and begin two consecutive words, the first identical letter was originally omitted and later squeezed in as a minuscule. By this line of reasoning the little *'aleph* of ויקרא (*vayyiqra'*, "called") is a late addition inserted to distinguish it from the *'aleph* that begins the next word אל (*'el*, "to").

We could, therefore, theorize that the original reading was ויקר משה (*vayyiqqar 'el moshe*, "He [God] manifested Himself to Moses"), with the verb presumably derived from the root ק-ר-ה (*q-r-h*, "occur, happen" [Qal], "encounter, manifest oneself" [Niph'al]). This would not be an irresponsible conjecture, for this is exactly how God's communication with the prophet Balaam is told in Numbers 23:4: ויקר אלהים אל בלעם (*vayyiqqar 'elohim 'el bil'am*, "God manifested Himself to Balaam" [see also 23:16]).

We thus see a surprising equivalence between Moses and Balaam. The verb ויקר (*vayyiqqar*, God having "manifested Himself") applies to both. And why shouldn't it? It is clear that from the Torah's perspective that the divine/human encounter is not restricted to Israelites. It is left for the rabbis to probe this phenomenon and to try to discover:

- whether there is any difference in how God communicated to Moses and to Balaam and other non-Israelite prophets;

---

136. Thus the conjecture by Ron, *Sefer Qaṭan ve-Gadol*, 88.

The Extraordinary Texts in the Torah

- what is gained meaning-wise by the addition of the *'aleph* in the case of Moses, to read ויקרא (*vayyiqra'*, "and He [God] *called*");
- whether ויקר (*vayyiqqar*) and ויקרא (*vayyiqra'*) are different forms of the same verb with similar connotations, or are two different verbs (as implied).

We find two views on these questions in the midrash. One holds that the same verb is intended for both: God called to Balaam just as he called to Moses. The difference is not that in Moses' case ויקר became ויקרא with the addition of the *'aleph*, but that in Balaam's case ויקרא became ויקר as the *'aleph* was lopped off. The truncation is to indicate that the divine calling to Balaam was clipped and incomplete. There was not the same fullness of communication with Balaam as there was with Moses and, for that matter, with all the prophets of Israel.

Alternatively, the pertinent verb derives rather from the root ק-ר-ה . What the text is suggesting is that Balaam's encounter with God was fragmentary because it was sporadic, a matter of chance or serendipity. God happened upon him, whereas God's link with Moses was steady and uninterrupted. Moses was, so to speak, always online with God.[137]

The point the midrash is making is that, however we explain it, God's relationship with Moses was unique compared to Balaam's and anyone else's, and it is the addition of the small *'aleph* in this first verse of Leviticus that establishes this. How this *'aleph* came to be is the subject of a debate between two exegetical giants who were father and son.

The medieval Talmudist Asher of Toledo (1250–1327) fancies Moses as remonstrating with God to keep him out of this first verse entirely. After all, Leviticus is a book for the *kohanim*, and Moses, unlike his brother Aaron, was not of the priestly order. So he felt that he really didn't need to be mentioned in this priestly book. (We also know that "Moses was a very humble man, more so than any other man on earth" [Num 12:3]). In this imaginary dialogue, God replies that there was no choice: it must be told that God imparted the laws of Leviticus to Moses. But that would require

---

137. See Vayyiqra' Rabbah 1:13. Rabbi Issachar of the Galilean town of Kefar Mandi offers a variation of this latter view. He connects the verb ק-ר-ה (*q-r-h*, "occur, happen") to the term for a nocturnal event, i.e., a seminal emission מקרה לילה (*miqreh layla*), an incident—or an accident—that renders a man (Balaam in this case) ritually unclean. This leads Rabbi Issachar to deduce that whereas God called to the prophets of Israel in purity and holiness, in the case of the prophets of the nations like Balaam, they heard the voice of God in an impure state resulting from an accident that defiled them. Rashi selects this approach in his opening comment on Leviticus 1:1.

writing ויקר (*vayyiqqar*, "He [God] manifested Himself") as with Balaam, and this was an equivalency God did not want to make. Accordingly, God instructed Moses to add an *'aleph* and write the manifestation as a clear *call*, i.e., ויקרא (*vayyiqra'*)—but to write the *'aleph* small to show that Moses, in his humility, held himself small.

Asher's son Jacob (the Ba'al HaṬurim) picks up this interpretation, but gives it a different twist. It was Moses, not God, who was ready to write ויקר (*vayyiqqar*), so as not to make himself greater than Balaam or other prophets to whom God appeared accidentally or in a dream. But God, knowing that his relationship with Moses was unlike that with any other mortal, instructed Moses to add the *'aleph* so as to show the distinction. And Moses, being the humblest man on earth, wrote it small.

This interpretation invites comparison with another irregularly written *'aleph* in the Bible, the one found in the opening verse of the book of Chronicles. That book begins with a genealogical listing of the progenitors of the human family, and the first verse reads and looks like this: אדם שת אנוש (*'adam shet 'enosh*, "Adam, Seth, Enosh"). Here the *'aleph* is written large, as the Masoretic note instructs. No explanation is given, but it could well be due to the sometime practice of writing the first letter of a book as a majuscule, as noted previously. More interesting, though, is the idea put forth in the Zohar that the *'aleph* is large because of how Adam, when he looked at the world into which he had been put, (rightly) viewed himself as the crown of creation. This is in contrast to Moses as we find him at the outset of Leviticus, outside the Mishkan and unable to enter. We were told in the last verses of Exodus that this was because of the cloud covering it. The Zohar reads this differently. Moses was *unwilling* to enter, even though he could have. He is unwilling because he knows that, for all his stature as an interlocutor with the divine, he is a mortal and he cannot encroach upon divine space. And so he waits until God calls to him from within the Holy of Holies to come inside and receive the laws that will be detailed in the book that will follow.[138]

The issue is ego. Moses has contained his ego. Among much else, the letter *'aleph* can signify the ego. It can stand for or indicate the two different Hebrew words for "I": אני (*'ani*) and אנכי (*'anoki*). When the "I" or the ego is diminished and contracted, then is it possible to hear the call of that which lies outside of or beyond the self. When, however, one is full of oneself,

---

138. Cited from the Zohar 3:53b in Ron, *Sefer Qaṭan ve-Gadol*, 92.

there is no room for anything else. That is the insight that the small '*aleph* encodes.

This opening verse of Leviticus raises some interesting questions about an exceedingly difficult and vexed issue: what does it mean to hear something that would make us know, or think we know, that we are being addressed by something or someone beyond us, by God, in the way that Adam and Abraham and Moses and Balaam felt themselves to be addressed by God? What is involved in such an experience? What is it that transforms this experience into a call?

The experience I am talking about is inherently subjective, private, and personal. It takes place in the innermost parts of one's being. It is not easily rendered into language, if it can even be rendered at all. And it is deeply problematical. How do we know for sure that what one is hearing is not some psychic construction or emotional aberration or psychological disorder? What happens when what is heard as a call from God contravenes ethical and moral norms?

Consider, for example, the story of the binding of Isaac, where a father hears a command from God to offer a sacrifice by killing his son. It is true that this command (if that is what it was) is quickly countermanded by a second call to refrain from killing—"*this has been a test!*"—still, the relationship of the divine call to the ethical is very much put in question.[139]

In short, how does one know—how do we know—that it is God who is calling? Carol Delaney cites the following trenchant words of Immanuel Kant:

> If God should really speak to man, man could still never *know* that it was God speaking. It is quite impossible for man to apprehend the infinite by his senses, distinguish it from sensible beings, and *recognize* it as such. But in some cases man can be sure the voice he hears is *not* God's; for if the voice commands him to do something contrary to the moral law, then no matter how majestic the apparition may be, and no matter how it may seem to surpass the whole of nature, he must consider it an illusion [emphasis his].[140]

---

139. This is the burden of Kierkegaard's *Fear and Trembling* (1843), where the ethical is suspended, superseded by obedience to divine authority. For a comprehensive analysis and searching critique of the Aqedah story and its cultural influence on the three monotheistic religions, see also Delaney, *Abraham on Trial*, especially 118–19, and her conclusion, 251–53.

140. Quoted in Delaney, *Abraham on Trial*, 123, from Kant's *The Conflict of the Faculties* (1798), which she characterizes as "a late and quite obscure little book."

But what if what one hears in the innermost recesses of the self is experienced as coming from a transcendent source outside the self, and is not contrary to the moral law, and prompts us to respond as Abraham and Moses did, with a reflexive, unhesitating הנני (*hinneni*, "Here I am!")?

The diminished *'aleph* in the first word of Leviticus points to the rudiments of an answer. It suggests that however and whenever we hear the divine, its call is not and cannot be about our ego needs. It doesn't matter if we hear it, or think we hear it, but once in our lifetime, or only occasionally, or even frequently and regularly. If it leads to or involves an "ego trip," then that call is suspect. If, however, we hear it in humility, with a diminished sense of our self-importance (though not in self-abasement or with any surrendering of our dignity) as Moses did, then we will respond in a similar way: with הנני (*hinneni*, "Here I am!").

Leviticus 6:2

צו את אהרן ואת בניו לאמר זאת תורת העלה הוא העלה על מוקדה על המזבח כל הלילה עד הבקר ואש המזבח תוקד בו

> *Command Aaron and his sons thus: This is the ritual of the burnt offering: the burnt offering itself shall remain where it is burned upon the altar all night until morning, while the fire on the altar is kept going on it.*

We now encounter another instance where the Masoretes mandated a small letter, and we know of no apparent reason that might explain it. Removal of the minuscular *mem* does not yield anything that resembles a word that could suggest an alternative reading. And so, as in other places, we toil to ferret meaning out of the text and the context.

When we first look at the verse and the passage in which it occurs we are tempted to abandon all hope of finding anything that would be interesting to anyone other than a cultural anthropologist or an historian of religion. We are, after all, situated in the most forbidding, figuratively speaking, textual landscape in the entire Pentateuch. We are reading the details of the various sacrifices that were offered in the Mishkan and, later, in the Temple. The verse we are looking at relates to the proper manner in which the *kohanim* (the priestly Temple officiants) were to perform the *'olah*. This term is generally translated as "burnt offering" and sometimes as "holocaust." These renderings are not incorrect, though they miss the etymological sense of the term.

The word for burnt offering or holocaust, *'olah*, is not derived from a root that means "to burn" but rather from the verb "to go up," which, however, is metonymically linked to burning by suggesting the idea that the whole sacrifice "goes up" in smoke.[141]

Unlike some of the other sacrifices, parts of which were to be eaten by the *kohanim* or the donors, the *'olah* was completely consumed by the fire on the altar.

That is the context of our verse. The verse itself is saying that the *'olah*, after it had been offered, must sit on the fire all night long until it has been totally incinerated.

The particular word that is the object of our attention, מוקדה (*moqdah*), is variously translated "where it is burned," "on its place of burning," "on the blazing-hearth," and "over its flame."[142] All accurately convey the idea that the *'olah* stays on the coals.

What, then, shall we make of the small *mem*? Only a sense for metaphor will help us here. We find it in the Hasidic masters, who were keenly aware of the mystical possibilities of everyday objects and deeds. Thus:

1. offering a sacrifice to God can be a metaphor for any act we perform that expresses our desire to serve God, to give something back to him for blessings received;

2. the fire on the altar is a metaphor for the passion we bring to our service.

Put these together, and we arrive at an insight about how we should approach our spiritual life and our service of God. Of course we must bring passion to it. Otherwise it is all for naught. I am always dispirited when, as happens too often, I visit a synagogue and everyone sits in studied indifference to what is going on. At such times I wonder why they are there at all, and I think of these lines from T. S. Eliot's "The Hollow Men":

> We are the hollow men
> We are the stuffed men
> Leaning together
> Headpiece filled with straw. Alas!
> Our dried voices, when
> We whisper together
> Are quiet and meaningless

---

141. Alter, *Five Books of Moses*, 564.

142. The renderings are, respectively, those of NJV, Richard Elliot Friedman, Everett Fox, and Robert Alter.

> As wind in dry grass
> Or rats' feet over broken glass
> In our dry cellar
>
> Shape without form, shade without colour,
> Paralysed force, gesture without motion;[143]

And then there are the synagogues I happen into where passion overflows to the point where it fairly assaults me. The decibel level leads me to wonder if there is some unrecorded teaching that the Ancient One of Israel is hard of hearing. I do know there is a verse "All my bones shall declare 'Lord, who is like You?'" (Ps 35:10), but this does not seem to imply bodily gymnastics while praying.

Why not a middle ground in our liturgical and our religious life: a fire burning within, molten passion about what we are doing—but an interior passion, enthusiasm and piety, inward and not on display. Hence the reduced *mem*: "the offering shall remain where it is burned." Or, as Moshe of Koznitz, son of the Magid of Koznitz said, "Let the coal be larger than the flame."[144]

Leviticus 11:42

.כל הולך על גחון ... לא תאכלום כי שקץ הם

Anything that crawls on its belly ... you shall not eat, for they are an abomination.

As we have seen (p. 77), Tractate Sofrim stipulates that the *vav* of גחון (*gaḥon*, "belly") must be enlarged, because it is the middle letter of the Torah.[145] The Masoretic tradition marks it as such. There is only one problem with this statement: it is incorrect. Over the centuries there have been a number of attempts to count the letters and words (not to mention the verses) in the Torah, and the various reckonings resulted in different totals! Different totals, of course, would result in a different determination of the middle letter. R. Jacob Schorr (1853–1924) did his own count and found

---

143. Eliot, "Hollow Men," lines 1–12.
144. Cited from Ron, *Sefer Qaṭan ve-Gadol*, 124.
145. Tractate Sofrim 9:2.

The Extraordinary Texts in the Torah

the middle letter to be located in Leviticus 8:28 in the *vav* of the word הוא (*hu'*, "it is").[146]

This discrepancy between what the Masoretic tradition mandates and what later scholars have found is worth exploring, for it brings to the fore several issues that relate to the transmission of the Torah's text. We have already had an inkling that this process was not nearly as smooth as hidebound traditionalists would like to think. We have, for example, noted the existence all along of variant textual traditions. We already see this in the following passage in the Talmud:

> Therefore were the early scholars called *sofrim*, for they counted every letter in the Pentateuch. They said that the *vav* of גחון *gaḥon* (Lev 11:42) is the middle letter of the Torah scroll, דרש דרש *darosh darash* (Lev 10:16) is the middle of the words,[147] and והתגלח *ve-hitgallaḥ* (Lev 13:33) is the middle of the verses. . . .
>
> Rabbi Yosef asked: "Is the *vav* of *gaḥon* on this side or on that side?" They answered him: "Let's bring a Torah scroll and count, the way Rabbi Rabba bar Bar Hana did [in another such instance when] they did not move from there until a Torah scroll was brought and counted."
>
> He [R. Yosef] replied: "They [the early *sofrim*] were experts in חסר *ḥaser (defectiva)* and מלא *male' (plene)* spellings, we are not" . . .
>
> Abaye said to him: "At least the verses we can count."
>
> [R. Yosef replied:] "No, in verses, likewise, we are not experts."[148]

Rabbi Yosef is alluding to the fact that some Hebrew words can be written in one of two ways: either with an additional letter or without. For example, in Genesis 23, where Abraham is bargaining with the Hittite chieftain Efron over the field that would become the ancestral burial place Machpelah, Efron's name is spelled in full as עפרון every time throughout the chapter, except in verse 16, where it is spelled defectively as עפרן.[149] In

---

146. Cohen, "On the Number," 14n4. [For still another calculation, see Andersen and Forbes, "What *Did* the Scribes Count," 315, with the claim that the first ה (*he*) in החזה in Leviticus 8:29 is the middle letter of the Torah.—G.A.R.]

147. [Note, incidentally, that this finding is incorrect. Andersen and Forbes, "What *Did* the Scribes Count?" 308, comment that דרש דרש in Leviticus 10:16 is actually 51.2 percent of the way through the Torah (by words), and that the actual middle word of the Pentateuch is ויקדשהו in Leviticus 8:15.—G.A.R.]

148. b. Qiddushin 30a.

149. Emanuel Tov observes a similar phenomenon in English where, for example,

explaining Rabbi Yosef's retorts that he and his contemporaries "are not experts in *defectiva* and *plene* spellings," Menahem Cohen writes:

> R. Yosef recognizes the possibility that the texts of the early *Sofrim* were not identical to the letter with the texts of his time and place. This he probably concluded from the fact that in Babylon itself [where he was situated] there were differences between the letter texts of different scrolls, and there was no one version which could be identified with certainty as the one which was before the early *Sofrim*. This is the plain meaning of the expression "we are not experts." . . .
>
> [And so] anyone who does not wish to ignore reality as it is reflected in all the periods of the Torah text's transmission will have to admit that any counting of letters in one generation or another can only represent the text in which it was counted and doesn't necessarily fit other books.[150]

We see this clearly in the inconsistency in where the Masoretes marked the middle letter and the middle word in the Torah on the one hand, and where they marked the middle verse on the other. With respect to the middle letter and the middle word they follow the Talmud's reckonings of these, noted in the passage by Cohen. But with respect to the middle verse they do not. The Talmud identifies the middle verse as Leviticus 13:33 (indicated by the word in it [והתגלח, *ve-hitgallaḥ*]). Tractate Sofrim, compiled presumably later than the Talmud, fixes it at Leviticus 8:15 or 8:23. The Masoretes, however, accepted neither of these determinations. They marked the middle verse of the Torah at Leviticus 8:8.[151] Why, then, this inconsistency, accepting the Talmud on letters (the *vav* that started this whole discussion) and words, but not on verses?

The answer is that, as Cohen tells us, the Masoretic rabbis understood:

> the possibility that the early *Sofrim* made a mistake in their count of the verses . . . [T]hey made a new count of the verses, the result

---

the word written as "favor" in the United States is spelled "favour" in the UK. Likewise, "catalog" vs. "catalogue" and "judgment" vs. "judgement." Tov (*Textual Criticism*, 210) further states: "With each successive transcription, the orthography of the biblical books was adapted either fully or partially to the system that was currently in practice in that period."

150. Cohen, "On the Number," 11–12.

151. [As a point of information, note that Andersen and Forbes, "What *Did* the Scribes Count," 307, consider Leviticus 8:9 to be the middle verse of the Torah.—G.A.R.]

of which contradicted what was said in the [Talmud], and this new result is what was accepted in the Masorah literature.[152]

The fact that Tractate Sofrim's count also differed from the Talmud's shows that the Masoretes were not the first or the only ones to be skeptical about the reckonings of the received tradition.

Why, then, did the Masoretes accept what the Talmud said about the middle letter and the middle word, but not what it said about the middle verse? More to the point, if the enlarged *vav* we are considering is not the middle letter of the Torah, why did the Masoretes persist in marking it as such? Cohen attributes this to the fact that although the Masoretes "counted all the letters and words of the Pentateuch several times and came up with several different results," they did not "recount the midpoint of the letters and words . . . because they didn't bother to repeat this tedious job, preferring instead to quote the [Talmudic statement]."[153]

What does all this say about the Masoretic tradition? That it is wrong? Unreliable?

I think that would be too harsh a conclusion. Let us remember that the early medieval scholars we call Masoretes took a text, or texts, that had been circulating for more than a millennium and stabilized them as best they could. The following words of Emanuel Tov are worth citing in their fullness, for they shed a great deal of light on what we've been looking at here. Let me note in advance that the word "corrupted" as Tov uses it is not a pejorative term. It has no moral overtones or implications. Tov writes:

> Most texts—ancient and modern—that are transmitted from one generation to the next get *corrupted* in one way or another. For modern compositions, the process of textual transmission from the writing of the autographs until their final printing is relatively short, thus limiting the possibilities of them becoming corrupted. In ancient texts, however, such as Hebrew-Aramaic Scripture, these corruptions (the technical term for various forms of "mistakes") were more frequent as a result of the complexities of writing on papyrus and leather and the length of the transmission process . . . The number of factors that could have created corruptions is large: the transition from the early Hebrew to the square script, unclear handwriting, unevenness in the surface of the leather or papyrus, graphically similar letters which were often

152. Cohen, "On the Number," 13.
153. Cohen, "On the Number," 13.

confused, the lack of vocalization, unclear boundaries between words in early texts [etc.]. . . .

Those who are unaware of the details of textual criticism may think that one should not expect any corruptions in . . . any . . . sacred text, since these texts were meticulously written and transmitted. The scrupulous approach of the *soferim* and Masoretes is indeed manifest in some of their techniques. . . . Yet, in spite of their precision, even the manuscripts that were written and vocalized by the Masoretes contain corruptions, changes, and erasures. More importantly, the Masoretes, and before them the *soferim*, made their contribution at a relatively late stage in the development of the biblical text, and before they put their meticulous principles into practice. Therefore, paradoxically, the *soferim* and Masoretes carefully preserved a text that was already corrupted [emphasis his].[154]

So the biblical text as we have it today, as it has been passed down—*because* it has been passed down—is imperfect, flawed. It is sublime in form and content, but it is not infallible.[155]

We can apply this conclusion to our tradition as a whole—the great body of text, ritual, ethics, and culture that our forebears lovingly preserved and bequeathed to us. The tradition is there for us: as ballast in which to anchor and structure our lives, as a wellspring from which to draw its teachings and insights. But it is not infallible. It is not above critique. It is a means to larger ends; it is not the end in itself. That is the import of the *vav* in גחון (*gaḥon*, "belly"). It is not the middle letter of the Torah, but it is still written large.

I will have more to say about it in this next section.

Leviticus 13:33

.והתגלח ואת הנתק לא יגלח והסגיר הכהן את הנתק שבעת ימים שנית

And he [the one with the scall] shall shave himself, but without shaving the scall; and the priest shall isolate him for another seven days.

As we have seen, there are on record no fewer than three determinations as to what the middle verse in the Torah is. The Babylonian Talmud (b. Qiddushin 30a) accords this verse that status. Tractate Sofrim says it is

---

154. Tov, *Textual Criticism*, 9–10.
155. See Levy, *Fixing God's Torah*. [bibliographic addition—eds.]

Leviticus 8:15 (or maybe 8:23) and stipulates that the first word in it, וישחט (*vayyishḥaṭ*, "and he slaughtered"), must be written large. That is not done in the majority of Torah scrolls. The Masorah annotates Leviticus 8:8 as the middle verse, but it does not mandate that any word or letter in it be enlarged. Yet curiously, the Masorah also seems to be respecting the Talmud's reckoning even though it may be wrong, for it marks the *gimel* in this verse as a majuscule (as represented)—but it gives no annotation to explain this.

In the face of this confusion and evident inaccuracy, our only recourse, if we are to discover something worthwhile in this enlarged *gimel*, is to follow a midrashic approach.

In itself this would be nothing new. The rabbis treat other such letters midrashically all the time, and in that spirit I myself have not been reluctant to jump into the play of midrashic signifiers. Midrash is not a closed process.

That brings me to an issue that that has been percolating throughout this chapter but which I have not yet noted or discussed: What happens when one wishes to proceed midrashically and finds nothing to play with in the verse or word or letter she is reading, nothing that sparks some imaginative twist that elicits from that particular text a teaching or an insight that was hitherto invisible or even unknown? In such a case, who or what is deficient: the reader or the text?

I would say the reader. Consider the enlarged *gimel* we are now looking at or the enlarged *vav* in the preceding discussion. There has been no shortage of commentators and homilists who have had no trouble bringing to light something of value they saw hidden in them. We are by now familiar with how they do this. They seize upon some aspect of the letter as the stimulus to the interpretations they are generating. A favorite is its numerical value or the gematria total of the word of which it is a part, or it could be some alliterative association that the letter triggers.

Examples:

- The letter *gimel* is the third letter of the Hebrew alphabet, and its numerical value is three. Three are the kinds of people who the Torah states must undergo a special shaving: the leper when his skin inflammation has not spread, the nazirite when he becomes contaminated by a corpse and has to start his vow all over again, and the Levites as part of their consecration process.¹⁵⁶ The *gimel* in this verse about the leper's shaving is made large so as to encode this teaching.

- The numerical value of the five letters of the word התגלח (*hitgallaḥ*, "shaved himself"; the initial *vav* is not included in this count) adds up to 446. The three letters of the Hebrew word מות (*mawet*, "death") also add up to 446. The enlarged *gimel* in the word serves to confirm the teaching that "three are considered as if they are dead: one who is poor, one who is blind, and a leper."¹⁵⁷

- The letter *gimel* stands for the mitzvah of גמילות חסדים (*gemilut ḥasadim*, "deeds of lovingkindess"), which is the central mitzvah in the Torah. That is why we see a large *gimel* at the center of the word in the verse that stands at the center of the Torah.

- The letter *vav* is the sixth letter in the Hebrew alphabet, and its numerical value is six. The *vav* in the middle word of the Torah, גחון (*gaḥon*; see p. 113), points to the sixth day of the month of Sivan, the day on which the Torah was given.

- The word גחון (*gaḥon*) means "belly," and the verse, as Rashi notes, is alluding to the snake, listed here among those crawling creatures that are not to be eaten. The *vav* is enlarged to replicate the original upright appearance of the serpent and thus remind us of the havoc it caused that led it to be cast down and forever crawl in the dust. Some say the *vav* alludes to six curses that were visited upon the snake.¹⁵⁸

I suppose each of us will have his or her own opinion about these inferences. Some will find them clever and insightful, some will find their homespun wisdom a bit cloying, and there will surely be some who find them overly pietistic, even corny. I tend toward the latter view.

This highlights a basic truth about midrashic and homiletic interpretation: it is inherently subjective. It is generated not by historical data or comparative cultural analysis, but by the personal life-situation and concerns, the fears and aspirations of the midrashic interpreter, and the community he or she addresses. That was true of midrash in the classical collections of the rabbinic period, and it is true for midrash as it has been created

---

156. See m. Negaim 14:4; and b. Nazir 40a.

157. b. Nedarim 64b. Actually, the text has the number as four, adding "one who has no children." [Perhaps Rabbi Diamond's point here was that a preacher could modify the source in order to make a point of his own. His intention here remains unclear.—eds.]

158. See Ron, *Sefer Qaṭan ve-Gadol*, 128–29 and 134–35.

The Extraordinary Texts in the Torah

in more recent centuries and in our time. These nuggets mined from the letters they explicate were surely meaningful to those who concocted them and those who heard or read them, and they probably continue to be so. To my more modernist sensibility they are, for better or worse, more quaint than compelling. And yet, as I've demonstrated, the size and shape of the *bet* in Genesis 1:1 or the little *'aleph* in Leviticus 1:1 speak to me clearly and substantially. Like beauty in the eye of the beholder, midrashic meaning inheres in the personal, communal, and generational context of the interpreter and his or her hearers and readers.

Numbers 14:17

ועתה יגדל נא כח אדני כאשר דברת לאמר

Therefore, I pray, let my Lord's forbearance be great, as You have declared, saying.

Deuteronomy 32:18

צור ילדך תשי ותשכח אל מחללך

You neglected the Rock that begot you,
you forgot the God who brought you forth.

Earlier in this chapter, I noted the idea that took hold among some commentators in the Middle Ages, namely, were one to traverse the biblical text from Genesis to Chronicles, one would find at various points each letter of the alphabet written once as a majuscule and once as a miniscule. The idea is more fanciful than real, principally because, as we have seen, there never was a fixed or predetermined number of letters that were to be written large and small.

Nevertheless, the notion that for each majuscule there exists a corresponding minuscule of the same letter sets up an interesting interpretive opportunity, especially if the two letters in question reside within the Torah text. This is the case with respect to two letters: 1) the ה (*he*), written small in Genesis 2:4 (בהבראם, *be-hibbar'am*, which has already been discussed) and written large in Deuteronomy 32:6 (ליהוה ה, *ha-la-yhwh*; to be discussed), and 2) the letter י (*yod*) in the two verses before us now.

Before we explore the two *yods* as a pair, we should note that there is no scribal or grammatical or other empirical issue that might account for why they are both written as they are. Nothing. Both are correct, parts of the verb forms they inhabit. Neither one could be thought to be spurious or superfluous. But there they are and have been for a very long time.

The respective contexts in which each of these *yod*s is embedded do point to a certain complementarity between them. Both concern the dynamics of how the people of Israel and God relate to each other.

The verse in Numbers is part of a passage that narrates one of the most tumultuous moments in that relationship. The scouts that Moses sent out to spy out the land of Canaan have returned, and their baleful report and discouraging prognosis have totally demoralized the people. They want to go back to Egypt. That is the last straw for God: after all that had been done for them they are still not signed up for the voyage to the Promised Land. Therefore, says God, "I will strike them with pestilence and disown them" (Num 14:12).

The relationship between God and Israel is at its lowest point since the episode of the Golden Calf. And just as he did then, so does Moses now intercede on the people's behalf. He beseeches God not to act on his anger.

> *If then You slay this people to a man, the nations who have heard Your fame will say, "It must be because the Lord was powerless to bring that people into the land He had promised them on oath that He slaughtered them in the wilderness." Therefore, I pray, let my Lord's forbearance [כח] be great.* (Num 14:15–17a)

And Moses then rehearses a truncated version of the attributes of God's mercy, just as he did in the aftermath of the Golden Calf.

Now the Hebrew word כח (*koaḥ*), which is what Moses is asking to be made great, means "strength." Milgrom explains its translation "forbearance" as "the strength to hold back from destroying Israel."[159] This is not incorrect, but it is too subtle for the context. Robert Alter's rendering makes it clearer what Moses wants here: "Let the LORD's power be great." Alter comments:

> Some interpreters, leaning on one marginal biblical parallel, claim that "power" here actually means "forbearance." Rashi more plausibly glosses "power" as God's power to do what He has said. That proposal makes particular sense in light of the jeering reference to God's inability, or lack of power, in the words attributed to the

---

159. Milgrom, *Numbers*, 111. He finds this usage in Job 6:12 and Nahum 1:3.

surrounding nations. That is, God, by standing by His word to Israel, will make the greatness of his power manifest.[160]

On this basis, writing the *yod* large in the word יגדל (*yigdal*, "may it be great") makes a lot of sense. *Yod* is, after all, one of the letters of the divine Name. A large *yod* here presents a wonderful consonance between what the verse looks like visually and what it is saying verbally. At this moment when the connection between God and Israel is tenuous, Moses is asking for God to show his power, to magnify his name that begins with *yod* and thus preserve or restore the relationship with his people.

The small *yod* in the verse in Deuteronomy 32 presents the converse of all this. Here we are in the middle of a poem, the final great utterance of Moses before he ascends Mount Nebo to die there. I pass over the view of most biblicists that this is actually a poem that pre-dates Deuteronomy and has been appropriated by the writer or compiler of that book who patched it in as Moses' swan song. The Torah asks that we read the poem as Moses' recapitulation in verse of the ups and downs of the relationship between God and Israel.

We are in the part of the poem where Moses is finishing his description of Israel's perfidious behavior (vv. 15–18). They have grown fat, have forsaken the covenant, and they have angered God by worshipping idols. And then this verse states the upshot of these actions: צור ילדך תשי ותשכח אל מחללך ("you neglected the Rock that begot you, you forgot the God who brought you forth").

Since it is the *yod* in the word תשי (*teshi*) that is the focal point, we ought to zero in on just what that word is conveying. That it means "neglected" is clear from the second half (stich) of the verse. This is biblical poetry, where the style mandates that the two (sometimes three) parts of the verse (called stichs) be parallel to each other in both form and content. In biblical poetry the second stich of a verse almost always echoes the first one, saying exactly the same thing or adding a slightly different nuance to it in different words. We can deduce that the word תשי (*teshi*) in the first stich, a verb here, means "neglected" from its parallel verb in the second stich ותשכח (*vattishkaḥ*, "forgot").[161]

---

160. Alter, *Five Books of Moses*, 751.

161. [The word תשי remains a *crux interpretum* in the Bible. Rabbi Diamond's analysis here follows the traditional view that the word is a verbal form derived from the root נ-ש-ה (*n-sh-h*, "forget"; thus ibn Ezra and Rashbam explicitly, and several other commentators, e.g., Rashi, implicitly).—G.A.R.]

But the word also has a secondary overtone that extends the range of implication. תשי (*teshi*) can also be seen as derived from the Hebrew verb ת-ש-ש (*t-sh-sh*, "be weak" [Qal], "weaken" [Hiph'il]).[162] Thus the midrashic gloss on the verse is "You have debilitated the power of the Creator."[163] Rashi picks this up in his comment on the verse. After duly noting that the primary meaning here is about forgetting, he parses Moses as saying: "When God sought to benefit you [Israel], you angered him and diminished his power to do good things for you."

Rashi does not connect either meaning with the small *yod*; did the manuscript he had not show it that way? But we can, and when we do, we find that it is the flip side of what we found in Numbers 14:17. There Moses asks God to magnify his power and so demonstrate to the nations and, more importantly, to Israel that the covenant with Israel still holds. Here Moses is saying that Israel's faithlessness has impeded God's power and diminished his role as their covenantal partner.

The numerical value of the letter *yod* is ten, and this fact predictably enables many commentators to upload material into both its small and large occurrences. Israel has weakened God by forgetting the Ten Commandments and/or by testing and trying God's patience ten times in the desert. Israel magnifies God's presence in the world whenever a community of Jews recites together the Qaddish with its ten expressions of praise:[164]

1. יתגדל (*yitgaddal*, "magnified")

2. ויתקדש (*ve-yitqaddash*, "and sanctified")

3. יתברך (*yitbarak*, "and sanctified")

4. וישתבח (*ve-yishtabbaḥ*, "and praised")

5. ויתפאר (*ve-yitpa'ar*, "and glorified")

6. ויתרומם (*ve-yitromam*, "and exalted")

7. ויתנשא (*ve-yitnaśśe'*, "and raised")

---

162. [This root does not appear in biblical Hebrew; instead, it appears for the first time in Tannaitic texts, for which see Moreshet, *Leqsiqon ha-Po'al she-Nitḥaddesh bi-Lshon ha-Tanna'im*, 397. But this fact does not create an obstacle to perceiving the meaning of "be weak, weaken" in תשי (*teshi*) in Deuteronomy 32:18. Most scholars assume that words attested for the first time only in post-biblical Hebrew may have been part of the Hebrew lexis already during the biblical period.—G.A.R.]

163. Vayyiqra' Rabbah 23:12.

164. Cited from Elazar Rokeach of Worms (c. 1176–1238), as cited in Ron, *Sefer Qaṭan ve-Gadol*, 146. See also 223.

The Extraordinary Texts in the Torah

8. ויתהדר (*ve-yithaddar*, "and honored")

9. ויתעלה (*ve-yitʻalleh*, "and honored")

10. ויתהלל (*ve-yithallal*, "and lauded")

God and Israel—actually God and humanity—are interdependent. The actions of one affect the other. If I may appropriate the oft-quoted words of President John F. Kennedy in his Inaugural Address: "Ask not what God can do for you; ask what you can do for God." This is a key idea in Jewish theology. We saw it in the linkage of the *nun* and the *resh* in Exodus 34:7 and 34:14 to produce נר (*ner*, "lamp/candle"). And now we see it encoded in the two interrelated *yod*s.

Numbers 25:12

לכן אמר הנני נתן לו את בריתי שלוֹם
Therefore say, "I grant him My pact of peace."

[N.B. We have not been able to locate a font with the "broken *vav*" form, so it appears with a strikethrough line, as a best approximation of its special quality. The form looks like this in a contemporary Torah scroll—eds.]:

Figure 7: The word שלום (*shalom*, "peace") in **Numbers 25:12**,
written with the broken letter *vav*.
[Image © Mordechai Pinchas (Marc Michaels), Sofer STaM,
used with kind permission (www.sofer.co.uk).]

In this book I have said a lot about scribes, the *sofrim* who from early in the history of Israel down to the present day copy out Torah scrolls, other biblical books such as Esther, *mezuzot*, and *tefillin*. As we turn to the irregular letter in this verse—and it is indeed irregular for it is neither a majuscule nor a minuscule, but rather a broken or cracked *vav*—let's hear from a practicing *sofer* himself:

> Throughout the *halakha* it is stressed that letters must be written as a complete *guf* (body) and if they are faded or partly illegible then the work is invalid.
>
> However, there is one exception where the scribe is mandated to make the letter incomplete. The letter in question is the *vav* in the word *shalom* in Numbers 25:12. This must be written with a break in the vertical line according to the Ritva (R. Yom Tov ben Abraham Ishbili, Spain c. 1250–1330).[165]

There is another opinion that holds that the *vav* should not be written this way but with its bottom half truncated, so that it looks like a small *yod*. And yet another that the *vav* should be written complete but as a minuscule. Commentators who follow these views then supply the conventional riffs on the various associations that the numerical values of these letters trigger.

The Masorah annotates the *vav* as broken, and that is how most Torah scrolls show it. Could this have something to do with the context in which this *vav* is written? The verse comes on the heels of a drastic action Pinḥas (Phineas) took at the sight of Zimri, a leader of the Israelite tribe of Simeon, and Cozbi, a Midianite princess, performing the sexual act in public, at the doorway of the Tabernacle. Pinḥas took matters into his own hands and killed them both with one thrust of a spear that skewered them in their coital union. It could be that the *vav* is written to represent visually the spear as it might have looked after Pinḥas had deployed it.

Pinḥas' act not only stopped the plague that had broken out among the Israelites in the wake of this moral outrage, it also earned him the reward of being the apotheosis of peace. The paradox of this could account for the broken *vav*. The *sofer* Mordechai Pinchas opines that

> the Massoretes must have been shocked by the violence of Pinchas' action as they made his blessing only partial through the broken *vav* which explains that true peace cannot be brought about through violence and that the two concepts are incompatible.[166]

This interpretation has been a staple of sermonizers for generations, and the relevance of its point has not diminished.

---

165. Pinchas, "Broken Vav," para. 1.
166. Pinchas, "Broken Vav," para. 11.

The Talmud advances a related idea. It regards the *vav*, its visual integrity impaired, as spurious. It reads the word without it, not as שלום (*shalom*, "peace"), but as שלם (*shalem*, "whole"). In this reading the broken *vav* is a visual metaphor not for the spear but for Pinḥas. By his extreme deed his moral wholeness was impaired. But a *kohen*, "priest," or any official or leader, who is not thus impaired will be *shalem* "morally whole."[167]

The truth of this teaching has been brought home to us too many times. How many political leaders, religious figures, athletes, artists, and public intellectuals have we seen who initially stood as solid, upright *vav*s and whose moral centers were corroded by their ethical and moral offences, and their stature collapsed?

One could also advance a reading that comes to just the opposite conclusion and endorses what Pinḥas did. The cracked *vav* is indeed spurious and should be deleted, to reveal Pinḥas as whole and the covenant with him as one of perfect peace. This would accord with the oft-cited words of Senator Barry Goldwater (1909–1998), that "extremism in the defense of liberty is no vice . . . and . . . moderation in the pursuit of justice is no virtue."[168]

Numbers 27:5

ויקרב משה את משפטן לפני יהוה

Moses brought their case before the Lord

Sometimes a letter written larger than the others seems by its size to be shouting out to us: "Hey, look at me!" That is how the elongated final *nun* in this verse strikes me. It invites us to pay attention to what the text at that point is telling us. Let us approach it accordingly.

The five daughters of Zelophḥad have approached Moses with a legal question. Their father has died, they have no brothers, they are unmarried, and there are no male heirs into whose hands the land can pass. They want to know if they, as women, can inherit from their father. Moses does not answer them. He "brings their case before the Lord."

This is where the text gets emphatic. "Their case" in the Hebrew is משפטן (*mishpaṭan*). The final *nun* is the form to indicate the feminine plural possessive. Were men speaking here, we would see the masculine

---

167. b. Qiddushin 66b.

168. Barry Goldwater, as stated in his acceptance speech as Republican candidate for President, 1964.

possessive *mem*, i.e., משפטם (*mishpaṭam*). The force of the enlarged final *nun* seems to be: "Dear reader: Please note the feminine here."

On one level we can explain why scribal tradition would want to make sure that we notice the *nun* of feminine form here. It could be mistaken for a *vav*. There is not much difference in appearance between the letter *vav* and final *nun*: ן/ו.

But there is in meaning. Written with a *vav* the word would be משפטו (*mishpaṭo*, "his case")—and that would make perfect sense. We'd think the text is saying that after hearing the five sisters, Moses puts his case, the case that they have brought to him, before the Lord. The enlarged final *nun*, however, makes it clear that it was "their" (the sisters') case. Accounting for the majuscule this way accords with one of the possible reasons why such letters are written: to make sure the text is read correctly, with the letter that, by its larger size, is highlighted. We saw this before with regard to Exodus 34:14 (אחר, '*aḥer*; as opposed to אחד, '*eḥad*).

But there is more here than the technicality of getting the word right, important as that is. Why make sure that we know that the case Moses hands off to God is "their" (the sisters') case? And come to think of it, why does Moses hand it off to God? Weren't there other officials to whom he could have assigned this case, the "chiefs of thousands, hundreds, fifties, and tens" (Exod 18:21, 25; Deut 1:15)? And didn't Moses say openly that he was the Chief Justice who would adjudicate the really hard cases: "And any matter that is too difficult for you, you shall bring to me and I will hear it" (Deut 1:17)?

The commentators propose a range of answers to these questions. A sampling:

- Moses actually knew what the law was in this case, but he deferred to God out of respect, in accordance with the principle that one does not teach the law in the presence of one wiser. The case had begun with the daughters coming before the "chiefs of tens." Those magistrates deferred to the "chiefs of fifties," who then deferred to the "chiefs of hundreds," and so on, up the line (see 27:2). When they got to Moses he, too, deferred—to the only higher authority left.[169]
- Moses knew the law, but he recused himself from judgment. When pleading their case the daughters had made a point of telling Moses that their late father "was not one . . . of Korah's faction, which banded

---

169. Bamidbar Rabbah 21:12.

together against the Lord, but died for his own sin" (27:3). This was a sincere attempt on their part to present their father in a good light, but Moses heard it as an attempt to sway him, and so he laid their case before God.

- Moses did not know the law and was genuinely stumped. [This was one of four such instances, the other three being: 1) what to do with the blasphemer (Lev 24:12); 2) what to do with the men who had become defiled and could not keep the Passover (Num 9:8); and 3) what to do with the man who went out and gathered wood on the Sabbath (Num 15:34).] A possible fifth such quandary was what to do with the couple copulating in front of the Tabernacle during the incident at Ba'al Pe'or (Num 25:6, and see Rashi on that verse).

- Moses did not know the law. He simply did not know if women were entitled to inherit. He had said that "any matter that is too difficult for you, you shall bring to me," implying that all fifty of the legendary gates of understanding were open to him. But in this case he was clueless. He did not know whether women could inherit in the same way as men could, and this was a clear sign that Moses had only reached the forty-ninth gate. Some say he could have reached the fiftieth, too, but God withheld that level of understanding from him in the light of his rather presumptuous statement that nothing was too difficult for him. (This view does not square with how Moses was described earlier: as the humblest man on earth [Num 12:3].) Now the numerical value of *nun* is 50. And so the *nun* here, in *their*, these women's case, is enlarged to indicate that Moses, even though he had passed through forty-nine gates of understanding, did not know a law that these women knew, that they could inherit their father's land, and he had to let God decide in their favor.[170]

These readings of the encounter of the daughters of Zelophḥad with Moses, interesting as they may be, do not satisfy. The first three do not even explain why the final *nun* is written large. But more significantly, they do not engage in any meaningful way the issue of gender that is at the heart of this incident. The last two begin to approach it and evince a vague awareness that it is there, but that is all. All of them originate in an interpretive

---

170. These views are developed by several commentators as collected in Ron, *Sefer Qaṭan ve-Gadol*, 164–72.

context that, for whatever reason, does not interrogate the assumptions about gender and power on which the narrative rests.

But gender is what this incident is about, at least at the level of the *peshaṭ*. That, I think, is the real point of the enlarged final *nun*. It denotes a feminine ending and it attracts our attention as such. A contemporary reading of Torah, therefore, cannot overlook the issues of gender and power that are raised in this legal encounter between five intrepid women and a supreme male authority figure.

At first blush this encounter looks like a gutsy challenge to male hegemony. We certainly shouldn't minimize the courage these women display in coming forward to assert their concern. But what really are they asking for?

> [T]he basic point at issue was the preservation of the father's name (27:4). The storyteller presumes an intricate connection between possession of land and preservation of family name. The women themselves are pictured as taking action for the sake of their father's name, not for the sake of their own opportunity to possess land.
>
> The story could be heard even in ancient Israel as a story of comfort for women who would not be left destitute, but it was preserved primarily as a story of comfort for men who had the misfortune not to bear any male heirs: their names would not be cut off from their clans.[171]

The wording of the law that comes down as result of the daughters' request confirms this. If a man dies with no sons, his property is *transferred* to his daughter, but if there are male heirs, whether sons or brothers of the father, the property is *given* to them (27:7–11). At the very end of Numbers (chapter 36), we see how this law will be played out. The heads of the clan of the tribe of Manasseh, to which Zelophḥad's daughters belonged, come before Moses in the same way with the same concern. Zelophḥad's daughters may indeed inherit their father's land, i.e., it may be transferred to them, but what will happen if they marry men from other tribes and that land will eventually be given to those tribes? The Manasseh tribal holding will ultimately be diminished. So God instructs Moses to tell the daughters that they can marry only within their tribe.[172]

That this is not a feminist outcome goes without saying. We cannot superimpose the values and the expectations of our modern or post-modern

---

171. Sackenfeld, "Numbers," 85.

172. For a full discussion of how the biblical law regarding the inheritance rights of women was modified in rabbinic law, see Hauptman, *Rereading the Rabbis*, 177–95.

post-Enlightenment western culture back onto the society of ancient Israel. But the story has nevertheless a certain resonance for contemporary Jewish men and women.

Why? I think it comes from the larger sense of the question the daughters of Zelophḥad put to Moses: "Can we inherit, too? Do we have a portion in what our father has left?" Today we hear this question not in its particulars, as an inquiry about real estate, but rather as a general one that Jewish women have asked, and are still asking, in our time: are we heirs to and full possessors of the tradition, i.e., the texts and the practices, that our ancestors have handed down, in the same way as men? Or have these texts and practices not really been given but only transferred to us as temporary conduits to future generations? To these important questions different answers will be proposed, to be sure. But the questions themselves should be triggered by this brash elongated, feminine final *nun*.

Deuteronomy 6:4

שמע ישראל יהוה אלהינו יהוה אחד

Hear O Israel! The Lord is our God, the Lord alone

SCRIBAL SECRETS

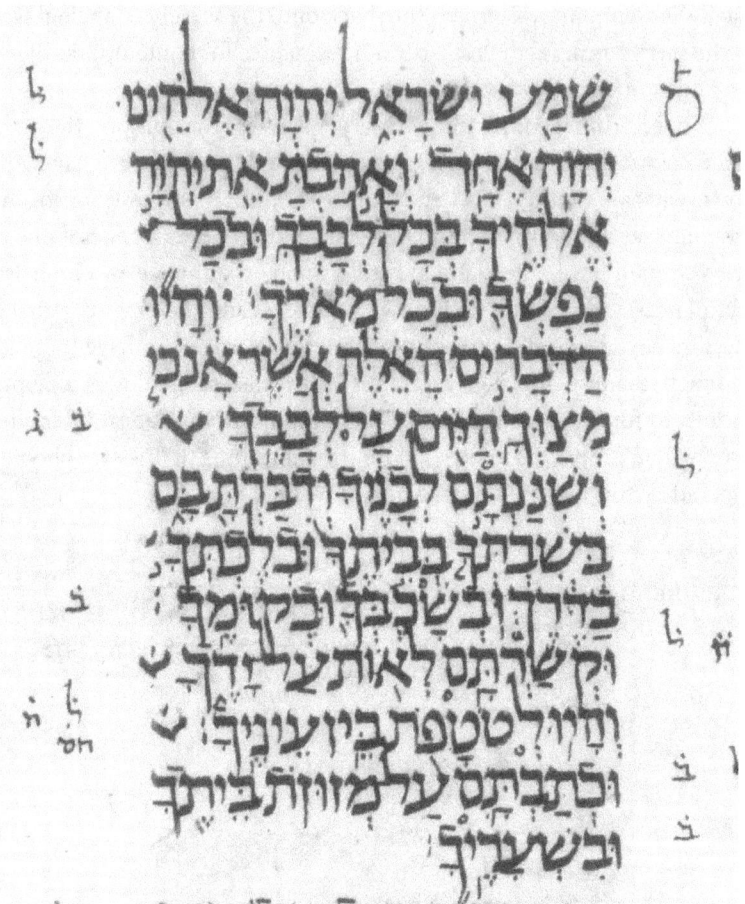

Figure 8: Deuteronomy 6:4–9, the Shemaʿ paragraph, as represented in the Leningrad (St. Petersburg) Codex, written 1009–1010 CE, Tiberias, Israel. Note the large ʿayin in the first word of the first line and the large dalet in the second word of the second line.
[Photograph by Bruce and Kenneth Zuckerman, West Semitic Research, in collaboration with the Ancient Biblical Manuscript Center. Courtesy Russian National Library (Saltykov-Shchedrin).]
See Figure 9 for even greater scribal/artistic accentuation of the two large letters.

Figure 9: Deuteronomy 6:4–9, the Shemaʿ paragraph, as represented in the Kennicott Bible, written 1476 CE, La Coruña, Spain, fol. 103r (upper-left portion of the page). Note the beautifully illuminated large ʿayin and large *dalet*, each of which extends to three lines of regular text.
[Used with kind permission of the Bodleian Libraries, University of Oxford. Photo: © Bodleian Libraries, University of Oxford.]

The Masoretic tradition did not abide by Tractate Sofrim's stipulation that all the letters of this verse must be written large. Only the ʿayin and the *dalet* are majuscules. When majuscules are noticed at all, these are the two that are probably the most widely discerned, since they appear in what is probably the most familiar verse in the Torah. They show us yet another instance where the largeness of each of the two letters can be exposited on its own terms and also in conjunction with the other. The ʿayin and the *dalet* each has its own set of connotations and when combined yield a whole new constellation of meanings. I presented these in the Preface, and thus there is no need here to repeat them here. I would only note that though the technical reason why each of these letters is written large—so as to ensure that they will not be mistaken for other look-alike letters—is compelling, the representational meanings that have accumulated about them have been perhaps even more influential. That is especially true of the idea that the two letters combined form the word עד (ʿed, "witness"). Whatever else the recitation of the Shemaʿ is, it is at heart the primal act of testimony by a Jew and by a community of Jews that the foundation of all foundations and the pillar of wisdom is to know that there is a Primary Being who brought into being all existence. All the beings of the heavens, the earth, and what is between them came into existence only from the truth of His being.

That is how Maimonides formulates the quintessence of Jewish creed in the very first words of his encyclopedic code of Jewish law, the *Mishneh Torah*.[173] As befits Maimonides, it is a very intellectual articulation of what it is a Jew is bearing witness to when he or she says the Shemaʿ. But the act of witnessing itself transcends human reason. We must say the Shemaʿ with every fiber of our being. If, as happens not infrequently, we are not up to the task at that particular moment, the two large letters that bracket the affirmation can serve to arouse our mindfulness.

[Most likely the tradition of writing the *ʿayin* and the *dalet* as majuscules arose through the following.

1. With the weakening of the *ʿayin* sound, under the influence of Greek and to some extent also Latin (which lack this phoneme), the sound approximated or even merged with the glottal stop *ʾaleph*. This would have led to a very similar realization of the two words שמע (*shemaʿ*, "hear") and שמא (*shemmaʾ*, "perhaps"). To ensure that the reader would realize that the former word was intended, and not the latter, the letter ע (*ʿayin*) was written large. After all, one would not wish to state, "Perhaps, O Israel, the LORD is our God, the LORD alone," for such an expression would constitute a heretical utterance!

2. As the author mentioned in the preface to this book (p. xviii), and as we saw regarding Exodus 34:14, the letters ד (*dalet*) and ר (*resh*) look very much alike. To avoid any potential confusion between אחד (*ʾeḥad*, "one") and אחר (*ʾaḥer*, "another") the tradition arose to write the ד (*dalet*) at the very end of this verse large.

In short, in Deuteronomy 6:4, the first majuscule is based on a potential confusion of sounds, while the second majuscule is based on a potential confusion of letters.—G.A.R.]

---

173. Maimonides, *Mishneh Torah, Sefer Maddaʿ, Hilkhot Yesode ha-Torah* 1:1.

The Extraordinary Texts in the Torah

Deuteronomy 9:24

ממרים הייתם עם יהוה מיום דעתי אתכם

As long as I have known you, you have been defiant toward the Lord.

Deuteronomy 29:27

וית‍שם יהוה מעל אדמתם באף ובחמה ובקצף גדול וישלכם אל ארץ אחרת כיום הזה

The LORD uprooted them from their soil in anger, fury, and great wrath, and cast them into another land, as is still the case.

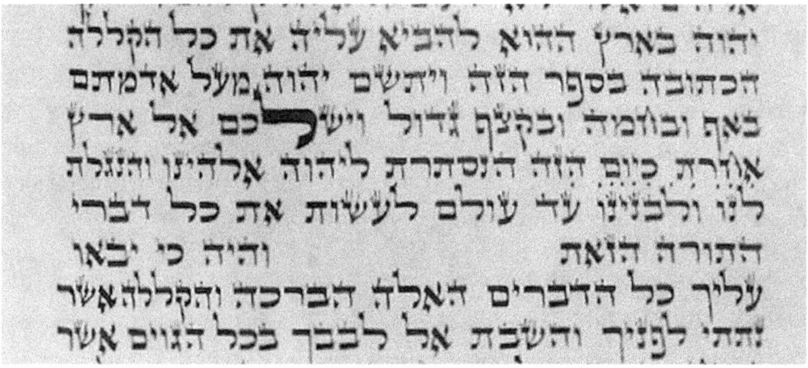

Figure 10: Deuteronomy 29:27 as represented in a contemporary Torah scroll. Note the large letter *lamed* in the word וישלכם.
The same image appears as Figure 3, regarding the dotted letters in the next verse.
[Torah scroll by scribe Rabbi Gustavo Surazski.
Scroll image courtesy of Temple Aliyah, Needham, Mass.]

Emanuel Tov has written that "the occurrence of some of these special letters is . . . probably random, that is, the special letters may have differed coincidentally from the surrounding ones, and hence they carry no particular message."[174]

On the one hand, that observation could apply to the two irregular-sized letters in these verses. On the other hand, one could argue that in the first of these verses, the minuscular *mem* does not differ coincidentally from the one that sits next to it; they are both integral to the verb ממרים (*mamrim*, "defiant"), and so, with no spaces between words in ancient manuscripts, one *mem* could have been dropped and the other done double duty.

174. Tov, *Textual Criticism*, 58.

Likewise, the large *lamed* in the second verse could be rescued from randomness by suggesting that its large size is a signal that it begins a new, i.e., second, word. Recall that Yeivin offered this as one possible function of majuscular letters. The verse comes at the end of a passage in which Moses is detailing what the nations will be told when they see the horrific devastation that will befall the land of Israel. Because the people of Israel have abandoned their covenant with God, "The LORD has uprooted them from their soil in anger, fury, and great wrath, and cast them [וישלכם] into another land."

If the *lamed* indicates a second word, then the last phrase of the verse would read ויש לכם אל ארץ אחרת (*ve-yesh lakhem 'el 'ereṣ 'aḥeret*, "but you will have God [in] another land"). Such a construction strains both the syntax of the Hebrew and plausibility.[175]

Neither verse has sparked much homiletic interpretation beyond the predictable five-finger exercises in gematria. The numerical value of the small *mem* in the first verse is forty (forty years in the wilderness), while the numerical value of the *lamed* in the second is thirty (thirty generations from Abraham to the Babylonian exile), and so on.

Deuteronomy 32:6

ה ליהוה תגמלו זאת עם נבל ולא חכם
הלא הוא אביך קנך הוא עשך ויכננך

Do you thus requite the Lord, O dull and witless people?
Is not He the Father who created you, fashioned you, and made you endure!

Now we have a verse where the majuscule in it could actually be functioning as a separate, independent signifier. It appears to belong to the word right after it, but it might not. It could be read as a letter that stands on its own as a locus of meaning. This is exactly how Tractate Sofrim 9:6 construes it.

In this passage, the letter *he* represents the interrogative marker. The phrase ה ליהוה תגמלו זאת (*ha-la-yhwh tigmelu zo't*, "Do you thus requite the LORD?") is indeed a question, in parallel with the second stich of the verse.[176]

---

175. See Tigay, *Deuteronomy*, 282. See also Ron, *Sefer Qaṭan ve-Gadol*, 206.

176. [The *he* at the beginning of this verse is doubly strange. Not only is it written large, it is written as an independent word, with a space between it and the following ליהוה—the only time any such thing occurs in the Bible. All other one-letter particles

The Extraordinary Texts in the Torah

In his penultimate peroration, the poem *Ha'azinu* (as Deuteronomy 32 is known, after its opening word in verse 1), Moses is rhetorically inquiring of the backsliding people, "Is this how you treat God?"

It is also possible to regard this *he* as the larger twin of a small *he* we looked at early on in this chapter, the minuscule *he* in Genesis 2:4 (בהבראם, *be-hibbar'am*, "when they were created"). This would not be a mere interpretational flourish; there is a clear connection between the two verses. The second stich shows this: "Is He not the Father who created you, fashioned you, and made you endure?!"

Both verses speak of the Creation, of God as the Creator, and of man as God's creation. The early narratives in Genesis make it clear that these three key elements in the cosmic equation—God, man, and the world—are intrinsically connected. Their fates are bound up in each other. We have seen this a number of times in the interpretations of several of these unusual letters. Now, in these closing passages of the Torah, Moses laments the rift between the parties.[177] The people have debased the divine image in which man was created and despoiled God's vision and expectations of this human being in which he set so much stock.[178]

In this context the interrogative signifier hits us with particular force: "Is this how you will treat God?" The question is addressed by Moses to Israel, but we may hear it addressed to the Jewish people in every generation. Indeed, we may hear it addressed to all of humanity in its collective presence in this world.[179]

There is much interrogation of God in our time, much dissatisfaction with how God runs the universe. It has been going on for a very long time. Job and Tevye come to mind as among the major cross-examiners, but western literature is filled with different ways of calling God on the carpet, some polite, some rude, some nasty.

The large interrogative *he* here can serve to remind us that in the biblical scheme of things, the questioning goes the other way, too. God has questions of man, of us. At the beginning of the Torah God asked איכה (*'ayyekka*, "where are you"; Gen 3:9). Now, near the end, God asks, through

---

(prepositions, definite article, interrogative marker, etc.) are always prefixed to the main word.—G.A.R.]

177. See n119 [p. 96].

178. So the commentator Ovadiah Sforno on this verse.

179. See the comments of Samson Raphael Hirsch in Ron, *Sefer Qaṭan ve-Gadol*, 217–18.

his proxy Moses "Is this how you requite me [for what I have bestowed upon you]?"

The dialogue between God and man is one of questions. That could be the ultimate implication of this large *he*. It is a sign that both parties, man and God, will have to continue living with their respective questions about each other.

* * *

Our trip through the Torah now ends, with eleven majuscules, eight minuscules, and one broken *vav* considered. These are the letters that have taken root in scribal tradition as requiring special inscription for whatever reason—and we have seen a variety of them—or for no apparent reason at all. These are the ones we are most likely to notice in Torah scrolls and in most printed copies of the Pentateuch. But there are others less frequently seen, majuscules and minuscules, and we should not be surprised when they do appear. They reflect less popular or local or particular understandings of how those letters should be written. The whole matter of special letters is, as should now be clear, the product of an open and fluid interpretive tradition.

In many ways that tradition has been the implicit subject of this book. The unusual letters, the dotted passages, the inverted nuns that I will discuss in the next chapter—these are the manifest subjects. Consideration of them forces us to see that it is the interpretive process itself that we are inquiring after.

Over and over we have seen two modalities in which this process, the perennial attempt to extract meaning from the texts of Torah, from its verses, words, and now, letters, has played itself out: a text-critical mode and a midrashic mode. This raises questions:

- Are these two separate and distinct interpretive modes? Or are they related? And if related, how?
- What do we get from each one? What don't we get? Each one yields meaning, to be sure, but what kinds of meaning? Objectively true meaning? Subjectively true meaning? How do these meanings differ?
- Are there other interpretive modes? What might they yield?

I will elaborate on these questions and attempt to articulate the rudiments of some working answers as I proceed.

The Extraordinary Texts in the Torah

3. THE MYSTERY OF THE INVERTED *NUNS*

The book of Numbers, *Sefer Bemidbar*, is the most variegated of the five books of the Torah. It contains priestly and levitical laws, narratives of the desert wanderings, census figures, special ritual procedures for women suspected of adultery and for individuals who wish to undertake special nazirite vows, the story of Balaam and his talking donkey, and all kinds of lists: of tribal gifts and marching formations, of levitical towns and cities of refuge, of the sacrifices to be offered on Sabbath and holidays, of the boundaries of the Promised Land, and more. Numbers also quotes snippets of archaic poetry, some from what was probably the Israelite literary canon (if we may speak of such) and some from the poetic canon of Israel's neighbors, the full texts of all of which have been lost.[180]

One such poem, of Israelite provenance, is the Song of the Ark that we find at the very end of Numbers 10:35–36:

ויהי בנסע הארן ויאמר משה קומה יהוה ויפצו איביך וינסו משנאיך מפניך
ובנחה יאמר שובה יהוה רבבות אלפי ישראל

When the Ark was to set out, Moses would say: Advance, O Lord!
May your enemies be scattered, and may your foes flee before You!
And when it halted, he would say: Return, O Lord,
You who are Israel's myriads of thousands!

It is not clear if this is a complete poem or only a fragment of a longer one. But it is a poem, as the parallelism and cadence indicate.[181] But its brevity is not the only feature that makes this poem distinctive. In the Hebrew text—on a Torah scroll, in medieval manuscripts, and in printed versions—the two verses are set off from the rest of the text and bracketed by what look like parentheses but which are really inverted *nun*s, i.e., the Hebrew letter *nun* turned upside down. Hence, the text looks like this:

ז ויהי בנסע הארן ויאמר משה קומה יהוה ויפצו איביך וינסו משנאיך מפניך
ובנחה יאמר שובה יהוה רבבות אלפי ישראל ז

---

180. Besides the one in chapter 10 which we will consider here, the other snippets all occur in chapter 21. The quotations there are from 1) "the Book of the Wars of the Lord" (vv. 14–15); 2) "the Song of the Well" (vv. 17–18); and 3) "the Song of Heshbon" (vv. 27–39). I have dealt with a dotted word in the latter fragment in Chapter II, Part 1, "Connecting the Dots"; see p. 68.

181. See Alter, *Five Books of Moses*, 733. Friedman takes issue with this view in his *Commentary on the Torah*, 459.

Scribal Secrets

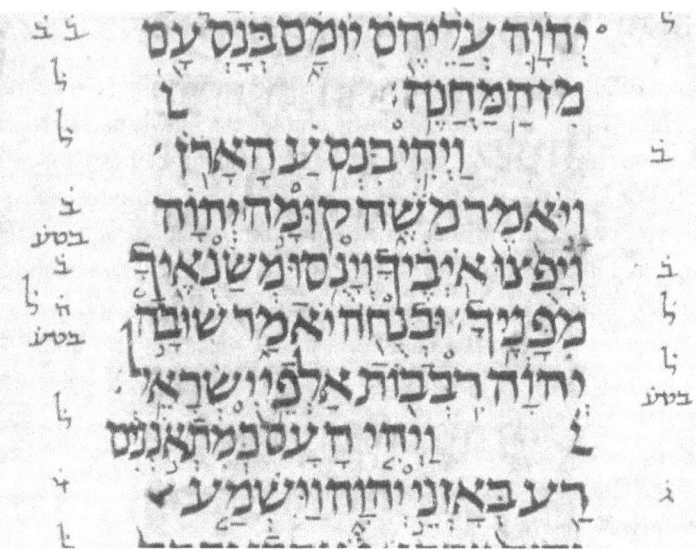

Figure 11: Numbers 10:35–36, as represented in the Leningrad (St. Petersburg) Codex, written 1009–1010 CE, Tiberias, Israel. The two verses are set off from the preceding text and the following text with the inverted *nun*s (or in this case, an approximation thereof) set within the white spaces which surround the passage.
[Photograph by Bruce and Kenneth Zuckerman, West Semitic Research, in collaboration with the Ancient Biblical Manuscript Center. Courtesy Russian National Library (Saltykov-Shchedrin).]

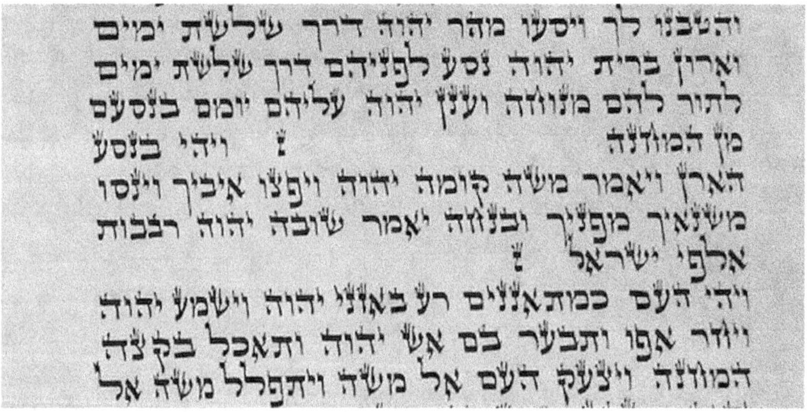

Figure 12: Numbers 10:35–36, as represented in a contemporary Torah scroll. Note the inverted *nun*s that demarcate the two verses.
[Torah scroll by scribe Rabbi Gustavo Surazski. Scroll image courtesy of Temple Aliyah, Needham, Mass.]

The Extraordinary Texts in the Torah

These inverted *nuns* are our subject here. In this chapter, I want to consider what they stand for and what they are doing in the text. Once again we will see that there are two stories here: the historical-critical one that biblical scholarship tells about the origins and purpose of these strange markings, and the midrashic-poetic one that commentators and interpreters over the centuries have read out of—or into—them. But before we can do any of that we need to get a fix on just what it is this poem or poetic fragment is saying.

A Battle Poem

Calling this text "The Song of the Ark," as modern scholars do, is appropriate, even though ancient Hebrew poems were not given titles. The subject is clearly the Ark of the Covenant, the chest into which were placed (according to Exodus 25:16 and 40:20) the two tablets of the Decalogue. The Ark had a dual function. As we learn in the verse just preceding the poem, the Ark served as a kind of GPS, guiding the people to their appointed stopping places: "They marched from the mountain of the LORD a distance of three days. The Ark of the Covenant of the LORD traveled in front of them on that three days' journey to seek out a resting place for them" (Numbers 10:33).

And, as we know from accounts later on in the Bible, the Ark accompanied Israel into battle as a visible manifestation not of God but of God's presence among the people.[182] This Song of the Ark reflects its latter function. Jacob Milgrom writes:

> Israel's religion ... was imageless from the outset ... and regarded the Ark not as a representation of the Deity but only as His footstool ... The image of God resuming His place on His throne after vanquishing His enemies (originally pagan nature gods) is found in Psalms 29 and 89 ... and was probably modeled after Canaanite prototypes that describe the march of the divine warrior god into battle and his enthronement as king of the gods upon his victorious return.[183]

In addition, Milgrom catches what I think is the key aspect of the poem: its petitionary nature.

---

182. Two well-known stories are Joshua 6 (the victory at Jericho) and 1 Samuel 4 (the defeat at the hands of the Philistines, including the capture of the Ark).

183. Milgrom, *Numbers*, 373–74.

> The song is only a prayer (the imperative "Arise," "Rest" [better: "Return"] are not written in the usual form *kum, shuv* but are lengthened to *kumah, shuvah* and thus may be expressing a wish). Moses petitions the Lord to arise from His throne and attack the enemy and then to return to His throne on the Ark-cherubim after the battle is over. There is no assurance that He will do either [for] ... the Ark was not conceived as the permanent residence of the Lord.[184]

Read this way, as a prayer, the first verse makes perfect sense. But what is the second verse saying? That is less obvious. To be sure, it is, in its first part, asking God to "return" to the Ark. But what does the last part, "Israel's myriads of thousands," mean? The New Jewish Publication Society translation cited above understands it as a phrase that elaborates on who the God invoked in the first line actually is. It supplies a phrase that is only presumed in the original: "You who are Israel's myriads of thousands." This sounds awkward, but it may be so only in English. In Hebrew, the locution may be a metonym, a word that denotes one thing but refers to a related thing. Milgrom explains: "Just as the prophets Elijah and Elisha are called "Israel's chariots and horsemen" (2 Kings 2:12; 13:14), so Israel's God is called "Israel's myriads of thousands.""[185] He also notes the early-sixteenth-century Italian commentator Sforno's insight that just as we have the depiction of Israel's God as "the Lord of hosts," an expression that occurs frequently in the Bible, so do we have here a less familiar one of God as the "the Lord of Israel's myriads of thousands."[186]

Robert Alter, whose ear for the nuances of biblical Hebrew is acute, is not at all certain that this is what the second verse is saying or how it should be translated. It's not clear to him that "Israel's myriads of thousands" is an epithet for God. The problem with the verse, he notes, is that in the Hebrew there is no apparent connection between "Return O Lord" and "Israel's myriads of thousands." This is what makes the verse so cryptic in the Hebrew original. He proposes that what's missing here is a preposition, specifically the preposition "to," which leads him to translate the verse, "Come back O Lord *to* Israel's teeming myriads."[187]

---

184. Milgrom, *Numbers*, 374.
185. Milgrom, *Numbers*, 81.
186. Milgrom, *Numbers*, 81.
187. Alter, *Five Books of Moses*, 733.

He bases this rendering on the fact that biblical poetic diction—especially in the case of the more archaic layer of Hebrew poetry—exhibits a great deal of ellipsis, which is, after all, a means of eliminating extra syllables and heightening the compactness of the utterance. It thus seems reasonable to infer that "to" is implied here.

Alter persuades me here. I find his version preferable. But no matter which translation we go with, it's clear what this poem, whether complete or fragmentary, is: an invocation of the God of Israel, whose presence is ensconced in the Ark, to make that presence manifest in battle on behalf of His people, and then to return to the Ark and abide in it in perpetuity.

In time the two verses transcended this original military meaning. Perhaps taking a cue from the two *nuns* that encase them in the Torah text, later Jewish tradition installed them in the synagogue service as brackets before and after the Torah reading. When the Torah scroll is taken out of the Ark the first verse is sung; when it is returned to the Ark the second verse is sung. The melodies (especially in the Ashkenazi tradition) for both are known even to casual synagogue goers. What the verses are saying in that context is something we shall ponder in the course of this discussion. But now let us turn from the poem itself to the inverted *nuns* that encase it.

The *Nuns*: Historical-Critical Views

As with the other markings we are considering in this book, we cannot say precisely when the inverted *nuns* were placed in the text. The rabbinic sources that deal with the passage do not tell us, nor do they speak explicitly of inverted *nuns*. Sifre says simply that the two verses were "marked."[188] The Babylonian Talmud states, "For this section [the two verses] the Holy One, blessed He, provided signs (סימניות, *simaniyot*) above and below it."[189]

Tractate Sofrim puts a human face on this matter. It instructs that in writing a Torah scroll "the scribe must provide [a sign in the form of] a shofar (horn) in the blank spaces of the section, "When the ark set forward etc.," at the beginning and at the end.[190]

---

188. Sifre Bamidbar, section 84, to Numbers 10:35–36.

189. b. Shabbat 115b–116a. So, too, Avot de Rabbi Natan A, ch. 34.

190. Tractate Sofrim 6:1. The translation here follows that of Lieberman, *Hellenism in Jewish Palestine*, 39. See his n. 12 for a detailed explanation of how he reads the passage and why he translates it this way.

In his authoritative discussion of the subject Lieberman identifies all these sources as referring to the Greek letters *sigma* C and its reversal, the *anti-sigma* Ɔ.[191] These, he says, were critical marks used by the scribes in the great schools of Alexandria to indicate that the text enclosed within them was not in its proper place.

Hebrew scribes employed these signs as well, but when their meaning was no longer understood, they came to be denoted by the Masoretes as inverted *nuns*. The modern parenthesis has developed from the use of the Greek *sigma* and *anti-sigma*, and this pair of signs likewise may indicate that the enclosed segment is not an integral part of the text.[192]

Now we are in a position to understand the two explanations for the inverted *nuns* that we find in the passage in b. Shabbat 115b–116a, the beginning of which I just cited. The full text reads as follows (I break it up into paragraphs and letter them for ease of reference):

A. "*When the Ark was to set out, Moses would say*": For this section [i.e., the two verses] the Holy One, blessed He, provided signs above and below it to show that this is not its correct place.

B. Rabbi [sc. R. Judah ha-Nasi = R. Judah the Patriarch] said: This is not the reason [for the signs]. It is rather [to show] that [this section] constitutes a ספר חשוב הוא בפני עצמו *sefer ḥashuv hu' bifne 'aṣmo* ("an important book unto itself").

C. With whom does the following statement of R. Shemuel bar Nachmani, [made] in the name of R. Yonatan, agree: [Scripture says] "*Wisdom has built her house, She has hewn her seven pillars*" [Prov 9:1]. These represent the seven books of the Torah. According to whom [is this statement]? Rabbi [Judah HaNasi].

D. Who [then] is the Tanna [the rabbinic teacher] who disagrees with Rabbi? It is Rabban Shimon ben Gamliel. For it was taught: Rabban Shimon ben Gamliel said: This section is destined one day to be uprooted from here and written in its proper place. And why was it written here? In order to separate the [narrative of the] first punishment from the [narrative of the] second punishment.

---

191. [Today, the *sigma* is written like this: Σ. But in antiquity, the form C (known as the "lunate *sigma*," based on its resemblance to the crescent moon) prevailed.—G.A.R.]

192. Tov, *Textual Criticism*, 51.

The Extraordinary Texts in the Torah

E1. What is [the narrative of] the second punishment? *"And the people took to complaining"* (Num 11:1).

E2. (And the narrative of the] first punishment? *"They marched from the mountain of the LORD a distance of three days"* (10:33).

E3. [On which verse] R. Hama the son of R. Hanina commented, "They marched [not away from the mountain of God, i.e., Mt. Sinai] but away from God [Himself]."

F. [So] where [then] is its place [this whole section, the two verses in 10:35–36]? Said R. Ashi: With [the part about] the banners.[193]

We see here two different views of why the inverted *nun*s are there. But they both agree that the two verses of the Song of the Ark inside the *nun*s are discontinuous with the narrative that precedes and follows them. They both understand that the poem "is an intrusion in its present setting."[194]

Let's look at the first view (A), which is expressed without attribution. Its proponent, Rabban Shimon ben Gamliel, is not identified until D. The view is that the *nun*s have been placed where they are in order to signify that the two verses of the poem have been transposed from someplace else in the Torah. Where the two verses have been transposed from is not made clear until F. They have been transposed, according to R. Ashi, from Numbers chapter 2, where the outline of the order of the Israelites' march from Mt. Sinai into the desert is given. Each tribe marches under its individual banner. R. Ashi is saying that the proper place of the Song of the Ark is after Numbers 2:17. That verse positions the Tabernacle within the march—and the Ark was a component of the Tabernacle complex.

(The medieval commentator Ḥizquni [thirteenth-century France] situates the Song later in Numbers, at 10:21. That would put it right after the section that describes the procession of the various Levitical clans which transported the Tabernacle and its sacred appurtenances. The Septuagint places the poem after 10:33, which, to my mind, makes it flow more naturally into the whole narrative.)

In any case, from wherever the Song of the Ark was moved, there seems to be an acknowledgement, however implicit, that the Torah text as we have it is not in its final state. That state, presumably, will be attained at some future time. When will that be? In his comment on the Talmudic passage, Rashi explains that it will be when "all [divine] punishments will be

---

193. b. Shabbat 115b–116a.
194. Leiman, "Inverted *Nuns*," 350.

abrogated and they [Israel] will not worry about them, and the Evil Impulse will have been annulled."[195] In the meantime, in the unredeemed time of this world, divine punishment (and, we should not forget to add, human transgression) is a reality.

The narratives in this part of the book of Numbers depict this reality. There were not one but two episodes of punishable conduct. Just before the Song, in 10:33, we learn that the Israelites marched away from Mt. Sinai. R. Hama (E3) interprets this to mean that they marched away from God Himself. What made this decampment sinful and, therefore, punishable only becomes clear later on, in the story of the angry confrontation with Moses over food at Qivrot ha-Ta'avah, told in 11:4–34.[196] That incident ends with the people being decimated by an unspecified severe plague, but it was the rebellious decampment that led to the plague, which was the first punishment (E2).

The second is sandwiched in between the two parts of the first, in the brief story told in 11:1–3. This is the complaint at Taberah, though just what the people are complaining about is not stated. Here, too, they are punished, this time by a disastrous fire (E1).

In this reading and configuration of the various narratives, the Song of the Ark is seen to intrude. Why? As R. Shimon ben Gamliel would have it, "in order to separate the first punishment from the second" (D). But why? Why was it so important for God or Moses or the Redactor—whoever arranged the text in its present order—to interpose the Song between the two episodes of Israel's sinfulness? R. Shimon doesn't say. We can only infer what his reasoning might have been from Rashi's comment about the difference between the moral purity of the messianic future and the implied contamination of the present: that it has something to do with not wanting to have to read about two punishments in a row.[197] Perhaps that would be too much to take. It's hard to say.

195. Rashi on R. Shimon ben Gamliel's statement in b. Shabbat 116a.

196. *Qivrot ha-Ta'avah* means literally "the graves of desire," though in Numbers 11:34 the term serves as the proper name of the place where the episode occurs.

197. In his commentary to Numbers 10:35, Naḥmanides proposes a different schema of punishments. He sees not two transgressions here but three. The first is the turning away from Mount Sinai (10:33), which he judges to have been a sinful act in its own right even though no specific punishment is detailed. He cites a midrash that compares this act to the behavior of a schoolchild who at the end of the lesson bolts from the classroom in fear of the teacher assigning more homework. The second transgression is the murmuring at Taberah told in 11:1–3. The third is the confrontation at Qivrot ha-Ta'avah (11:4–34). In this reading, the Song of the Ark comes between the first and the second

This first explanation for the placement of the Song of the Ark, and for the whole purpose of the inverted *nun*s, presupposes an understanding by the rabbis that the Torah's text was alterable. If the Song can be "uprooted and [later] written in its proper place" (by whom?), then the text as we see it today is not in the final or perfect state that it will achieve in the future, presumably the messianic future.

The eminent Talmudic scholar Rabbi David Weiss Halivni calls this state "maculate." This might sound like a strange word to use in this context, but it has connotations that are helpful. "Maculate" and its opposite, the more familiar "immaculate," both derive from the Latin word *macula*, meaning "spot" or "stain." When Halivni calls the Torah's text maculate, he means that when it was originally given to Moses at Sinai, it was pure and unsullied by any contradictions, inconsistencies, or scribal errors, i.e., it was immaculate. In the course of time, as the biblical record makes clear, Israel fell back into idol worship and the careful transmission of the holy writ was neglected and the text became blemished. It was not until after the Babylonian Exile, in the time of Ezra and his contemporaries (fourth century BCE), that the text of the Pentateuch was re-constituted into more or less the form in which we find it now. The words and verses of the Torah bear the consequences of this neglect and the reconstitution it necessitated. They frequently display evidence of the processes of the human literary endeavor to repair the blemishes—composition, editing, redaction—and scribal devices like inverted *nuns*. These scribal and editorial fingerprints comprise the stain wrought by maculation. I must stress here that when Halivni says that the Torah's text is maculate he is not casting aspersions on its spiritual or theological power or even its authority (though fundamentalists will claim that he is). He is saying, openly and unabashedly, that the Torah's words and verses, as they issued from the divine mind, passed through the imperfect prism of human inspiration and creativity on their way to the written word.

Halivni's account of maculation is a signal contribution to a contemporary understanding of the Torah, for it integrates—and more aptly, reconciles—two perspectives on the Pentateuch that have long been considered to be mutually exclusive: on the one hand, the insights of source criticism and the documentary hypothesis which fuels it; and on the other hand, the age-old postulates of the traditional Jewish view of the Torah

---

and all three are given in the order in which they occurred, and there is no need to make the strained connection between 11:4–34 and 10:33.

as the unmediated word(s) of God uttered and dictated to Moses at Sinai. This first explanation for the inverted *nun*s, attributed in the Talmud to the venerable R. Shimon ben Gamliel, is, then, an important expression and acknowledgement of the maculate nature of the Torah text. Although R. Shimon reads that text within an historical and interpretive horizon quite different from ours, his notion that the Torah text is alterable enables us to feel that the distance between his time and the time of his rabbinic contemporaries, great as it is, is not as unbridgeable as we may think.

    Let's turn now to the second explanation, Rabbi Judah ha-Nasi's idea that the inverted *nun*s indicate that the poem lying between them represents a discrete scroll or book (B). Does this also mean to say that the Song of the Ark is an intrusion, and therefore, a kind of blemish on a text that was presumed to be immaculate? The answer depends on what we think Rabbi Judah has in mind when he calls the poem ספר חשוב הוא בפני עצמו (*sefer ḥashuv hu' bifne 'aṣmo*, "an important book unto itself"). His statement could be translated "it [the two verses enclosed within the inverted *nun*s] is *thought to be* a book unto itself," or more likely, "it is *a significant* book unto itself." However we render it, the statement hangs there laconically without specification or elaboration. But it is picked up in Midrash Mishle, the midrash on the book of Proverbs. And there its suggestiveness is ratcheted up because that source adds one word, ונגנז (*ve-nignaz*), thereby reading: ספר חשוב הוא בפני עצמו ונגנז (*sefer ḥashuv hu' bifne 'aṣmo ve-nignaz*), essentially, "It was a separate book and was withdrawn."[198]

    The word *nignaz* here means "withdrawn" in the sense that the text in question was taken out of circulation and sequestered, possibly in a *genizah*, the archive or storehouse in ancient and medieval synagogues (and some contemporary ones, too) where old or defective sacred writings, such as old prayerbooks and Bibles that were tattered beyond repair, were placed. The allusion in Midrash Mishle is to the idea, expressed in b. Shabbat 30b, that certain books or writings that were denied the status of holy writ and were excluded from the biblical canon because of their problematical content or spurious (non-Mosaic) authorship had to be removed from circulation and deposited in a *genizah*. This happened with the book of Ben Sira, though there were apparently other attempts, unsuccessful ones, to dislodge the books of Proverbs and Ecclesiastes. Midrash Mishle's version of Rabbi Judah's statement thus presents us with a fascinating mystery: just what was

---

198. The translation follows Leiman, "Inverted *Nuns*," 350.

The Extraordinary Texts in the Torah

this book that was enclosed within the inverted *nuns*? Why was it withdrawn? And when? And by whom? It doesn't say.

The mystery was compounded in 1897 when, as Leiman reports:

> Elkan Adler published an eleventh-century MS [manuscript] which he had discovered a year earlier in the Cairo Genizah. It contained the following passage:
>
>> Some Midrashim ... state: Why did the sages place inverted *nuns* before the verse: *The people took to complaining* (Num. 11:1)? The sages thereby declared:
>>
>> The entire Torah consists of the prophecy of Moses except for these two verses (i.e., Num. 10:35–36) which are from the prophecy of Eldad and Medad. Therefore they were enclosed with a curved *nun* and inserted into the Torah.[199]

Leiman continues:

> In the light of the Adler manuscript which clearly ascribes Num. 10:35–36 to Eldad and Medad ... Lieberman somewhat reluctantly proposed in 1950 that the *Midrash Mishlê* passage be rendered as follows:
>
>> [These two verses] stem from an independent book which existed but was suppressed (i.e., declared apocryphal).[200]

This is quite different from the translation I cited previously. Lieberman explains, "It appears that the Rabbis alluded to the apocryphal book of Eldad and Medad, an excerpt of which was allegedly attached to the Bible."[201]

This is a sensational claim. If it is true, and the Song of the Ark is not only a discrete scroll or book but was written by a hand other than that of Moses and was interpolated into the book of Numbers, we have here what would appear to be *prima facie* evidence that the Torah text as we read it now was not cut from whole cloth but is rather an assemblage of texts. How many texts? In the Talmudic passage we've been looking at (C), Rabbi Shemuel bar Nachmani says seven, that is to say: Genesis, Exodus, Leviticus, the beginning of Numbers, our two verses, the rest of Numbers, and Deuteronomy.

---

199. Leiman, "Inverted *Nuns*," 351.

200. Leiman, "Inverted *Nuns*," 351.

201. Lieberman, *Hellenism in Jewish Palestine*, 41n28, cited by Leiman, "Inverted *Nuns*," 351–52.

Moreover, if this mysterious book within the inverted *nun*s, whether it is a fragment from a lost book of the prophecies of Eldad and Medad or something else, was indeed "attached" or interpolated into the Pentateuch, the implication clearly is that a human hand or human hands were at work here, assembling, editing, and/or redacting. Whether this is what Rabbi Judah had in mind when he first made his statement or, more likely, is what Leiman describes as "a very early and rare medieval instance of the denial of Mosaic authorship of a portion of the Torah,"[202] we have again the sense that Halivni's idea of the maculate nature of the Torah's text is not a modern one.

But let us not get carried away. It is possible, I would say likely, that none of these speculations are true. When he calls the two verses between the *nun*s a "book unto itself," Rabbi Judah may mean nothing more than that they comprise a discrete literary unit. In rabbinic parlance the word ספר (*sefer*) does not necessarily refer to what we today know as a book. It could denote what we would call a text or a document. If that is his intention, Rabbi Judah could be saying nothing more than that the two verses simply constitute a very short text that appears in the Torah exactly where they belong: where Israel is finally arrayed in the ordained marching order and sets out from Sinai. This is just how Rashi explains Rabbi Judah's comment.

There are several indications that this is the correct way to understand Rabbi Judah. Mishnah Yadayim 3:5 determines that a text becomes a *sefer* when it contains 85 or more letters. That is the threshold for defining a text as a discrete literary unit. The basis for this ruling is—you guessed it—the Song of the Ark, which contains 85 letters. Moreover, when Midrash Mishle states that the *sefer* that is the two verses of the Song "was a separate book and was withdrawn" it does not mean that they "stem from an independent book which existed *but was suppressed*," as Lieberman translated (and the emphasis is his), but that these two verses were [or, better, are] an independent book, large enough *to qualify for storage*. The word ונגנז *nignaz* is a technical term in talmudic law and refers to the process by which sacred objects which have outlived their usefulness are retired. Such objects may not willfully be destroyed or discarded. They are to be stored away or buried in a manner which allows them to decompose naturally.[203]

---

202. Leiman, "Inverted *Nuns*," 351.

203. Leiman, "Inverted *Nuns*," 353–54. Leiman writes: "The seemingly difficult ונגנז [*ve-nignaz*] is not difficult at all when properly vocalized: read ונגנז [*ve-nignoz*] (Niph'al participle), not ונגנז [*ve-nignaz*] (Niph'al perfect)."

The Extraordinary Texts in the Torah

Leiman concludes persuasively that the putative book of the prophecies of Eldad and Medad that the fragment Elkan Adler found in the Cairo Genizah speaks of is a figment of a medieval midrashic imagination. It is based on a misreading of the verb *nignaz* in Midrash Mishle's report of Rabbi Judah's original statement that the two verses constitute "a *sefer* unto itself." There are, then, no implications in that statement that the inverted *nun*s come to tell us that the Song of the Ark was interpolated from some non-Mosaic outside source, or even that it was transposed from some other part of the Torah, as Rabban Shimon ben Gamliel would have it. If the Song is a discrete *sefer*, and the book of Numbers is now not one but three "books," and the Torah now comprises not five but seven "books"—no big deal. The Talmud is comfortable with that even though the tradition continued to speak of *ḥamishah ḥumshei torah*, the five books of Moses.

Construed this way, the distance between the interpretive world of the rabbis and ours is undiminished. Only the first understanding of the inverted *nun*s, the one put forth by Rabban Shimon ben Gamliel, allows us to think that Sages anticipated what we have come to know, or think we know, about how the Torah came to be.

The *Nun*s: Midrashic Views

As we see from the foregoing, the historical-critical approach to the inverted *nun*s is grounded in the actualities of scribal practice in Near Eastern antiquity. In contrast to it, the midrashic approach looks at the *nun*s without recourse to their historical context. Whereas the former approach is empirical, the latter is imaginative. Surprisingly, there is little material on the *nun*s in the classical midrashic texts, but there have been attempts by latter-day homileticians to discover meaning in what the *nun*s suggest verbally and visually, i.e., what they sound like and what they look like. Building on what I've found of such attempts, I offer the following as a way to interpret the *nun*s midrashically.[204]

Nun = Fish

---

204. The following paragraphs are derived from essays on the internet by Rabbi Norman Lamm, Rabbi Shlomo Riskin, and Rabbi Moshe Bogomilsky. [Unfortunately, as far as we can determine, none of the websites accessed by Rabbi Diamond while writing this section of the book appear to be currently still working.—eds.]

Scribal Secrets

The Jewish mystical tradition sets up a beautiful interpretation of the *nun*s. To see how it works we have to take note of some specific conceptual steps on which the interpretation is built:

1. In Aramaic, the word *nun* means "fish." This is probably because earlier versions of the letter *nun* (נ) looked something like a fish.
2. In Hebrew the word for fish is דג (*dag*).
3. At the end of the book of Genesis, the aged Jacob takes his two grandsons, Manassah and Ephraim (Joseph's sons), on his knees and he blesses them as follows:

> *The God in whose ways my fathers Abraham and Isaac walked, the God who has been my shepherd from my birth to this day; the angel who has redeemed me from all harm—bless the lads. In them may my name be recalled, and the names of my fathers Abraham and Isaac, and may they be teeming multitudes upon the earth.* (Gen 48:15–16)

It is the last line of this blessing that interests us here. In Hebrew it reads: וְיִדְגּוּ לָרֹב בְּקֶרֶב הָאָרֶץ (*ve-yidgu larov be-qerev ha-'areṣ*, "And may they be teeming multitudes upon the earth"). Nahum Sarna comments that the Hebrew verb וְיִדְגּוּ (*ve-yidgu*) is "a unique verb apparently formed from *dag*, 'fish,' a symbol of proliferation and multiplicity."[205]

In fact, Targum Onqelos renders the key phrase into Aramaic as follows: וכנוני ימא יסגון (*u-khenune yamma yisgon*, "and may they proliferate like the fish of the sea"). Onqelos thus connects this part of Jacob's blessing back to the covenantal promise made to Abraham that his descendants would be "as numerous as the stars in the sky and the sand on the seashore" (Gen 22:17). If fish here is a metaphor for the Jewish people, we could say that it points not only to the promise of their collective survival as a people, but to the idea that the primary mode of Jewish existence is not individual and private but communal and collective. Like fish we swim in schools.

To this associative mix let us add one more ingredient: the visual fact that in the Torah the *nun*s are *inverted*. As fish, they are swimming against the current. The ability to do this is thought to be the ultimate indicator of a fish's viability. The metaphor works perfectly for the people of Israel, who have been described, in the words of the title of a book written years ago,

---

205. Sarna, *Genesis*, 328.

as "the people of eternal dissent."[206] That has been their—our—millennial role: to say "no" to all ideologies and individuals who have purported to announce or represent redemption to a world that is profoundly unredeemed, and to the cultures and values upon which they are based. I think of the words of the *Alenu* prayer that concludes every single Jewish worship service, whether on weekdays, Sabbath, or festivals:

> It is our duty to praise the Master of all . . .
> who has not made us like the nations of the world . . .
> who has not designed our lot to be like theirs,
> nor our destiny like all their multitudes . . .
> We hope, therefore, LORD our God,
> soon to behold see the glory of Your power . . .
> when the world shall be perfected under the sovereignty
> of the Almighty . . .

Now let us bring all this to bear on the Song of the Ark and the *nun*s that surround it. The poem itself is about the Ark, which contains "the two tablets of the covenant," the foundational text on which Israel's existence is predicated. The Ark and the tablets within it are at the center of the poem. The *nun*s surround the poem (and thus the Ark and the tablets) not merely to protect them but more importantly to modify them, like parentheses upon the words in a sentence, or to act upon them, like mathematical operators upon the operands they bracket. Midrashically, the *nun*s represent the Jewish people. We could diagram it this way:

> [The Song of the Ark]
> The Jewish (The Ark of the Covenant) People
> The Jewish (The Ark [The Tablets of the Law] of the Covenant) People

This configuration invites us to ponder the relationship of the Jewish people to the Torah. Consider: Without the *nun*s, the Song of the Ark stands alone, without a context. Like the bracketed material in a sentence, its sense depends on what lies on either side of it, the surrounding words within which it is nested. Like all bracketed material, it could be removed from the sentence and the sentence would still stand. But the meaning of the sentence would not be quite the same. It would be less rich and less nuanced. Likewise, if the reverse were the case and the words around the parentheses were deleted, the material inside would stand alone. But they would stand without a context.

---

206. See Polish, *Eternal Dissent*.

So what modifies what? Does the material outside the parentheses qualify or operate upon what is inside them? Or does the bracketed material at the core of the sentence or formula determine the meaning or the power of what brackets it? It boils down to the question I heard many years ago from one of my teachers, Dr. Mordecai Kaplan: Do the Jewish people exist for the sake of the Torah? Or does the Torah exist for the Jewish people? This is possibly the central existential question for Jews in our time, forced upon us by the challenges and the promises of modernity. The question addresses us as Jews, both in our individuality and in our collectivity. In modernity Jewish peoplehood is no longer necessarily coterminous with Torah, and that, to appropriate some words of Martin Buber from another context, is "the exalted melancholy of our fate."[207] In modernity there is no consensus on what Jewish peoplehood entails.

Another Interpretation: *Nun* = Bow

Genesis tells us that when the Great Flood ended, a great rainbow appeared in the sky. It was a sign from God and a promise:

> *I have set My bow in the clouds, and it shall serve as a sign of the covenant between Me and the earth. When I bring clouds over the earth, and the bow appears in the clouds, I will remember My covenant between Me and you and every living creature among all flesh, so that the waters shall never again become a flood to destroy all flesh.* (Gen 9:13–15)

God here is making a universal covenant with the entire human family. The world will never again be destroyed by water. (Note: nothing is said here about fire.) Ḥizquni, in a wonderful example of midrashic thinking, explains (at Genesis 9:13) that when a bow appears upside down, this is an indication of peace, for when archers shoot, the string [of the bow] faces them and the bow [itself] faces the enemy. And the string of this bow [i.e., the rainbow] faces us.

In other words, the rainbow that came out after the Flood looked like an archer's bow that the archer inverted to indicate the cessation of hostilities. (Let us remember that in the Middle Ages soldiers were bowmen, not riflemen or tank gunners, and in his time Ḥizquni would very likely have been able to observe them in action.)

Naḥmanides elaborates on Ḥizquni's explanation (again, at Genesis 9:13):

---

207. Buber, *I and Thou*, 21.

The Extraordinary Texts in the Torah

> Should you want to know how the rainbow can be a sign, the answer is that . . . every visible object that is set before two parties to remind them of a matter that they have vowed between them is called a "sign," and every agreement is called a "covenant."[208]

He cites as examples the stone pillars that Jacob erected as a sign of the covenant between him and Laban (Gen 31:46–52), and, more to the point here, circumcision as a bodily mark of the covenant between God and Israel (Gen 17:9–12). Naḥmanides concludes: "When the . . . rainbow is seen in its inverted form, it is a reminder of peace,"[209] and a sign of the covenant between God and humanity.

The inverted *nun*s can be read in this way, too, as inverted bows and what they connote. They are symbolic signifiers, pointing to the idea that the proper context of the Ark and what it contains is peace. The covenant between God and Israel—which the contents of the Ark, the two tablets of the Decalogue, represent—is itself circumscribed by the universal covenant of peace between God and the human family that the rainbow represents.

Another Interpretation: The *Nuns* = Inversion

But the semiotics of the *nuns* can lead to quite the opposite conclusion. They can be derived not from what they resemble as letters, whether fish or (rain)bow, but from how they appear in the text: inverted.

And the Song of the Ark is located within this inversion. The Song is in the upright position, its words thus legible, and the *nuns* around them are upside down. It is this disjunction that we must ponder.

Now the *nuns* are telling a different story about the context in which the Song appears, the reality within which it is sung. They are telling us that it is an inverted reality, where everything is topsy-turvy. Things are not as they should be; they need to be set aright. This is the world in which we live, this imperfect and unredeemed world. It is imperfect because, if the Ark is to move forward, Israel has to pray that its enemies will be scattered (the first verse of the Song). It is unredeemed because we still have to pray that the divine presence will return to the people of Israel and again abide among them (the second verse of the Song). This is the world that the *nuns* intimate. Were they right side up, they would not be in the text at all.[210] The Song of the Ark would have a different content.

208. Chavel, *Genesis*, 137.
209. Chavel, *Genesis*, 138.
210. They would take their rightful place right side up in the alphabetically incomplete Psalm 145 (the acrostic beginning with the letter *ʾaleph*), in which the line which should commence with the letter *nun* is conspicuously absent.

One of the postulates of classical midrash is that each interpretation stands on its own, has its own hermeneutical dynamics and cogency. That is certainly true of the three readings of the *nun*s I have given here. Each one works on its own terms. Yet in a way that is natural and was wholly unintended on my part, the three can be seen to relate to each other and to follow an interesting progression. In the first reading the *nun*s are an objective correlative for the people of Israel. The association fits very well. In the second the *nun*s suggest something more universal. They point beyond the Jewish people to the postdiluvian covenant that, as Genesis tells us, was made, and still obtains, between God and the human family. In the third the *nun*s have implications for all who are part of that family. They summon us all to overturn them and restore them to their natural position. This is a task that still awaits completion.

4. ADVENTURES IN SPACE

This chapter is still in process. It will comprise brief discussions of other para-textual features that need to be noted, including a) open and closed sections (*parshiyot petuḥot* and *setumot*), with attention to how white or blank space can produce meaning; b) the brick-like layout of the Song of the Sea in Exodus 15; and c) the stanza layout of the Song of Moses in Deuteronomy 32. [Alas, this section was not completed at the time of the author's untimely death.—eds.]

CHAPTER III

Reading the Torah Today

HISTORICAL TRUTH AND MIDRASHIC TRUTH

[This chapter was left unfinished, with the author's note, "Material needs to be added that nuances and deepens the discussion." Except as noted, it has been printed here in the manner it reached our hands.—eds.]

Having now looked at the ten dotted passages in the Torah and the unusual letters—the large, the small, the two inverted, and the one broken—we can rightly ask: what does it all mean? What implications, or even conclusions, can we draw from this exploration of these textual phenomena? What are the truths and insights that history gives us about these extraordinary texts, and what possibly different truths and insights do we get from midrash about them—and not only about them?

I can say it now: this examination of these extraordinary texts in the Torah has been an heuristic device that has enabled us to raise these questions. We must now apply them not only to the dots and unusual letters, but to the more familiar parts of the Torah's text: the narratives, the laws, the rituals, the poems. The issues that this inquiry brings to the fore relate to the whole enterprise of reading Torah in our time.

The key word here is *text*. Early on, I noted that the dots and unusual letters that we have been studying are integral to the Torah's text. Scribal tradition makes this clear and Jewish law mandates that it be maintained.

It is only because they are a part of the text that these features warrant any consideration at all.

These markings are only actualized visually, through the act of reading; they would not be known to us from hearing the Torah read aloud in the synagogue. This underlines a fundamental fact about Torah itself: it has two distinct, though interrelated, modes of existence: a text to be heard, to be communicated by chanting, and a text to be read, to be introjected by study and reflection. It is a text in both modalities, the auditory and the visual, because the Torah is actualized in or through both of these.

The two modalities are intrinsically different experiences. Hearing the Torah is done communally—on Shabbat, on festivals, and on Mondays and Thursdays, the two weekdays when people used to gather in the marketplace. Hearing the Torah is a group experience, a liturgical act performed only in a minyan. As such it recapitulates the event at Sinai. It is, or can be, a self-conscious theological moment for the individuals who are part of the congregation and for the congregation as a whole. Reading Torah is a different experience. It can be done in private or in a group setting. In either case it is *talmud torah*, an act of study in which the mind is deployed in the service of the heart. The intellectual and the existential are intertwined, and it is sometimes hard to know which aspect of the self is setting the agenda.

This twofold nature of how the Torah comes to us is rooted in the ancient dichotomy between the oral and the written, between chanting the Torah for listeners to hear and writing it down for readers to interpret. We already see this in the book of Deuteronomy (5:1), where comprehension of the reality of the One God through hearing (*Shema' Yisra'el*, "Hear O Israel") is balanced by the equally crucial need to understand the implications of this reality through ongoing study of a written text. While the Torah may originally have been a text that literate bards wrote out for themselves from which to chant (a practice that continues even today in the public reading in the synagogue), its textual nature, articulated in the book of Deuteronomy and developed by the rabbinic tradition, requires that it also be interpreted. Jose Faur names the period between the destruction of the Second Temple (70 CE) and the compilation of the Mishnah by Judah HaNasi (Judah the Prince), which he dates around 189 CE, as the key period when this development took hold. That, he says, is when:

> it became imperative to distinguish between "written" and "oral" texts. This difference was postulated on the basis that only the Scripture possesses a "written" text, that is, a "Masorah" or duly

registered text, that could be expounded at the orthographic level, independently of its linguistic sense. Hence a profound concern developed with the written aspects of the Scriptures: the orthography of words, defective and full spelling, and calligraphic ornamentations. These became "significant"; they could acquire meaning through canonical exegesis.[1]

[At this point, Rabbi Diamond included the following three sentences, though he never returned to these thoughts in order to flesh out additional meaning.—eds.]

The same is true of the textual phenomena we have been considering.

The exegesis Faur is talking about does not just come about. It requires reading.

What kind of reading? With what ends in mind? With what assumptions about the text?

HISTORY AND MIDRASH, PESHAṬ, AND DERASH

[This book is devoted to the study of anomalies in the written text of the Torah. As we have seen, the existence of such features quickly caught the eye of alert rabbinic readers; convinced that such details were bearers of meaning, they set out to uncover their significance. Such a process demanded not only close attention but also *method*: the extraction of meaning from the text could not be a haphazard process. The study of Scripture required technique and rules of procedure: these might be only tacit, but they were necessary.

In the present concluding chapter, two such methods will be examined, one historical and the other homiletic. The traditional names for these, as presented in the earlier chapters, are *peshaṭ* and *derash*.—R.G.]

Let us here recall the description I gave in the introduction of the two kinds of reading and discussions that go on in the Shabbat morning minyan in which I participate. I noted there that anyone who would frequent that minyan over a period of time would notice that the membership includes two kinds of readers. There are some who tend to view the weekly Torah portions primarily through the prism of history and historical analysis. And there are others who are more attuned to the ways in which midrash and the major Jewish commentators spin the text. This divide in my minyan harks

---

1. Faur, *Golden Doves with Silver Dots*, 84.

back to an older debate about how the Torah is to be read, one that goes back to rabbinic times and was continued in the Middle Ages. This is the debate about the relative merits of two presumably different ways of reading Bible: *peshaṭ* and *derash*. It is interesting that the *Etz Hayim* Humash, which many members of the minyan use, bifurcates its commentary in just this way, though this arrangement is seldom mentioned or acknowledged in the discussions.

What exactly *peshaṭ* and *derash* denote is not easily stated, for their meaning has shifted over the centuries. Today *peshaṭ* is generally understood to be the plain, simple meaning of the text. But David Weiss Halivni, who has tracked the evolution of these two reading practices, cautions that this definition of *peshaṭ*, while not incorrect, "is entirely the invention of the medieval exegetes. It has no basis in the Talmud."[2] In the Talmud, as Halivni shows, *peshaṭ* referred to the meaning of the text that accrues from its context. It was only in the Middle Ages that it was defined more narrowly as the meaning determined by the lexical denotation of the words and by parsing grammar and syntax. *Derash*, on the other hand, was always understood to be what Halivni calls the "applied" meaning, that is, the meaning that results when various interpretive techniques are applied to the text. For Rabbi Akiva ben Yosef in the first part of the second century CE, *derash* meant that not only context but everything in the text could be—had to be—plumbed for significance: individual words and letters, every feature or irregularity of inscription or expression, even the filigreed crowns that ornament the tops of the letters in the Torah scroll. All were fair exegetical game. The great medieval commentator Rashbam (Rashi's grandson Rabbi Shemuʼel ben Meir, Franco-Germany, ca. 1085–ca. 1174), whose interpretive agenda was to lay out the *peshaṭ*, says that the meaning produced by *derash* is deduced from "redundancy of the verses, or from peculiarities of language in which the plain meaning is written."[3]

The discussions in my minyan, however, and the interpretive divide we have seen played out in the preceding chapters, show us that the *peshaṭ/derash* dichotomy needs to be updated for our time. This is because the terms of the divide have expanded as our understanding of the hermeneutical process has deepened. If *peshaṭ* refers to the context of what we are reading in the Bible, as it did to the rabbis, or even if it refers only to the

---

2. Halivni, *Peshat and Derash*, 53

3. Rashbam, opening comment on Genesis 1:1. See also Halivni, *Peshat and Derash*, 82.

Reading the Torah Today

plain sense of the text, as it did to the medieval commentators, our concept of *peshaṭ* today needs to be expanded to encompass historical understanding. Our modern and/or post-modern interpretive state of mind requires it. Likewise, *derash* today entails the play of imaginative and intuitive energies on more than the minutiae of the Torah's language; it needs to connect the text to the broader screen of contemporary personal, communal, and societal concerns.

The modern situation is more challenging in another respect as well. In rabbinic antiquity and the Middle Ages *peshaṭ* and *derash* were not seen as mutually exclusive ways of reading, but simply as two different ones; but in our time they are. The interpretive scene today is divided between what are termed two distinct reading communities—historians and historicists on one side, and literary, semiotic, and rhetorical theorists on the other. Whereas medieval *pashṭanim* (seekers after *peshaṭ*) like Rashbam respected the truth claim of *derash* as put forth by *darshanim*, their modern equivalents, the historians, and the modern and post-modern theorists of meaning, each claim exclusionary rights to the truth its interpretive methodology furnishes. Each one contends that it alone captures or discovers the meaning of the text it is reading. The very concept of a text has been expanded to include not only a written document or literary creation but an event, a movement, or an ideology—indeed, anything that generates meaning.

The historians stake their claim on the fact they deal with documented facts: "This is what the text says; this is what we know happened." They hold themselves to be dealing with an objective reality. The literary theorists are not impressed with this hard-nosed empiricism. They maintain that while we will certainly bump into furniture when we walk through a dark room, when it comes to non-material entities like written texts and human events, there is no objective reality, only subjective human constructions, i.e., interpretations, of it. Such constructions are not necessarily willful or wrong, but they are always embedded in, contingent upon, and qualified by the personal and social context in which they are generated.

At bottom this debate is a philosophical argument about whether there is an objective reality. On one side stand the empiricists and positivists, who say that there is. On the other side are the existentialists and phenomenologists who say that all reality is subjectively experienced. To explore these differences would take us into the realms of ontology and epistemology, an adventure that lies beyond the scope of this book and this writer and would, in any case, take us away from the matter at hand, which is how we read the Bible.

Let us, then, zero in on just how the historicists and the midrashists respectively put forth their claims that they are each reading the biblical text in the fullest, most correct and authentic way. Writing about professional historical practice in general, Peter Novick notes:

> The assumptions on which it rests include a commitment to the reality of the past, and to truth as correspondence to that reality; a sharp separation between knower and known, between fact and value, and above all, between history and fiction.[4]

We can understand why historians feel that they alone possess the keys to the kingdom of meaning. Jacob Meskin, though not a historian himself, represents this sensibility beautifully.

> Is not history the final bar before which both religious stories and secular narratives must be brought? Is not exactly this the foundation of the distinctively "modern" world ushered in by the Enlightenment? It is acceptable to object to biases on the part of certain historians; it is acceptable to object to whole schools of historical writing, on the grounds that they are ethnocentric, or blind to gender; it is even acceptable to worry about the possibility that history may be little more than a tool for exercising power and abetting conquest. But is it acceptable to challenge the historical worldview itself, to explore alternatives to looking at reality in a historical way? Modernity itself seems to be founded on this historical worldview. How could there also be a *separate* dimension of meaning and analysis which [is] inassimilable to the discourse of history and the historian's method? And if there were such, would it not threaten the basis of modern, secular culture?[5]

Literary theorists and semioticians would answer that there are other dimensions of meaning beyond the historical; that it is indeed acceptable to challenge the historical worldview; that the modern has been superseded by an emerging new reality we still know only as post-modern and post-secular. They say this because Marx's description of modernity as "all that is solid melts into air" applies even more accurately and forcefully to post-modernity. For it has become clear to post-modernists that although facts are essential to historical interpretation, they are not enough to prove

---

4. Peter Novick, cited in Berkhofer, *Beyond the Great Story*, 47–48.
5. Meskin, "Textual Reasoning," 169.

an interpretation . . . The problem with historical facts, as with histories themselves, is that they are constructions and interpretations of the past.⁶

Such a position rests on an understanding of human cognition quite different from that of empirical historians. Whereas the latter presume a Cartesian separation between the knower and the known, as Novick noted, the post-modernists do not. They maintain that all knowledge is subjective, the nature of the known is always qualified by the knower.

This position collapses the distinction between *peshat* and *derash*. It says in effect that all *peshat* is *derash* and that *derash* can be—not is, but can be—*peshat*. Meaning is plastic, contingent, and relative, and truth is contextual.⁷

It is unlikely that this epistemological divide will be or can be bridged. Many historicists tend to belittle the midrashic enterprise as fanciful, soft, even silly. From their side the midrashists look upon the historically-minded as one-dimensional, locked in to a narrow, reductive parsing of the text and of reality.

Occasionally one finds refreshing acknowledgement that it is not a case of either/or. Cyrus Gordon concludes his introduction to *The Bible and the Ancient Near East*, a widely read presentation of the Bible's historical, linguistic, and cultural context, with this judicious observation:

> Although objectivity is essential for the historian, the reconstruction of history will always have a personal element. The capacity to see implications and relationships, the judgment which decides that certain elements are more important than others, and the ability to reconstruct an evolving and continuous whole demand genuine creativity on the part of the historian.⁸

It is time to return to the pluralistic perspective of the rabbis and the medievals. They understood that an exclusivist interpretive stance of any kind is inadequate to the kind of text the Bible presents. To apprehend and comprehend it requires the full range of what the human mind and heart can do. In neurological terms, historical thinking is left-brained, midrashic

---

6. Berkhofer, *Beyond the Great Story*, 53.

7. The implications of this position are certainly problematical. They lead to the question of whether there is or can be any absolute. Post-modern ethicists and theologians have been working on this question for some time now. See, among others, the work of Mark C. Taylor and John D. Caputo.

8. Gordon and Rendsburg, *Bible and the Ancient Near East*, 32.

thinking right-brained. They deploy different faculties and sensibilities approximately as follows (and I do not claim this as an exhaustive list):

Historical thinking: Left Brain	Midrashic thinking: Right Brain
objective	subjective
logical	intuitive
empirical	metaphysical
analytical	poetic
factual	imaginative
evidence-oriented	insight-oriented
sequential patterns	symbolic patterns
cautious	daring
serious	playful

We could even correlate nomenclature with this binary structure. When we read historically we are more likely to call the five books of Moses the Pentaeuch; when reading midrashically we'd probably feel more comfortable calling it the Torah or the Humash.

So if history and midrash each have distinct contributions to make when it comes to reading the five books, however we refer to them, what might these be? I see three:

- different understandings of what the text is;
- different understandings of the past;
- different kinds of truth about the world and our place in it.

Let's look at these.

THE TEXT

We have seen from the foregoing chapters that the raw material of the text is a different entity in the hands of the historian than it is in the hands of a midrashist. It is this very difference that enables one to do with the text what the other would not and to discover in it what the other could not.

For the historian the biblical text is an object, much like a human body on the operating table would be for a surgeon. It has to be so if a dispassionate, objective analysis or procedure on it is to happen. (It is not clear, however, whether every biblical historian is as aware as every surgeon that the object before him or her is a living entity.) In Buberian terms, the historian relates to the text as an "It," not as a "Thou."

And so the work proceeds. The text is read as a document that has to be placed in the geographic, linguistic, cultural, and political context in which it was written. To be understood properly, it has to be treated comparatively. To read the Bible historically *ipso facto* requires a modicum of knowledge about the ancient Near East, particularly of Mesopotamian and Egyptian civilizations and their institutions and legal systems. A sense of how biblical Hebrew is related to west Semitic languages, especially Ugaritic, while not a prerequisite, is certainly a desideratum. So, too, is a working knowledge of what the findings of the major archaeological discoveries have been and what they imply for how we must read the Bible. These would include the discoveries at Ebla and Ugarit (Ras Shamra) in the northern Levant, Mari and Nuzi in what was Mesopotamia, Amarna in Egypt, and, of course, the Dead Sea Scrolls in modern-day Israel.

The suffix "critical" is often applied to this kind of reading. I have repeatedly heard it described as "historical-critical" or "text-critical." This doesn't necessarily mean an antagonistic attitude on the part of the historicist, but rather an interrogative one. To read the biblical text critically means to read it outside the pre-understandings of theology or religion, be they Jewish or Christian (though one must certainly know what those pre-understandings are), and without any agenda of advancing the social or political interests of those reading communities. Solid historical inquiry requires that the chips fall where they may as far as those interests and the theology underlying them go. This is not new. In the Middle Ages the determination of the *peshat* of certain verses in the Torah led to readings of them that sometimes were at odds with the halakhic rulings that rabbinic *derash* had read out of—or into—them. The great *pashtan* Rashbam occasionally went out of his way in his commentary on the Torah to assure his contemporaries that his quest for *peshat* had not led him to heterodox conclusions or behaviors.[9]

For the contemporary midrashist the biblical text has an entirely different ontological status. While it may not be the concretization in words of

---

9. See his comments to Genesis 1:1 and 37:2. Rashbam is undoubtedly referring to *midrash halakha*, the hermeneutical methods by which halakhic teachings are extracted from the verses in question. I do not think Rashbam was as forbearing toward the interpretations yielded by *midrash aggadah*, which are non-performative, non-binding, and looser. See Lockshin, "*Peshat* and *Derash* in Northern France," the introductory essay to his annotated translation of *Rashbam's Commentary on Deuteronomy*, especially 17 n68.

a supernatural divine revelation that it was for the rabbis, it is nonetheless a living organism that speaks to the individual and the community who hear and read it. In Buberian terms the text is a dialogical partner, a "Thou" that addresses the "I" of the hearer(s) and faces the "I" of the reader(s). Here, too, there is interrogation, but it is interrogation of a different order. Here it is not only the reader who asks questions of the text; the text asks questions of the reader. The questions asked, and the answers given, when they are given, are quite different from those that occur in historical reading.

Another way to see the difference between historical and midrashic reading is to frame it in terms of the distinction the literary theorist Roland Barthes (1915–1980) made between a *work* and a *text*. A *work* is considered

> as a closed, finished, reliable representational *object* . . . [whereas] the modern notion of a *text* [is] considered as an open, infinite *process* that is both meaning-generating and meaning-subverting. "Work" and "text" are thus not two different kinds of object but two different ways of viewing the written word.[10]

By this distinction we would have to say that even though most biblical historians refer to the Bible as a text (the branch of biblical scholarship with which this book is most concerned is known as textual criticism), they really relate to it as a work.

THE PAST

The historicist objectification of reality encompasses not only the texts transmitted or preserved by the past, but also the past itself. Indeed, the past *is* the grand text which historical inquiry seeks to interpret.

Historians are aware that the past the Bible presents to us is not "what really happened." What we are reading in the Torah and in many later books of the Bible is a highly stylized version of what really happened, the spin the biblical writers and redactors have put on lived events. Martin Buber, applying what he learned from nineteenth and early twentieth century biblical criticism, calls this version "saga," which, he says, is to be distinguished from "history."

> The literary character within which our historical mode of thinking must classify [biblical] narrative is the saga; and a saga is

---

10. Johnson, "Writing," 40.

generally assumed to be incapable of producing within us any conception of a factual sequence.[11]

The task of the historian is to strip away the layers of saga presented in the biblical text and get down to the kernel of lived historical actuality. Time here is linear; from the perspective of now, one gains a perception of then. The historian "objectifies the past so as to make readers believe that the text does not intrude between their apprehension of the past and the past itself."[12]

Buber himself, while he certainly respected the scientific aspirations of biblical criticism, nevertheless cautioned against thinking these aspirations could be satisfied by the mere quest for facticity. If facts are the quarry of historical research, then the saga itself, the transmutation of lived human events into poetry or narrative or even law, is itself an empirical reality and must be studied on its own terms.

The meeting of a people with events so enormous that it cannot ascribe them to its own plans and their realization, but must perceive in them deeds performed by heavenly powers, is of the genuine substance of history.

We shall not regain an historical nucleus of the saga by eliminating the function of enthusiasm from it. This function is an inseparable element of the fragment of history entrusted to our study . . .[13]

Whether Sinai was a volcano cannot be determined historically, nor is it historically relevant. But that the tribes gathered at the "burning mountain" comprehended the words of their leader Moses as a message from their God, a message that simultaneously established a covenant between them and a a covenant between him and their community, is essentially an historical process, historical in the deepest sense . . .

> There is no other way of understanding history than the rational one; but it must start off with the overcoming of the restricted and restrictive ratio, substituting for it a higher, more comprehensive one.[14]

If history is what happened, saga is how the people remembered—and continue to remember—what happened. The saga that is the Bible is really

---

11. Buber, *Moses*, 13.

12. Berkhofer, *Beyond the Great Story*, 59.

13. [We assume that the ellipses here and at the end of the next paragraph indicate that the author wished to expand on these thoughts.—eds.]

14. Buber, *Moses*, 17.

a manifestation of Jewish collective memory, and in explaining it this way Buber adumbrates the dichotomy developed later in the twentieth century by Yosef Yerushalmi between history and memory.[15]

But once we grasp saga as the textualization of experience, we begin to take leave of the domain of history and approach the boundary of midrashic cognition. We begin to see the difference between going beneath the surface of the text to recover the objective event or events that were experienced in the past, and plumbing the depths of the text midrashically so as to re-create those events and subjectively experience them in the present.

Midrashic time is different from historical time. Historical time is linear. There is a clear sense of before and after. In midrash then and now are coeval. The rabbis certainly knew that their present was preceded by a past, but in their interpretive perspective "there is no before or after in the Torah."[16]

Unlike the biblical writers, the rabbis seem to play with Time as though with an accordion, expanding and collapsing it at will. Where historical specificity is a hallmark of the biblical narratives, here that acute biblical sense of time and place often gives way to rampant and seemingly unselfconscious anachronism.[17]

Abraham and Sarah are alive and present to the rabbis and, as we read about them, to us. The Sinai experience is ever-present to our consciousness because its implications are ongoing. **Even the smallest details can contribute to this outcome.** The large *bet* with which the Torah begins discloses something about the reality we are born into; the dots over Esau's kiss tell us something about how we as individuals are to negotiate our passage through that reality; and the inverted *nuns* suggest some meanings about our collective life as Jews within that reality.

In its larger sense the perspective of midrash is ahistorical and, at times, metahistorical. Events are seen *sub specie aeternitatis*. The modernist Hebrew poet Uri Zvi Greenberg expressed it thus:

אשר יהיה בעתיד, כבר היה לפנים
ואשר לא היה לא יהיה לעולם.
על כן אבטח בעתיד, כי שוויתי את דמות
העבר לפני: זה מראה ונגון.
סלה והללויה ואמן.

15. Yerushalmi, *Zakhor*.
16. b. Pesaḥim 6b; Midrash Tanḥuma, *Terumah* 8; among others.
17. Yerushalmi, *Zakhor*, 17.

What will be in the end has already been in the past.
What has never been will never be.
Therefore do I trust in the future, for I have set the face
of the past before me: this is my vision and my song.
Selah. Halleluya. Amen.[18]

TRUTH

In the light of the different ways in which history and midrash understand the biblical text and the biblical past, can we say that one of them provides a truer reading of the Bible than the other? With regard to the various extraordinary texts we have studied, can we say that the text-critical account of their origin and function is truer than the interpretations given them by midrashists and homilists? Or is the reverse the case?

We have to be careful here. It is not clear that we can or should accept the premise of these questions—that there is one essential interpretive truth to be found. Even if there were, such truth would not be as objective as we would think or as we might like it to be. It would be dependent on the values, the expectations, the politics, the theology (however inchoate or unarticulated)—the whole complex of inter-related factors that go into what a given reader or reading community brings to the text and to the world in which it is being read.[19]

We will not gain much if we construe the relationship between history and midrash as a hermeneutical prizefight in which the objective is for one of them to deliver a knockout blow to the other so that a winner can be declared and everyone can go home and read in accordance with the victor's principles and assumptions. If we are to speak of interpretive truth at all, it is better to speak of it as the truth of *meaning*, the sense that what is being told or shown or affirmed makes sense, interprets reality adequately and satisfactorily to that particular reader or reading community. Meaning thus construed is various. There is meaning that accrues from marshalling facts, analyzing them, and assessing their implications, and there is meaning the imagination brings back after it has soared unfettered into realms beyond the text.

Let us step back for a moment from the issues involved in reading the Bible and consider the butterfly. Who would we think most correctly or

---

18. Greenberg, *Rehovot Hanahar*, 37.
19. See Berkhofer, *Beyond the Great Story*, 74.

accurately understands it, gives the truest account of what it is: a lepidopterist or a poet? The lepidopterist knows a great deal about the butterfly she is studying. Much of her knowledge comes from analyzing a dead specimen under a microscope or pinning its body to a corkboard so that she can show how body and wings interact with the laws of aerodynamics in such a way that the butterfly flies. The poet, however, comprehends the living butterfly in its flight and finds its whole meaning in contemplating the wonder of its flight. Are we to say that one of these two ways of apprehending a butterfly is superior to the other, that one "reads" the butterfly more truly than the other? Would it not be better—dare I say "truer"?—to say that each of them discovers and communicates equally important truths and insights about the butterfly?

My argument here is that if we are to read the Bible adequately and satisfactorily we need the meanings that both history and midrash can give us.

Our post-Enlightenment brains are hard-wired to process reality historically. When we read the Bible we instinctively want to know the temporal coordinates of a given figure or event or law, even if the text does not provide them. We have a sense that there is a before and after in the Torah and in the whole scheme of the anthology that is the Bible.

Historical criticism supplies this perspective. It inserts the 24 books into the historical and cultural matrix of the ancient Near East and reads them in that context. It helps us when we know that the creation and flood stories in Genesis were written after and in response to such Mesopotamian epics as Enuma Elish, Atrahasis, and the story of Gilgamesh. We gain valuable—crucial—insights into Judaism when we see how the Torah's account of these mythic events departs from those works. A lot is gained from knowing that the books of the Pentateuch are not cut from whole cloth, but are rather an amalgam of texts that speak in different voices with different outlooks, biases, and priorities. The textual polyphony that source criticism makes audible helps us to anticipate and appreciate the variegated nature of the Judaism that will develop out of biblical religion. These are all meanings that only a historical approach can provide.

I would, therefore, agree with the philosopher Emmanuel Levinas when he wrote that "No one can refuse the insights of history." Yet in the very next sentence he says, "But we do not think they are sufficient for everything."[20] The practitioners of historical scholarship in the nineteenth

---

20. Levinas, *Nine Talmudic Readings*, 5.

Reading the Torah Today

and twentieth centuries thought that they were. They were certain that the empirical positivism of their methodology was the royal road to meaning when studying the Bible or other canonical texts of Judaism or the Jewish experience as a whole. They even called what they were doing the "science of Judaism" (*Wissenschaft des Judentums*). Considering the apologetics and the obscurantism they were struggling against, they had good reason to do so.

In the twenty-first century, however, such a position is at best an anachronism. The assumptions and methods of historical reading constitute only one interpretive code. I will state my further agreement with the contention that any text, including and especially biblical text, "possesses many more meanings than the explicit factual message historians claim as the core of historical understanding."[21] As we see from the case of the butterfly, meaning is polyvalent. How it is determined is governed by the interpretive code used to discover or uncover or recover it. I speak here primarily of meaning as it applies to written texts, though the same, I think, holds for meanings communicated by the non-literary arts such as painting, sculpture, dance, and film.

The meaning that midrash gives us is of a different order from that of history. I speak here of rabbinic midrash, specifically rabbinic midrash in its aggadic mode, where its energies are directed not towards determining the halakhic import of the text it is interpreting, but toward the existential import of that text. Midrash trades not on the factual details behind the text, but on the presumption of the reality in history of a living, ongoing interpretive community it calls "Israel" that it takes to be addressed by the text. While it often speaks to the concerns of the individual member of that community, its perspective is collective, the collective memory and aspirations of that community. The truths midrash communicates situate the reader within the community and the drama of its existence on the stage of human history. Consider the midrashic parsings of the inverted *nuns* compared to what text-criticism makes of them. Or the midrashic connotations of the large *bet* of Genesis 1:1 and the small *alef* of Leviticus 1:1. Or what the dot over the word רחוקה *reḥoqa*, "distant," in Numbers 9:10, might suggest about someone who is far away from where the exodus from Egypt is being re-enacted, i.e., from where Passover is being ritually commemorated. These are all meanings that only a midrashic approach can provide.

---

21. See Berkhofer, *Beyond the Great Story*, 74.

Scribal Secrets

But midrash has its limitations, too, and they are the obverse of those of history. If the interpretive horizons of history can be constricted by a presumed objectivity, those of midrash can become diffuse by their essential subjectivity. Midrashic readings may be ingenious or charming, but what we want most from biblical interpretation is that it be not so much ingenious or charming as compelling. Because they are subjectively determined, midrashic readings run the risk of being private constructions which may be compelling to their originator but may not be to others. (I must here own up to the possibility that this may be true of the midrashic takes I have offered in the preceding chapters.) But the problem doesn't end here, because the very notion of being compelling is itself a subjective criterion.

Another difference between history and midrash lies in how they each engage the larger issues of the Jewish problematic as they well up from the biblical text. This is so because their respective interpretive agendas are fundamentally different from, and sometimes in tension with, each other. A historical approach to the Bible, as previously discussed, operates outside the beliefs and interests of Judaism or Christianity and may at times come to conclusions that are at odds with those beliefs and interests.[22] Midrash, on the other hand, is energized by those very beliefs. The meanings it generates serve to articulate and affirm them. Each approach has its own integrity and is sufficient unto to itself—but only to itself. To the reader who wants to read the Bible with both mind and heart—and is this not the desideratum?—both are necessary. To be sure, having one's reading informed by both history and midrash means taking on the dissonances that will arise between them and the disquiet these can create. But as the saying goes, "the game is worth the candle." And there is the added consolation of F. Scott Fitzgerald's dictum that "The test of a first-rate intelligence is the ability to hold two opposing ideas in mind at the same time and still retain the ability to function."

This prompts the question whether these are the only two ways of reading the Bible available to us. What about the four interpretive modes propounded by medieval exegetes encompassed by the four-letter acronym *PaRDeS* (פרדס), the Hebrew word for orchard (related to "paradise")? In this scheme the Bible's text is seen as a bountiful orchard filled with all kinds of luscious and nutritious fruit, and the four letters stand for four

---

22. For a seminal treatment of this issue, see Yerushalmi, *Zakhor*, 81–103 and the discussions it provoked (noted in Yerushalmi's preface to the 1996 edition of *Zakhor*).

ways in which the fruit can be picked, i.e., four different modes by which meaning is discovered or recovered from the text:

פשט	Peshaṭ	the literal meaning or plain sense of the text
רמז	Remez	literally "hint"—the symbolic or allegorical meaning
דרש	Derash	the midrashic or homiletical meaning
סוד	Sod	literally "secret"—the secret or mystical meaning

Peshaṭ and *derash* have already been discussed, and I have made the case for their continued utility as interpretive categories. But with *remez* and *sod* things are not so clear. Like *peshaṭ* and *derash*, their meanings have fluctuated over time, as have the exact ways in which they have been applied. What is clear is that these two interpretive approaches have never been accorded the same status as *peshaṭ* and *derash*. They are certainly not part of the standard repertoire of biblical interpretation. *Remez* and *sod* came to the fore as exegetical modes only with the rise of Kabbalism in the post-Talmudic period. They may be Jewish appropriations of Christian ways of reading the Bible in the Middle Ages, when allegory and anagogy were prime engines of meaning. They only cohere within the ideas and worldview that underlie the Jewish mystical tradition. If one does not stand within that tradition or does not predicate one's view of the biblical text on a supernaturally revealed origin (I do not mean to equate the two positions), *remez* and *sod* are inoperative as ways to locate meaning.

A case in point is *gematria*, the technique of computing the numerical value of a word or phrase in the Torah and then connecting it to another word or phrase with the equivalent value. I'm not sure if such interpretive play is classified as an aspect of *remez* or if it belongs to *sod* or whether it still falls within the purview of *derash*. Whatever it is, the ingenuity of *gematria* can be impressive, as we have seen from its application to some of the large and small letters. But can any reader who does not regard the provenance of the Torah as beyond the human reality honestly believe that the meanings yielded by *gematria* were intentionally encoded in the text? To such a reader *gematria* for all its cleverness is contrived, which is another way of saying that it is not compelling.

And so with *remez* and *sod* being problematical, PaRDeS is not a credible or useful interpretive system. In any case it has never been regarded as authoritative or mandatory. But *peshaṭ* and *derash* remain as two basic ways of extracting meaning from the Bible. In their updated and expanded manifestations they give us plenty to work with. The essential enterprise of *peshaṭ* as the great medieval commentators developed it, to capture as precisely as possible the plain sense of the text, is still the starting point for any reading of the Bible. If historical criticism is now the primary method by which the text is rendered intelligible, a host of approaches are included under its rubric: Semitic linguistics, archaeology, social anthropology, gender and cultural criticism, computer science—all the disciplines and tools that modern and postmodern humanistic study, the social sciences, and even the hard sciences have developed and continue to develop.

    Midrash likewise is not a monolithic way of reading. It can still include interpretive moves our rabbinic forebears made: parsing individual letters, words, and phrases; pondering the implications of juxtapositions in the text; getting into the heads of the biblical characters; constructing dialogues between them. But as I've noted, it can entail more than that. A midrashic approach can be sensitive to the larger issue or issues played out in the text, be they theological, moral, political, or psychological. It can speak to the current perceived condition of one's community, of society, of the Jewish people. It can bring the text to bear on personal and domestic concerns. It does not even have to be bound by a commitment to explicate the text's intended meaning. Midrash can use the text as the rabbis often did: as a pretext for what they wanted to say. In its widest sense midrashic reading authorizes the poetics of individual and collective Jewish memory.

    Peshaṭ and *derash*, history and midrash, then, are generic terms, each encompassing a variety of reading agendas and strategies. I'd like to think that this is what the rabbis meant when they said שבעים פנים לתורה (*shiv'im panim la-torah*, that "the Torah has seventy faces").[23] The glory of my own minyan is that it has made room for both.

---

23. Bamidbar Rabbah 13:16.

Bibliography

Alter, Robert. *The Five Books of Moses: A Translation with Commentary*. New York: Norton, 2004.
Andersen, Francis I., and A. Dean Forbes. "What *Did* the Scribes Count?" In *Studies in Hebrew and Aramaic Orthography*, edited by David Noel Freedman et al., 297–318. Winona Lake, IN: Eisenbrauns, 1992.
Berkhofer, Robert, Jr. *Beyond the Great Story: History as Text and Discourse*. Cambridge: Harvard University Press, 1995.
Buber, Martin. *I and Thou*. Translated by Ronald Gregor Smith. London: Continuum, 2004.
———. *Moses: The Revelation and the Covenant*. Oxford: East & West Library, 1946.
Buber, Salomon, ed. *Midrash Sekhel Ṭov*. Berlin: Itzkowski, 1900.
Butin, Romain. *The Ten Nequdoth of the Torah; or, The Meaning and Purpose of the Extraordinary Points of the Pentateuch*. Reprint. New York: KTAV, 1969.
Camus, Albert. *The Myth of Sisyphus and Other Essays*. Translated by Justin O'Brien. New York: Random House, 1955.
Carr, David M. *Writing on the Tablet of the Heart: Origins of Scripture and Literature*. New York: Oxford University Press, 2005.
Chavel, Charles B. *Ramban (Nachmanides) Commentary on the Torah: Genesis*. New York: Shilo, 1999.
Cohen, Menachem. "On the Number of Verses, Words and Letters in the Bible." http://cs.anu.edu.au/~bdm/dilugim/StatSci/middle_english.pdf.
Cross, Frank M. "Ammonite Ostraca from Heshbon: Heshbon Ostraca IV-VIII." *Andrews University Seminary Studies* 13 (1975) 1–20.
Delaney, Carol. *Abraham on Trial: The Social Legacy of Biblical Myth*. Princeton, NJ: Princeton University Press, 1998.
Eliade, Mircea. *The Sacred and the Profane: The Nature of Religion*. Harper Torchbooks 81. New York: Harper & Brothers, 1961.
Faur, José. *Golden Doves with Silver Dots: Semiotics and Textuality in Rabbinic Tradition*. Bloomington: Indiana University Press, 1986.
———. "Reshima me-ha-'Otiyot ha-Gedolot ve-ha-Qeṭanot she-ba-Miqra' me-ha-Geniza ha-Qahirit" [A List of the Large and Small Letters in the Bible from the Cairo Geniza]. *Proceedings of the American Academy for Jewish Research* 35 (1967) 1–10.
Fox, Everett. *The Five Books of Moses*. New York: Schocken, 1995.
Freedman, H., and Maurice Simon. *Midrash Rabbah*. Vol. 1. New York: The Soncino Press, 1983.

Bibliography

Frensdorf, Solomon, ed. *Sefer Okhlah ve-Okhlah*. Reprint. New York: KTAV, 1972.
Friedman, Richard E. *The Bible With Sources Revealed: A New View Into The Five Books of Moses*. San Francisco: Harper, 2003.
———. *Commentary on the Torah with a New English Translation*. San Francisco: Harper, 2001.
———. *Who Wrote the Bible?* New York: Harper, 1987.
Garr, W. Randall. *Dialect Geography of Syria-Palestine, 1000–586 BCE*. Philadelphia: University of Pennsylvania Press, 1985.
Ginsburg, Christian D., trans. *Masoret ha-Masoret*. New York: KTAV, 1968.
Gordon, Cyrus H., and Gary A. Rendsburg. *The Bible and the Ancient Near*. 4th ed. New York: Norton, 1997.
Greenberg, Uri Z. *Rehovot Hanahar* [The Streets of the River]. Vol. 5 of *Kol ketavav* [His Collected Works]. Jerusalem: Mosad Bialik, 1992.
Hakohen, Mordecai. *'Al HaTorah*. Jerusalem: Orot, 1956.
Halivni, David W. *Peshat and Derash: Plain and Applied Meaning in Rabbinic Exegesis*. New York: Oxford University Press, 1991.
Hauptman, Judith. *Rereading the Rabbis: A Woman's Voice*. Boulder, CO: Westview, 1998.
Israel, Felice. "The Language of the Ammonites." *Orientalia Lovaniensia Periodica* 10 (1979) 143-59.
Johnson, Barbara. "Writing." In *Critical Terms for Literary Study*, edited by Frank Lentricchia and Thomas McLaughlin, 39-49. Chicago: University of Chicago Press, 1990.
Kelley, Page H., et al. *The Masorah of Biblia Hebraica Stuttgartensia*. Grand Rapids: Eerdmans, 1998.
Leiman, Sid Z. "The Inverted *Nun*s at Numbers 10:35-36 and the Book of Eldad and Medad." *Journal of Biblical Literature* 93 (1974) 348-55.
Levenson, Jon D. "Genesis." In *The Jewish Study Bible*, edited Adele Berlin and Marc Zvi Brettler, 53-54. 2nd ed. New York: Oxford University Press, 2014.
Levinas, Emmanuel. *Nine Talmudic Readings*. Translated by Annette Aronowicz. Indianapolis: Indiana University Press, 1990.
Levy, B. Barry. *Fixing God's Torah: The Accuracy of the Hebrew Bible in Jewish Law*. New York: Oxford University Press, 2001.
Lieberman, Saul. *Hellenism in Jewish Palestine*. New York: Jewish Theological Seminary, 1950.
———. *Tosefta ki-Fshuṭah*. Vol. 4. New York: Jewish Theological Seminary, 1962.
Lockshin, Martin I. "*Peshat* and *Derash* in Northern France." In *Rashbam's Commentary on Deuteronomy*, 1-25. Providence, RI: Brown Judaic Studies, 2004.
Matt, Daniel C., trans. *The Zohar: Pritzker Edition*. Vol. 2. Stanford: Stanford University Press, 2004.
Meskin, Jacob. "Textual Reasoning, Modernity, and the Limits of History." In *Textual Reasonings: Jewish Philosophy and Text Study at the End of the Twentieth Century*, edited by Peter Ochs and Nancy Levene, 162-74. Grand Rapids: Eerdmans, 2002.
Milgrom, Jacob. *The JPS Torah Commentary: Numbers*. Philadelphia: Jewish Publication Society, 1990.
Moreshet, Menahem. *Leqsiqon ha-Po'al she-Nitḥaddesh bi-Lshon ha-Tanna'im*. Ramat Gan, Israel: Bar-Ilan University Press, 1980.
Niditch, Susan. *Oral World and Written Word: Ancient Israelite Literature*. Louisville: Westminster, 1996.

Bibliography

Ouaknin, Marc-Alain. *The Burnt Book: Reading the Talmud*. Translated by Llewellyn Brown. Princeton, NJ: Princeton University Press, 1995.

Pinchas, Mordechai. "The Broken Vav—*vav k'tia*." http://www.sofer.co.uk/broken-vav.

Plaut, W. Gunther, ed. *The Torah: A Modern Commentary*. Rev. ed. New York: Union for Reform Judaism, 2005.

Polish, David. *The Eternal Dissent: A Search for Meaning in Jewish History*. London: Abelard-Schuman, 1960.

Rendsburg, Gary A. "Notes on Genesis XXXV." *Vetus Testamentum* 34 (1984) 361–66.

———. "What We Can Learn about Other Northwest Semitic Dialects from Reading the Bible." In *Discourse, Dialogue, and Debate in the Bible: Essays in Honour of Frank H. Polak*, edited by Athalya Brenner-Idan, 160–78. Hebrew Bible Monographs 63; Amsterdam Studies in Bible and Religion 7. Sheffield: Sheffield Phoenix Press, 2014.

Ron, Zvi. *Sefer Qaṭan ve-Gadol* [The Book of Small and Large]. San Diego: Rossi, 2006.

Sabato, Haim. *Aleppo Tales*. Jerusalem: Toby Press, 2005.

Sackenfeld, Katharine D. "Numbers." In *Women's Bible Commentary*, edited by Carol A. Newsom et al., 49–56. Rev. ed. Louisville: Westminster John Knox, 2012.

Samuel, Maurice. *Certain People of the Book*. New York: Knopf, 1967.

Sarna, Nahum M. *The JPS Torah Commentary: Exodus*. Philadelphia: Jewish Publication Society, 1991.

———. *The JPS Torah Commentary: Genesis*. Philadelphia: Jewish Publication Society, 1989.

Schniedewind, William. *How the Bible Became a Book: The Textualization of Ancient Israel*. Cambridge: Cambridge University Press, 2004.

Schnitzer, Shemu'el. "'Otiyot Gedolot u-Ze'irot ba-Miqra" [Letters Large and Small in the Bible]. *Bet Mikra* 27 (5742/1982) 257–65.

Slouschz, Nahum. *Thesaurus of Phoenician Inscriptions*. Tel Aviv: Devir, 1942.

Sperling, S. David. "Modern Jewish Interpretation." In *The Jewish Study Bible*. New York: Oxford University Press, 2004.

Steiner, George. *No Passion Spent: Essays 1978–1995*. New Haven: Yale University Press, 1996.

Talmon, Shemaryahu. "Prolegomenon." In *The Ten Nequdoth of the Torah or The Meaning and Purpose of the Extraordinary Points of the Pentateuch*, by Romain Butin, xviii–xxv. New York: KTAV, 1969.

Tawil, Hayim, and Bernard Schneider. *Crown of Aleppo: The Mystery of the Oldest Hebrew Bible Codex*. Philadelphia: Jewish Publication Society, 2010.

Tigay, Jeffrey H. *The JPS Torah Commentary: Deuteronomy*. Philadelphia: Jewish Publication Society, 1996.

Tov, Emanuel. *Textual Criticism of the Hebrew Bible*. 3rd rev. ed. Minneapolis: Fortress, 2012.

van der Toorn, Karel. *Scribal Culture and the Making of the Hebrew Bible*. Cambridge: Harvard University Press, 2007.

Würthwein, Ernst. *The Text of the Old Testament: An Introduction to the Biblia Hebraica*. Translated by Errol F. Rhodes. 2nd ed. Grand Rapids: Eerdmans, 1995.

Yeivin, Israel. *Introduction to the Tiberian Masorah*. Translated and edited by E. J. Revell. Missoula, MT: Scholars, 1980.

Yerushalmi, Yosef H. *Zakhor: Jewish History and Jewish Memory*. Seattle: University of Washington Press, 1982.

Zornberg, Aviva. *The Particulars of Rapture: Reflections on Exodus*. New York: Doubleday, 2001.

Index of Scriptural Passages

Genesis

	37, 37n10, 43, 47, 85, 87, 119, 147
1:1	3, 76, 77, 81, 83, 86, 87, 88n104, 94, 95, 119, 158n3, 163n9
2:4	79, 86, 93, 94n111, 94n113, 96, 119
3:9	135
4:1	48
9:13	152
9:13–15	152
9:24	48n32
12:2	96
12:10–20	40
16:5	30, 38, 99
16:6	40
17:9–12	153
18:9	30, 37n11, 41, 42n19
18:10–15	40
18:27	97
19:33	30, 37n11, 44, 45, 72
19:35	45, 47
21:9–14	41
21:12	40
22:17	150
23	113
23:2	86, 98
23:16	113
24:1	98
25:1	98
25:22	101
26:34–35	100, 100n127
27:45	101
27:46	79, 79n83, 86, 99, 100n127
31:46–52	153
33:4	2, 31, 35, 37n11, 49, 50n36, 51n37
37:2	66, 163n9
37:12	31, 37n11, 63
41:18	65n62
45:14–15	51n37
48:15–16	150

Exodus

	37, 37n10, 105, 147
15	154
18:20	53n41
18:21	126
18:25	126
25:16	139
34:7	86, 102, 103, 123
34:14	86, 102, 103, 123, 126, 132
40:20	139

Leviticus

	37, 37n10, 147
1:1	3, 79, 81, 86, 106, 107n137, 119
6:2	79, 86, 110
8:8	114, 117
8:9	114n151
8:15	76, 77, 83, 113n147, 114, 117
8:23	76, 77, 83, 114, 117
8:28	113
8:29	113n146
10:16	113, 113n147

Index of Scriptural Passages

11:42	76, 77, 78, 83, 86, 112, 113
13:33	83, 86, 113, 114, 116
24:2	104
24:12	127

Numbers

	37, 37n10, 120, 137, 147
2:17	143
3:14	67
3:14–17	67
3:16	67
3:39	31, 66
4:34	67
9:6–7	52
9:8	127
9:10	31, 37n11, 39n13, 52, 53
9:13	53
10	137n180
10:21	143
10:33	139, 143, 144, 144n197
10:35	144n197
10:35–36	3, 7, 18, 137, 141n188, 143, 147
11:1	143, 147
11:1–3	144, 144n197
11:4–34	144, 144n197
11:34	144n196
12:3	107, 127
14:12	120
14:15–17	120
14:17	76, 77, 86, 119, 122
15:34	127
21	137n180
21:14–15	68, 137n180
21:17–18	68, 137n180
21:24	74
21:26–29	69
21:26	68
21:27	70n70, 74
21:27–39	137n180
21:28	70
21:29	70n70
21:30	31, 67, 68, 70, 74
23:4	106
23:16	106
25:6	127
25:12	76n78, 86, 123
27:2	126
27:3	127
27:4	128
27:5	80, 80n88, 86
27:7–11	128
28	71
28:5	71n72
28:13	72
28:21	72
28:29	72
29	71
29:4	72
29:10	72
29:15	31, 71, 72
36	128

Deuteronomy

	14n10, 37, 37n10, 57, 62, 85, 121, 147, 156
1:15	126
1:17	126
2:9	67
5:1	156
6:4	76, 77, 78, 80, 80n88, 86, 102, 129, 132
9:24	80, 80n88, 83, 86, 133
17:16	53n41
29:17	57
29:17–20	57
29:20–27	57
29:27	57, 76, 77, 78, 86, 133
29:28	2, 18n20, 31, 37n11, 38, 56, 57, 58
30:11–14	62
31	57
32	121, 135, 154
32:1	135
32:6	76, 76n78, 77, 78, 86, 119, 134
32:15–18	121
32:18	76, 77, 78, 79, 86, 119, 122n162
34:12	76, 78

Index of Scriptural Passages

Joshua
6   139n182

1 Samuel
4   139n182

1 Kings
    47
4:3   13n7
14:21   47

2 Kings
2:12   140
13:14   140
22:8–10   14
22:9   13n7

Isaiah
    105
33:20   44
43:10   105

Jeremiah
36:10   13n7

Nahum
1:3   120n159

Psalms
18:29   104
28   139
35:10   112
89   139
145   153n210

Proverbs
    87, 146

9:1   142
20:27   104

Job
6:12   120n159

Song of Songs
    87

Ruth
    47
4:13–22   47

Ecclesiastes
    146

Esther
    123

Daniel
    30

Ezra
7:6   17

Nehemiah
8:8   17, 18

1 Chronicles
    87, 108, 119
1:1   81

Matthew
1:7   47n31

Luke
3:31   47n31

Index of Ancient and Medieval Sources

Avot de Rabbi Natan A
- 34 — 18n20, 61n58, 71n71, 141n189

Avot de Rabbi Natan B
- 60n52, 61n58
- 37 — 18n20

Babylonian Talmud

Berakhot
- 45b — 21n26

Shabbat
- 30b — 146
- 115b–116a — 141n189, 142, 143n193

Pesaḥim
- 93b — 54n44
- 6b — 166n16

Megillah
- 3a — 18n21
- 11b — 76n78

Ketubot
- 106a — 19n24

Nedarim
- 64b — 118n157

Nazir
- 23a — 46n27
- 40a — 118n156

Qiddushin
- 66b — 76n78, 125n167
- 30a — 13n8, 83, 113n148, 116

Bava Qamma
- 93a — 99n125

Bava Meṣi'a'
- 87a — 43n20

Bava Batra
- 16b — 98n122
- 78b–79a — 70

Sanhedrin
- 43b — 58, 59n51, 61n57
- 116a — 144n195

Menaḥot
- 29b — 7n5, 95n115

Bekhorot
- 4a — 67

Bamidbar Rabbah
- 46n26
- 3:13 — 4n1, 18n20, 61n58
- 13:16 — 172
- 21:12 — 126n169

Ba'al HaṬurim
- 50n36, 88n104

Ben Sira
- 146

Bereshit Rabbah
- 42, 46, 46n26, 87
- 1:10 — 88n102, 88n104
- 12:9 — 96n118
- 12:10 — 95n114, 95n116
- 19:30 — 70n70
- 48:15 — 42n19
- 51:9 — 46n28

Index of Ancient and Medieval Sources

Bereshit Rabbah *(continued)*
78:9   50n36

Ge'ulat ha-Ger
     96n117

ibn Ezra, Abraham
     51, 51n37, 121n161

Jerusalem Talmud
     Megillah
         1:8 (71c)   76n78

Leqaḥ Ṭov
     61n57

Ma'or va-Shemesh
     97n121

Maimonides
     132
     Mishneh Torah
         27
         Sefer Madda', Hilkhot Yesode ha-Torah
            1:1   132n173
         Sefer Ahavah, Hilkhot Sefer Torah
            7:8   75n77
            2:9   75n77
            8:4   28n39
         Sefer Qorbanot, Hilkhot Qorban Pesaḥ)
            5:8   54n44

Massekhet Sefer Torah, see Tractate Sefer Torah

Massekhet Sofrim, see Tractate Sofrim

Masoret ha-Masoret
     25

Me'or Ha'Afelah
     96

Midrash Mishle
     26:24   40n14, 146, 147, 148, 149

Midrash Tanḥuma, *Terumah*
     8   166n16

Midrash Tehillim
     123:2   105n135

Minḥat Shai
     84

Mishnah
     Pesaḥim
         9:2   54
     Mo'ed Qatan
         3:4   19
     Negaim
         14:4   118n156
     Yadayim
         3:5   148

Naḥmanides
     70n70, 144n197, 152, 153

Nefuṣot Yehudah
     46   104n133

Pesiqta de Rav Kahana
     12:6   105n135

Rashbam
     121n161, 158n3, 163n9

Rashi
     37, 38, 42n19, 43n20, 70n70, 107n137, 121n161, 122, 127, 144, 144n195

Sefer Okhlah ve-Okhlah
     25, 25n36, 81, 83

Śekhel Ṭov
     46, 66

Sifre Bamidbar
     39, 39n13, 45, 46, 50, 54, 59, 60, 62, 65, 72
     69   39n13
     84   141n188

Sifre Devarim
     40n13

Śifte Ḥakhamim
     67

Targum Onqelos
     150

Index of Ancient and Medieval Sources

Tractate Sefer Torah
    20, 22

Tractate Sofrim
    22, 76, 79, 80, 81, 83, 87, 87n101, 88, 89, 112, 114, 115, 116, 131, 141
  6:1   141n190
  9:1   76
  9:2   76, 112n145
  9:3   76
  9:4   76
  9:5   76
  9:6   76
  9:7   76

Tur, Yoreh De'ah
  275   75n77

Vayyiqra' Rabbah
  1:13   107n137
  19:2   103n132
  23:12   122n163

Zohar
    43, 43n21, 44, 47, 96, 105, 108
  1:91b   96n119
  1:93a   96n119
  1:101b   43n22
  1:110b   47n29
  3:53b   108n138

Index of Authors

Alter, R., 40, 48, 57, 69, 70, 111 141, 120, 121, 137, 140
Andersen, F. I., 113, 114

Berkhofer, R., 160, 161, 165, 167, 169
Buber, M., 152, 165
Buber, S., 46
Butin, R., 34, 42, 53, 54, 57, 60, 61, 62, 71

Camus, A., 91, 92
Carr, D. M., 12, 13
Chavel, C. B., 153
Cohen, M., 113, 114, 115
Cross, F. M., 74

Delaney, C., 109

Eliade, M., 91

Faur, J., 80, 157
Forbes, A. D., 113, 114
Fox, E., 111
Freedman, H., 88
Frensdorf, S., 25, 83
Friedman, R. E., 4, 70, 94, 111, 137

Garr, W. R., 74
Ginsburg, C. D., 25, 26
Gordon, C. H., 161
Greenberg, U. Z., 167

Hakohen, M., 51
Halivni, D. W., 158
Hauptman, J., 128

Israel, F., 74

Johnson, B., 7, 164

Kelley, P. H., 79, 94

Leiman, S. Z., 143, 146, 147, 148
Levenson, J. D., 100
Levinas, E., 168
Levy, B. B., 116
Lieberman, S., 16, 19, 22, 35, 36, 54, 141, 147
Lockshin, M. I., 163

Matt, D. C., 43, 44, 47, 96
Meskin, J., 160
Milgrom, J., 52, 53, 54, 66, 67, 68, 120, 139, 140
Moreshet, M., 122

Niditch, S., 12

Ouaknin, M.-A., 10, 11

Pinchas, M., 124
Plaut, W. G., 57
Polish, D., 151

Rendsburg, G. A., 73, 74, 102, 161
Ron, Z., 79, 84, 85, 96, 97, 98, 99, 102, 104, 106, 108, 112, 118, 122, 127, 134, 135

Sabato, H., 28

Index of Authors

Sackenfeld, K. D., 128 171
Samuel, M., 101, 102
Sarna, N. M., 48, 104, 150
Schneider, B., 28
Schniedewind, W., 12
Schnitzer, S., 22, 79, 83, 84, 85, 87
Simon, M., 88
Slouschz, N., 74
Sperling, S. D., 8
Steiner, G., 92, 93

Talmon, S., 36, 49, 61, 64
Tawil, H., 28

Tigay, J. H., 5, 57, 134
van der Toorn, K., 12, 13, 14, 15, 16, 17
Tov, E., 11, 20, 21, 94, 113, 115, 116, 133, 142

Würthwein, E., 13, 25

Yeivin, I., 11, 12, 23, 27, 28, 78, 80, 81, 87, 134
Yerushalmi, Y. H., 166, 170

Zornberg, A., 99

www.ingramcontent.com/pod-product-compliance
Lightning Source LLC
Chambersburg PA
CBHW051739230426
43670CB00012B/2089